D0915713

Educators in the Catholic Intellectual Tradition

EDUCATORS IN THE CATHOLIC INTELLECTUAL TRADITION

Edited by
John L. Elias
and
Lucinda A. Nolan

SACRED HEART UNIVERSITY PRESS
FAIRFIELD, CONNECTICUT
2009

Copyright 2009 by the Sacred Heart University Press

All rights reserved. Except for brief quotations in a review, this book, or parts thereof, must not be reproduced in any form without permission in writing from the publisher. For information, contact the Sacred Heart University Press, 5151 Park Avenue, Fairfield, Connecticut 06825

Parts of the chapters "John Lancaster Spalding: Prelate and Philosopher of Catholic Education." by Lucinda A. Nolan, "Thomas E. Shields: Progressive Catholic Religious Educator," by John L. Elias, and "Sister M. Rosalia Walsh and the Parish Catechetical Apostolate," by Lucinda A. Nolan, appear in essays by the respective authors in the Christian Educators of the Twentieth Century online project. Parts of "Sister M. Rosalia Walsh and the Parish Catechetical Apostolate," by Lucinda A. Nolan, also appear in an article by the author in *Religious Education* 102 (2007): 314-27. Parts of the chapter "George Johnson: Policy Maker for Catholic Education," by John L. Elias ,appear in an article by the author in *Religious Education* 104 (2009). Parts of the chapter "Mary Perkins Ryan: Visionary in Modern Catholic Religious Education," by Ann M. Heekin, appear in an article by the author in *Religious Education,* 103 (2008): 196-217.

Library of Congress Cataloging-in-Publication Data

Educators in the Catholic intellectual tradition / edited by John L. Elias and Lucinda A. Nolan.
    p. cm.
  Includes bibliographical references and index.
  ISBN 978-1-888112-18-4
  1. Catholic Church—Education. 2. Catholic teachers—United States—Intellectual life. 3. Catholic intellectuals—United States. I. Elias, John L., 1933- II. Nolan, Lucinda A., 1947-
    LC485.E38 2009
    370.088'282—dc22   2009024659

This book is dedicated to the lifelong work of Gerard S. Sloyan, priest, professor, scholar and friend, whose unquenchable search for knowledge, love for the Church, and enduring sense of hope have guided countless religious educators into the new millennium.

Contents

Introduction
John L. Elias and Lucinda A. Nolan   1

John Lancaster Spalding:
Prelate and Philosopher
of Catholic Education
Lucinda A. Nolan   20

Edward Pace: Pioneer Psychologist,
Philosopher, and Religious Educator
John L. Elias   49

Thomas E. Shields:
Progressive Catholic Religious Educator
John L. Elias   75

George Johnson:
Policy Maker for Catholic Education
John L. Elias   103

Virgil Michel: Prophet of
Liturgical Education and Reform
Jacqueline Parascandola   131

Sister M. Rosalia Walsh and
the Parish Catechetical Apostolate
Lucinda A. Nolan   162

Jacques Maritain and His Contribution to the Philosophy of Catholic Education in America
Luz M. Ibarra 189

Neil G. McCluskey: A Public Voice for Catholic Education
Harold D. Horell 219

Mary Perkins Ryan: Visionary in Modern Catholic Religious Education
Ann M. Heekin 245

Shaping the Christian Century: The Vision of Gerard Sloyan
Philip A. Franco 271

References 297

Contributors 319

Index 321

Preface

We have written this book to assist educators in understanding how the Catholic faith and intellectual tradition have been and might continue to be handed on in an open and critical manner. After an introduction that highlights the work of educators in the first nineteen hundred years of Christianity, we treat a selection of twentieth-century American Catholic educators who have added to this rich tradition. We have chosen to include Jacques Maritain of France in this volume because of his many years of teaching and lecturing in this country and the influence his writings have had on the development of a Catholic philosophy of education in the United States.

Both of us as well as the other contributors to this book have been associated, as professors or graduates, with the Graduate School of Religion and Religious Education of Fordham University, Bronx, New York.

We offer special thanks for bringing this book to completion to David Coppola of Sacred Heart University, a dear friend and colleague. We thank Sid Gottlieb of the Sacred Heart University Press for handling countless editing and publishing details. James Morgan offered his characteristically fine work in editing the manuscript. We are also most appreciative of Edna Paulson's excellent work on the index for the book.

We thank our colleagues at Fordham University and The Catholic University of America for the rich intellectual climate they have provided. We are especially grateful to our spouses, Eleanor Flanigan and Robert Nolan and our adult children: John's Rebecca and Chris, Rachel and Russ, and Cindy's, Robert and Marine, Lesley and Mike and Kevin, all of whom continue to bring so much joy to our lives.

During the writing of this book, both of us were blessed and inspired by the births of first grandchildren: for John, Julia Violet Elias Dodson; for Cindy, Noah Xavier Giovannelli. Perhaps this book might inspire their parents, Christopher Dodson and Rebecca Elias, and Lesley and Michael Giovannelli, as well as other parents and educators in their task of nurturing the coming generations in religious faith.

John L. Elias
Fordham University

Lucinda A. Nolan
The Catholic University of America

Introduction

JOHN L. ELIAS AND LUCINDA A. NOLAN

The Catholic intellectual tradition is both rich and varied. It is a living tradition that continues not only as a body of work, but as a way of "doing things that is the outcome of centuries of experience, prayer, action and critical reflection" (Hellwig 2000, 3). Included within this tradition are works of history, theology, literature, philosophy, and social science. The artistic tradition is replete with architects, novelists, poets, artists, and playwrights. In fact there is no area of human endeavor and culture that does not find expression within the Catholic intellectual tradition. A distinctive feature of this tradition is Cardinal Newman's ideal of "the integration of the arts and sciences by the believing mind under the guiding light of theology" (McCool 2000, 39).

Within this vibrant tradition there are also works that reflect deeply on ideas and practices of education and pedagogy. This is not surprising, since the Catholic Church has always placed a high value on the development, maintenance, and growth of its tradition as it is handed down from generation to generation. One of the primary tasks of any religious body is to introduce new generations to the lore and practices of its life as well as sustain individuals throughout their lives. This education in the faith takes place in many venues, customary theologies, philosophies, and practices that are a part of the Catholic intellectual tradition and the means of handing it on.

This book contains a collection of studies of prominent educators who have made significant contributions to handing on the Catholic intellectual tradition in the United States. These men and women have enriched this tradition by careful attention to educational theories and methods that find their origin in the Jewish and Christian past. Ancient

Israel was assiduous in handing on the Torah or Law, the prophets dramatically called people back to the practices of the covenant, and the sages gave practical advice for everyday living. The Acts of the Apostles and the Letters of Paul chronicle the careful attention to safeguarding and transmitting teachings in the early apostolic Christian communities.

The Catholic intellectual tradition in education embraces a rich heritage garnered from its Jewish and Greek roots; the early apostolic communities; the writings of the patristic age, scholastic philosophers and theologians; Renaissance humanists; educators in religious orders of men and women; popes; Cardinal Newman; and Thomistic philosophers such as Jacques Maritain and Etienne Gilson. Contributors to this tradition in the past three centuries have been mainly European scholars. However, in the past two centuries educators in the United States have made notable contributions to the task of handing on the Catholic intellectual tradition.

When examined closely, it becomes evident that United States educators have made significant contributions. In an era that has witnessed the emergence of Catholic Studies programs in U.S. Catholic colleges and universities and discussions about the Catholic identity of all Catholic institutions, it is necessary to identify these key contributors as well as the nature and parameters of their influence on Catholic education. However, before turning to this task we review in brief some of the more significant educational developments in the Catholic intellectual tradition.

The Emergence of the Catholic Intellectual Tradition in Education

Preaching and teaching as forms of education make up a great deal of the Christian Scriptures. Jesus was a rabbi (teacher), a prophet, and a sage. He sent his chosen apostles and disciples on teaching missions. The Acts of the Apostles is largely a description of the preaching and teaching of Peter and Paul, as well as other disciples of Jesus. Paul's letters to the Churches reflect the deep concern of early Christians for educating in the faith and sustaining the newly formed communities in the Christian way of life. The Pastoral Letters assign particular importance to orthodoxy in teaching, the handing on of right or correct teachings.

The Church of Alexandria made a profound contribution to Christian teaching through its renowned catechetical or theological school that provided education for advanced students of Christianity through study of the Scriptures. The most notable educators in this school were Clement (150-220) and Origen (d. *c.* 254). Clement's *Pedagogus* (2004), written circa 170, describes Christian learning as coming from the close relationship between Christ the teacher and the Christian student. Origen taught all the subjects of the classical or secular school as preparatory to philosophical and theological studies. Gregory of Neocaesarea praised Origen's respect for freedom in learning, "We went into and examined with entire freedom all sorts of ideas, in order to satisfy ourselves and enjoy to the full those goods of the mind" (In Murray 1957, 157).

In the fourth century the Church at Jerusalem was graced with an excellent teacher in Cyril of Jerusalem, whose *Instruction for Those about to be Illumined* (1986), composed circa 348, provided a thorough course of instruction in the faith for inquirers and catechumens. The course consisted of daily homilies given during the liturgies of Lent. The forty days of training was comprised of eighteen lectures, which complemented ascetical practices. In this way Cyril did not teach or preach by words alone but also through these moving religious experiences.

A prominent educator in the eastern part of the Roman Empire was Basil, Bishop of Caesarea (329-379). Before entering the monastery he studied rhetoric and philosophy. His monastery prided itself on integrating scholarship with contemplation. Though many Western fathers in the patristic era, notably Jerome, Tatian, and Tertullian, opposed classical learning as harmful to the life of faith, Basil wanted his monks to be educated in Greek classics, even though he recognized some of the difficulties with these classics. His views were expressed in the tract, *Address to Young Men on Reading Greek Literature* (1933).

The greatest educator from the patristic period was no doubt Augustine of Hippo (354-430), a teacher of rhetoric before he became a bishop. In a number of treatises he described the role and functions of teachers and catechists. His truly great classic *The Confessions* (2007), written in 397, described his self-education and development which lasted throughout his entire life. In marvelous prose Augustine related how he came to religious faith through study, prayer, and exposure to the example of Christians. He also contributed to Christian education through his *De Magistro* (1995a), composed in 389, a philosophical treatise on how one learns; *De Catechizandis Rudibus* (1946), composed in 398, an instruction on how catechumens should be educated; and *De Doctrina Christiana* (1995b), a discourse on how the Scriptures are to be interpreted and their truth communicated. The first three books of this treatise were written in 397 while the fourth was written in 426. In all his works Augustine stressed that God was the interior teacher of the soul who prompts all learning.

Augustine's gift to Christianity was a veritable theology of education. All his key educational concepts are connected with his theology of faith, understanding, free will, grace, sin, and love. His theology of education is aptly summarized here: "Education for Augustine moves from doubt to understanding and faith. His view of education has a supernatural basis since its ultimate end for the Christian is the possession of eternal happiness. For the attainment of this happiness the intellectual activity of learning is the engine" (Elias 2002, 39).

Augustine has enriched Christian education by affirming that education is essentially the search for wisdom to lead a life centered on God. He came to the conclusion that though he was versed in the classics himself, the classical writers are of little help in the search for true wisdom about God. The Bible became the center around which Christian learning crystallized for him. Augustine's views in matters of faith shaped and determined much of Christian theology until the emergence of the great medieval theologies.

The medieval scholastic period also had its share of noteworthy educators that contributed to the Catholic intellectual tradition in education. One such teacher was Peter Abelard (1070-1142). At the beginning of his *Sic et Non*, written in 1120, Abelard announced that "by doubting we come to inquiry and by inquiry we perceive the truth." Thomas Aquinas shared this same optimistic opinion in his *Summa Theologica*, written between 1266 and 1272. The scholastic method allowed practitioners to save the appearances of the ancient authorities while, at the same time putting forward original solutions of their own whenever the sources required further explication (Clancy 1997, 34).

Abelard, anticipating by centuries the far-ranging probing of the Enlightenment *philosophes*, insisted on the priority of understanding over faith, reversing the axiom of Anselm: "I believe so that I may understand." It was Abelard's view that nothing can be believed unless it is first understood and that it was of no use for anyone to tell others something which neither he nor those he taught could grasp with the intellect. He was a Socratic teacher in the classroom who constantly probed questions of theology. Faith for him was often the best hypothesis or estimate.

Abelard believed in the importance of studying the classics in order to foster religious literacy. He contended that Paul and Augustine had made large contributions to understanding Christian doctrine because they were saturated with secular literature before their conversion to Christianity and so had learned how to better express themselves. Abelard concluded, "I therefore judge that the study of secular letters is especially commended by divine dispensation" (Clanchy 1997, 57).

The essence of the scholastic method of education was not to explicate the spirituality of the Scriptures line by line, as the monks did, but to pose wide-ranging questions and then answer them from logical principles as if for the first time. The most famous scholastic question was Anselm's *Cur Deus Homo?* Why did God wish to redeem humanity by becoming incarnate, when it could have been done by any prophet or angel?

Abelard did not invent the scholastic method. In the 1070s, Anselm remarked that his audience demanded that "nothing whatsoever should be asserted here on the authority of Scripture; everything is to be argued by individual and specific investigation." There were thus limits to the faith seeking understanding. Interrogation and response was accepted as an academic procedure before Abelard. Abelard did not clearly express that he understood the limits of understanding seeking faith (Clanchy 1997, 83).

There were two types of teaching in the medieval scholastic world, depending on whether one followed Socrates or Cicero. The Socratic Method of questioning dialogue stimulated clever students, but it could leave weaker ones confused and the syllabus short-changed. While the Ciceronian approach of carefully delivered discourses surveyed the subject elegantly and comprehensively, it did not allow for disagreement, nor did it always capture the audience's attention. Socratic teaching is erratic and inspirational where a Ciceronian approach is professional and practiced. Over the ages most teachers have used both modes: the Ciceronian lecture for surveying a subject and the Socratic seminar for discussion (Clanchy 1997, 85).

Bernard of Clairvaux (1090-1153), rejecting the scholastic method in his attack on Abelard, wrote to the pope,

> Away, away with any idea that the Christian faith should have its limits in the estimates of those academics who doubt everything and know nothing. I go secure in the sentence of the Master of the Gentiles, and I truly know that I shall not be confounded. (In Clanchy 1997, 35)

To Abelard he wrote "You whisper to me that faith is an estimate and you mutter about ambiguity to me, as though nothing were certain" (Clanchy 1997, 35).

The greatest of the scholastics and perhaps the greatest contributor to the Catholic intellectual tradition was Thomas Aquinas (1225-75). Aquinas moved beyond the paradoxical *Sic et Non* of Abelard to build a synthesis of learning from experience and learning from faith, which has characterized Catholic education ever since. In 1879 Pope Leo XIII made Thomas's theology the official norm for Catholic theology. This papal action did much to promote Thomism but may in the end have led to its rejection by many contemporary Catholic philosophers and theologians.

While Thomas introduced Aristotle into Christian theology, he did not depart totally from the Platonism of Augustine. What is prominent in his thought is a great respect for natural knowledge alongside revelation, an appreciation for the natural conditions of human life, a healthy belief that all truths that humans can arrive at are God's truth, and finally a conviction that all truths are capable of being reconciled with one other. While Thomas is not quite in vogue among Catholic theologians today, every age is in need of someone who can build a creative synthesis between faith and culture as Thomas did. We are in need of someone who possesses his intellectual spirit, robust faith, and broad sympathy with the thought of the day.

Thomas's contribution to Catholic educational theory lay in his careful analysis of human teaching and learning. For him learning takes place through one's own discovery or through instruction by a teacher.

Teaching is thus a dynamic process in which there are two causes: the teacher and the active mind of the student. Christian educators before Aquinas, notably Origen and Augustine, had been reluctant to give the human teacher the title of true teacher because of their belief that God alone illuminates human understanding. Aquinas, however, in his treatise *De Magistro* (Mayer 1929), written in 1272, viewed the teacher as the instrumental or intermediary cause of learning.

Aquinas also contributed to education in the Catholic intellectual tradition an optimistic view of the possibilities of human intelligence; a notion that the inculcation of habits and dispositions develop the power of the soul; an emphasis on the importance of sense experience in the life of the mind; and the idea that human intelligence has influence over all aspects of life. He also suggested the overarching aim for all Christian education: the fusion of faith and reason, religion and culture (Donohoe 1958, 105-08).

Various religious orders of men and women nurtured prominent educators in the Catholic educational tradition to hand on the guidelines for faith and conduct to institutions for general education. Aquinas is representative of the Dominican Order of Preachers, who together with the Franciscans Friars were the most influential educators at the renowned University of Paris.

An older religious order that made significant contributions to the educational tradition of the Church was the Benedictines. While education was not a main feature of the Rule of St. Benedict, the rule did seem to presuppose educated monks. While medieval monasteries were surely places of learning, their learning was different from scholastic learning. The Benedictine tradition made a unique contribution to Catholic thought when it suggested that "an intellectual tradition springs from and flourishes within a larger context: concrete practices, an environment, sets of relationships, an atmosphere" (Driscoll 2000, 56). Elements of the Benedictine tradition include its attitude toward time, relationships, and community. Learning takes place through *lectio divina*, the slow meditative reading of the Scriptures and early church spiritual writers. Thus prayer and contemplation are essential practices in a person's education. The use of sermons and spiritual talks as vehicles for education also originated within the monastic context (LeClercq 1959, 72).

According to Thimmish (1972), Jean Leclercq, the outstanding historian of monastic education, has observed that monastic culture during the Carolingian Renaissance in the eleventh and twelfth centuries was increasingly

> personal and creative but more literary than speculative, concerned more with experience than with abstract thought, more with esthetics than with dialectics. He sees this culture as distinct in its time from both nascent scholasticism and a new current of secular humanism. This monastic humanism, as he calls it, read the authors of classical antiquity in an explicitly Christian framework, moralizing them as necessary. It valued the whole quality of life, the prose of daily work and mutual service as well as the poetry of graceful writing and psalmody and contemplation. It integrated the life of the mind with the steady and demanding round of work and prayer that the Rule of Benedict calls a school of the Lord's service. (Thimmish 1992)

Another distinctive Catholic approach to education emerged during the Italian and Northern Renaissance (1320-1600). Medieval Catholicism witnessed the birth of the university, especially the theological and arts faculties at the University of Paris. The educational achievement of Renaissance humanism was the Catholic secondary school. Furthermore, Francisco Petrarch (1304-74), Petrus Paulus Vergerio (1370-1445), Desiderius Erasmus (1466-1536), Thomas More (1478-1535), and John Colet (1467-1519) developed the stimulating scholarship taught to the young in humanist schools. Of the Renaissance educational theory it has been said:

> Combined with continued faith in the Christian tradition as articulated by Augustine, as communicated in Jerome's Bible, as rationalized by Thomism, as synthesized by Dante, this was to be the essence of western civilization down to the early decades of the twentieth century. (Cantor 1993, 561)

The humanist approach that has been the most powerful embodiment of the Catholic intellectual tradition has been a mainstay in the Jesuit school and college, which have flourished for centuries throughout the world. The Jesuits published a *Ratio Studiorum* in 1599, "considered the most comprehensive and certainly the most enduring set of regulations for the conduct of education ever compiled" (Castle 1958, 7). The *Ratio* contained rules for administrators and teachers. It prescribed an ordered sequence of studies and methods for various grades and levels. Inspired by Renaissance humanism, it presented a rigorous seven-year program of classical studies to be taught in secondary schools and colleges. The document was optimistic in calling for the transmission of the wisdom of the Western culture, a synthesis of secular culture with Christian life. True to its scholastic roots "it emphasized a mental training in logical argument: thesis, evidence, objections, discussion and final proof" (Bryk et al. 1993, 19).

The real spirit of Jesuit education, however, is found in Ignatius Loyola's *Spiritual Exercises* (1522-24), the constitutions of the society, and the *pietas literata* of Renaissance humanism. Piety and virtue were fostered through attendance at liturgies, learning of Christian doctrine, daily prayers, examination of conscience, confession, meditation, and prescribed readings, including the lives of the saints. While classical authors made up a large part of the curriculum of the secondary school, Jesuit colleges gave pride of place to the philosophy and theology of Thomas Aquinas. Eventually Jesuit education influenced the educational endeavors of many religious orders of men and women (Elias 2002, 99-104).

The *Ratio* prescribed three stages of education: humanistic, philosophical, and theological. The goal of the humanistic stage was *eloquentia perfecta*, to speak Latin fluently and persuasively. The philosophical stage focused on the thought of Thomas Aquinas. The theological stage, which was also dominated by the teachings of Thomas, was the most important stage to which the others were ultimately directed.

While the Jesuits focused primarily on schools and colleges, elementary or primary schools were the special province of the Brothers of the Christian Schools. Jean Baptiste de la Salle (1651-1719) dedicated the order to the education of poor boys. In his *The Conduct of Schools* (1695) he stressed reading, writing, singing, and religion. The curriculum also included the learning of trades. This handbook emphasized the authority of the teacher and classroom management, which were especially necessary because of the large classes that the brothers taught. Strict religious and moral training was also provided. Detailed instructions were given on the religious formation of the young boys through the catechism. Rewards and punishments were introduced as important elements of pedagogy. De la Salle also established a school for training teachers, whose profession he viewed in an exalted manner as co-workers with Christ in saving souls.

The Catholic intellectual tradition in education received another classic expression in the writings of Cardinal John Newman, notably *The Idea of a University* (1893; rpt. 1982). Newman's ideal bore fruit, however, not in the university which he attempted to establish in Ireland but in his Oratory School in Birmingham, England. Since then his idea of a Christian liberal education has been the educational ideal for numerous schools, colleges, universities, and seminaries in the western world. Newman set before educators the goal of fostering thinking persons for participation in society, whose lives are to be formed by Christian theology. Education for Newman had both intellectual and moral functions. Newman aimed at

> Improving the condition, the status, of the Catholic body . . .
> by giving them juster views, by enlarging and refining their
> minds, in one word, by education. . . . From first to last,
> education, in this large sense of the word, has been my line.
> (Newman 1957, 259)

In his lectures, Newman explained that theology should have a prominent place in all educational institutions. If a university is to be true to its promise to teach all knowledge, it must teach theology. University education should also include a liberal education that views all knowledge as constituting a unity. For Newman the content of theology was the patristic tradition, especially the writings of Clement of Alexandria and Origen. To this he added the educational theory of Augustine of Hippo. Teaching in Catholic schools for Newman is a sacred calling in which teachers supplement the efforts of the interior divine teacher by their example and influence. This education was to be intellectual, religious, and moral as well as include the secular arts and sciences (McCool 2000, 43). At the university level, Newman was more concerned with the transmission of a general Christian culture than he was in the production of specialized research.

The Catholic intellectual tradition in education achieved in the writings of Popes Leo XIII (1810-1903; pope from 1878-1903) and Pius XI (1857-1939; pope from 1922-39) a powerful synthesis of theology, culture, and education that lasted until the second half of the twentieth century. In *Aeterni Patris* (1879) Leo XIII inaugurated a revival of Thomism which influenced all aspects of Catholic intellectual life. Pius XI applied this synthesis to education in his highly influential encyclical, *Divini Illius Magistri*, issued in 1929. This letter made the case for the teaching mission of the Church and rejected certain elements of the new education which were being promoted in schools in Europe and the United States. The document stressed the rights of the church and the family in education while conceding some rights to the states. Newman's vision of the chief characteristic of Catholic education as the integration of theology and culture is prominent in the document:

> It is necessary that all teaching and the whole organization of the school, and its teachers, syllabuses and textbooks in every branch, be regulated by the Christian spirit, under the direction and maternal supervision of the Church, so that religion may be in very truth the foundation and crown of the youth's entire training; and this in every grade school, not only the elementary, but the intermediate and the higher institutions of learning as well. (No. 44)

The encyclical described the ultimate purpose of education in terms that resonate with the Catholic intellectual tradition. It should be directed at the formation of the supernatural person "who thinks, judges and acts constantly and consistently in accordance with right reason illumined by the supernatural light of the example of Christ; in other words, to use the current term, the true and finished [person] of character" (No. 51). This purpose is achieved by appealing to students' natural abilities, experience in the world, and social and economic life, all developed by the power of the supernatural.

The philosophy and theology expounded in this encyclical dominated all discussions of Catholic education until at least the

1960s. As late as 1956 Redden and Ryan could still make this statement about the role of Thomism and neo-scholastic philosophy in Catholic education:

> The only complete, adequate, natural way of thought is scholastic philosophy, which supplies the rational foundations for our supernatural way of life and way of thought. There may be other non-scholastic ways of thought but none of them is complete and adequate, even if it be presupposed they are sound. . . . The *Philosophia Perennis* . . . furnishes basic criteria for differentiating the truth from the false and for passing judgment on all philosophies of education. (1956, vii)

Thus neo-scholasticism supplied the theological framework of Catholic education, which was guided by a particular vision of the origins, nature, and destiny of human persons. Christianity was the basis for an adequate and sound education. John Courtney Murray (1904-67), a prominent Jesuit theologian, went so far as to say that only Christian theology provides the knowledge that determines the goals, context, unity, and intelligibility of education. For Murray the whole person is Christian and Catholic: "the equivalence of these three terms is the basic tenet of the Christian educator" (Veverka 1993, 527.)

Besides the encyclical, the most enduring educational work of the Thomistic revival is Jacques Maritain's *Education at the Crossroads* (1943). This work will receive extensive treatment in this book from Luz Ibarra. While a Frenchman by birth, Maritain (1882-1973) spent many years in academic positions in the United States and was very influential in presenting a Thomistic philosophy of education that attracted great attention from Catholic as well as other educators.

Until the 1960s, neo-Thomistic philosophy as propounded by Maritain and other philosophers was the underlying philosophy of Catholic education in the Catholic world. Neo-Thomism provided a bulwark for Catholics against engaging the complex, relative, and ambiguous in modern thought. Halsey (1980) termed this a triumphal ethos that dominated the entire American Catholic experience before 1960. However, Catholic education theory as rooted in Thomistic philosophy experienced many challenges in the last half of the twentieth century (McCool 2000; Elias 1999, 2002). This Thomistic synthesis has been challenged within the Catholic community itself. It is charged with being based solely on a classicist culture of Greece and Rome, which was erroneously presented as a universal culture. The Jesuit theologian Bernard Lonergan (1973) has questioned this universality because of studies in history and the social sciences which demonstrate a multiplicity of cultures.

Since Vatican II (1962-65), many Catholic philosophers and theologians have largely abandoned the Thomistic synthesis, including its philosophy of education, in the name of contemporary biblical and historical studies as well as other philosophical systems. They are less committed to the patristic tradition and to Greek metaphysics. In fact, the last two popes have clearly not been greatly committed to Thomistic thought (Kerr 2006). Furthermore, Vatican II gave little attention to Thomistic or neo-Scholastic philosophy and theology.

While there are some Catholic scholars who still adhere to Thomism, their writings tend to deal with historical issues and do not to any great extent engage modern problems. Other philosophies have become more dominant among Catholic philosophers including analytic philosophy, existential phenomenology, and even postmodernism. Modern philosophers

> Question whether any philosophy, even aided by theology, can validate a worldview, an integrative interpretation of the universe. The vastness of the universe, the limited nature and uncertainty of human knowledge, the partial and historical character of every viewpoint make any universal worldview philosophically impossible. (McCool 2000, 48)

Many Catholic scholars have bemoaned the lack of commitment to neo-scholasticism as the intellectual foundation of Catholic education. This is so largely because nothing has seemed to have taken its place. Gleason (1995) sees this lacuna as a crisis, since it leaves Catholic educators without a unifying philosophy for their educational endeavors.

After Vatican II, the Catholic intellectual tradition in education became decidedly more theological than philosophical. *Gaudium et Spes* (1965), the Pastoral Constitution of the Church in the Modern World, became the new theological basis for Catholic education, with its statements on the relationship between faith and culture, dialogue with those outside the Catholic community, its emphasis on human freedom, and the commitment to service, especially to the service of the poor. It was this document that lay at the basis of the Land O' Lakes statement that defined Catholic education in United States Catholic universities as exploring with freedom of inquiry the religious heritage of the world through constant discussion without theological or philosophical imperialism (O'Brien 1994, 49).

Education in the Catholic Intellectual Tradition in the United States

Until the mid-1960s Catholic education in the United States was almost synonymous with Catholic schooling in church-established institutions. Parish schools, secondary schools, colleges, universities, and seminaries were the chief focus of the hierarchy and the Catholic people. Most of the educators treated in the present volume wrote about these institutions. It is only around the time of the Second Vatican Council with the writings of Mary Perkins Ryan, Gerard Sloyan, and Gabriel Moran, that Catholic education included the education of young people not in Catholic educational institutions and the education of adults. This change was accompanied by a virtual abandonment of the traditional neo-Scholastic or Thomistic philosophy of education that was the intellectual foundation for Catholic educational institutions.

The nineteenth century saw the emergence of Catholic intellectuals, usually members of the hierarchy, with one notable exception, Orestes Brownson (1803-76). He decried the low academic achievement of parish schools and argued that Catholic attendance at public schools would strengthen the public schools. He was more interested in having the laity "develop their intellectual skills and to play active roles in American society" (Walch 2003, 57). The Church's interest in Catholic education was restricted to the development of the Catholic schools, seminaries, and a small number of Catholic colleges for men and women. Debates ranged over whether Catholics should establish their own schools or make use of public institutions whose education would be supplemented by the instruction in Christian doctrine. Those who favored Catholic institutions largely prevailed.

An early voice promoting the fostering of Catholic intellectual life was Bishop John Spalding of Peoria, who campaigned for the establishment of a Catholic university along the lines of the Catholic University of Louvain, where he did advanced studies. Lucinda Nolan treats the educational efforts of Bishop John Lancaster Spalding (1840-1916), the most prominent Catholic educational philosopher at the end of the nineteenth century into the twentieth century.

The greatest boost to Catholic intellectual life in the United States came with the establishment of the Catholic University of America in Washington, D.C., in 1888. The founding of Catholic University was significant for a number of reasons. First of all, "Catholics needed a university of their own to mobilize the intellectual resources of their tradition and bring them to bear on contemporary issues" (Gleason 1995, 7). Catholic University was able to promote the Thomistic revival inaugurated by Pope Leo XIII. Ideally, the university was also to be the place where the debates among conservative and liberal Catholics could be given a scholarly hearing. Many of the educators included in this collection were influenced by this development. While Archbishop Spalding was not directly influenced by the revival, his education certainly was. His essays and lectures contained many elements of the Thomistic tradition on faith and reason, reason and revelation, revelation and culture. To be sure, Spalding was at the center of the debates about "Americanizing" and "modernizing" Catholicism in this country.

Three twentieth century professor-educators at Catholic University of America were directly influenced by the Thomistic revival. Monsignor Edward Pace (1861-1938), who had a personal relationship with Leo XIII from his student days in Rome, was greatly instrumental in promoting Thomistic philosophy including Thomistic philosophy of education. Father Thomas Shields and Monsignor George Johnson brought Thomism to bear on the entire system of Catholic education in the United States. John L. Elias writes in this collection on Shields (1862-1921), Pace, and Johnson (1889-1944). Each helped to shape Catholic education in the first half of the twentieth century. These men were considered liberal or progressive in their educational theories and practices and each published widely in many fields. All were keenly interested in Catholic schooling and brought a strong psychological emphasis to their writing. In addition,

Pace was the foremost Thomistic philosopher of Catholic education. Shields together with Pace inaugurated *The Catholic Educational Review,* which provided a forum for themselves and many other Catholic educators. George Johnson, the major Catholic spokesperson of his time, guided the Church's educational enterprise through the difficult years of the Depression and the Second World War.

Jacqueline Parascandola's chapter on Virgil Michel (1890-1938) relates his direct and enduring influence on catechetics and religious education through his leadership in the liturgical renewal movement in the early twentieth century. Michel studied with Shields and Pace at Catholic University and is indebted to them for many of his ideas on education. Dom Virgil's vision of liturgy as source and summit for the Christian life originated with his studies in Europe and culminated in his remarkable contributions to catechetical renewal in this country through his teaching, writing, and publishing. The liturgical movement had an intellectual and educational component fostered through liturgical weeks, the journal *Orate Fratres* (later renamed *Worship*), and liturgical arts. Jacqueline Parascandola identifies personalist philosophy, belief in the formative power of liturgy, and commitment to social justice as major components of Michel's thought.

A definitive statement of the Thomistic approach to Catholic education is found in the writings of Jacques Maritain. Luz Ibarra establishes in her essay that the French-born philosopher and political thinker Maritain, though not a citizen of the United States, was the most influential Thomist in the U.S. in the twentieth century and occupies a well-earned place in the volume for his scholarly contributions in writing and lecturing as visiting professor in this country. His Terry lectures given at Yale University, published as *Education at the Crossroads* (1943), brought the Thomistic philosophy of education to the attention of many within and outside the Catholic Church. This philosophy of education prevailed in Catholic education until the 1960s. Maritain promoted an integral humanism in education designed to enable students to realize their potential intellectually, morally, and spiritually. Ibarra makes the case that this philosophy deserves to be retrieved in order to shape contemporary endeavors at all levels of education in the Church.

Lucinda Nolan's chapter on Sister M. Rosalia Walsh (1896-1982) of the Mission Helpers of the Sacred Heart examines the development in the early decades of the twentieth century of a catechetical ministry to Catholic children who attended public schools. Sister Rosalia, writing extensively on psychology of education and methods of teaching, furthered the cause of better preparing catechists for working with children. Nolan's essay defines Walsh's role in introducing the Munich Method and in supporting the establishment of the Confraternity of Christian Doctrine in the United States. Sister Rosalia was herself a beneficiary of the vision of Spalding and Shields who advanced the cause for university education of women religious in the United States.

Harold Horell's study of the career of Neil McCluskey shows that though rooted in the Thomistic philosophy of Catholic education, he assimilated into this intellectual synthesis relevant ideas drawn from his criticism of prominent educators in the United States including Horace Mann, William Harris, and John Dewey. In his attention to moral education, adult education, and Catholic higher education, McCluskey manifested the pragmatic dimension that has characterized United States educators. McCluskey was instrumental in developing the Land O' Lakes Statement (July, 1967), which has greatly influenced the nature and direction of Catholic higher education in the United States. The Statement provoked a decades-long debate about the appropriate character and purview of American Catholic higher education in relation to the hierarchy.

The final two educators treated in the collection, Mary Perkins Ryan (1912-1993) and Gerard Sloyan (b. 1919), began the process of going beyond the Thomistic synthesis to explore other dimensions of the Catholic tradition. They explored biblical, historical, and liturgical dimensions that were not prominent in Catholic educational thought. Both of them were heirs to the new theologies developed in France and Germany during the World Wars. Sloyan was also conversant with the theories and practices of United States education.

Ann Morrow Heekin picks up the later years of the liturgical movement in her reflections on Mary Perkins Ryan's work in writing and publishing in the 1960s and 1970s. In today's terminology Ryan might be described as a pastoral theologian, since she was intensely interested in relating theology to the life and practices of the church. Like Virgil Michel, Ryan (1912-1993) saw the liturgy as central in the Church's catechetical endeavors. Ryan was also influenced by the writings of the French theologians who moved away from the Thomistic synthesis to focus on the Scriptures and writings of the early church fathers. As an author and editor, Ryan brought attention to the pastoral nature of catechesis and the importance of adult education. In a highly controversial book, *Are Parochial Schools the Answer?* (1964), she argued that Catholic schools could not and should not bear the burden of all of Catholic education. Heekin's chapter highlights Ryan's struggles and efforts through collaboration with many of the outstanding persons in Catholic religious education to advance catechetical renewal into the post-Vatican II years, while making the claim that history has not afforded her due recognition.

Twentieth-century Catholic religious education owes an immense debt of gratitude to Gerard Sloyan, whose lifetime endeavors have touched nearly every aspect of theology. The last chapter, written by Philip Franco, frames Sloyan's remarkable career. Having pursued recent scholarship and a personal interview with the Catholic University of America professor, Franco highlights for the reader the many disciplinary realms that have benefited from Sloyan's efforts over the last six decades including liturgy, scripture, ecumenism, preaching, ecumenism, religious education and catechetics. It is fitting that his story closes this collection, though in no way is his story closed. Franco's chapter ends with a section on Sloyan's continuing efforts in a field he has been so instrumental in shaping.

The need for scholars and teachers such as those presented here has never been greater than it is today. The whole of the Catholic intellectual tradition, as a body of work, a "way of looking at things", and a "way of doing things," is dependent on men and women who like those celebrated in this collection are committed to the task of passing on the tradition.

While the book ends with the impressive work of Father Sloyan, the tradition of education in the Catholic intellectual tradition has continued throughout the second half of the twentieth century into the twenty-first century. Influential educators in higher education have included Theodore Hesburgh, Paul Reinert, and Roy Deferrari. Catechetical and religious education scholars have included Gabriel Moran, Maria Harris, Berard Marthaler, Francis Buckley, Mary Charles Bryce, Mary Boys, and Thomas Groome. The work of these and many others has been fostered by Catholic educational institutions of higher education such as Catholic University of America, Fordham University, Boston College, Dayton University, the University of San Francisco, and Loyola University in Chicago. The contribution of Catholic educators to the Catholic intellection tradition continues today in the work of young scholars attending these and other Catholic institutions of higher education. Remembering, handing on, and contributing to this rich traditional heritage remain a task of significant importance for us all.

John Lancaster Spalding: Prelate and Philosopher of Catholic Education

LUCINDA A. NOLAN

> Religion is judged by its influence on faith and conduct, on hope and love, on righteousness and life–by the education it gives.
>
> –John Lancaster Spalding (1905, 129)

No single bishop in the history of the American Catholic hierarchy has commanded the respect and attention of scholars in the area of religious education as much as John Lancaster Spalding (1840-1919), first bishop of Peoria, Illinois. While written essays and lectures give the reader of history a record of his philosophy of education, he was no mere theorist. Through the decades of his religious life which spanned the years between the Civil and First World Wars, Spalding collaborated on the production of the *Baltimore Catechism* (1885), was instrumental in the founding of the Catholic University of America, heralded women's education, edited textbook series, and modeled the pedagogies he extolled in his writings. While falling short of developing a systematic philosophical treatment of education, Spalding nevertheless stressed the importance of religious education and the roles of family, church, state, and school in the development of Christian moral values throughout his long career (De Hovre 1934, 173).

Following a brief biography, this chapter examines the philosophical underpinnings of Spalding's writings on education and concludes with the identification of his major contributions to Catholic religious education in this country. The case for the singularity of this bishop's concern for Catholic education in the

United States is its core focus. The author is indebted to many fine historians who have built up a substantial body of work on this giant of the American Catholic Church. Included in this group of scholars are John Tracy Ellis, Merle Curti, and Franz Hovre, as well as several scholars who have done dissertation studies on of the life, educational theory, and social ideas of Spalding. In 1961, in the Gabriel Richard Lecture to the National Catholic Education Association, John Tracy Ellis said:

> Both by the spoken and written word, employed over a period of forty years, John Lancaster Spalding earned the distinction of having made the most significant contribution to education of any single member of the American Catholic community, as well as having won an honored place in the general educational picture of the United States of his time. (1961, 50)

The Spaldings and American Catholicism

The Spalding and Lancaster families arrived in the United States around 1650, having left England most likely as a result of the persecution of Catholics in England at the time. The Lancaster family traced its roots to Edward III of England (Schroll 1944, xv). Both families resided in the Maryland colony and both families, some two hundred years later, moved west to Kentucky as part of the Maryland Colonization League. Kentucky, in the vision of these early Catholic pioneers, was to be "the cradle of Catholicity in the West" (Schroll 1944, 27). In 1839, John's father, Richard Martin Spalding, a landowner and politician, married Mary Jane Lancaster and together they raised a large family. John, the eldest, was born in Lebanon, Kentucky, on June 2, 1840. Young John was privileged to be a member of such an old and well-established American Catholic family. The Spalding family's long-time residency was a rarity amid the large number of foreign-born priests in this country at the time.

The education of John Lancaster Spalding was overseen first by his mother and later by his uncle on his father's side, Bishop Martin John Spalding of Louisville. Mary Jane Lancaster Spalding schooled young "Lank" until he was twelve years of age. For a woman of that time, she was well educated. An early graduate of Loretto Academy, her academic achievements attest to her gift of remarkable intelligence. Throughout her life, she held education as one of life's highest values. Mary Jane Spalding taught John that "the purpose of human life is to know truth, to love goodness, to do right, that so, having made ourselves god-like, we may be forever be with God" (Spalding 1890, 151). John Lancaster Spalding attributed his love of things of the mind to his upbringing and later scholars would give credit for his advocacy of women's education to Mary Jane Spalding's influence (Schroll, xvi).

Spalding attended St. Mary's College in Lebanon, Kentucky (a secondary school in today's terms) and later Mount St. Mary's College, a *petit séminaire,* in Emmitsburg, Maryland (Sweeney 1965, 37). In 1858, he transferred to Mount St. Mary's of the West in Cincinnati, Ohio. Spalding later graduated from Mount St. Mary's of the West as the class valedictorian.

The sharp and intelligent mind of young Spalding was channeled early into the arts of debate and rhetoric and it was evident that he would excel at oration. It is not known at exactly what point he determined to study for the priesthood, but it was largely his admiration for his uncle Martin Spalding and his observations of the clerical lifestyle that led him to become a candidate for the diocese of Louisville (Sweeney, 43). In the fall of 1859, following the advice and arrangements of his uncle, Spalding sailed for the American College of the Immaculate Conception in Louvain, Belgium. Martin Spalding had been influential in the founding of the American College in Louvain and it must be noted that it later served as a model in the vision of both the uncle and his nephew for an American Catholic university. John Lancaster Spalding exhibited an exceptional intellect and was soon enrolled in the more advanced courses of study at the Catholic University of Louvain.

In the summer of 1862, while still studying in Europe, John Lancaster Spalding had occasion to attend a meeting of the Catholic Union at Aix-la-Chapelle (Sweeney 1965, 53-54). The Catholic Union was an assembly of lay social groups that had been forming since 1848 throughout the German states. These groups of church and national leaders gathered to discuss issues of Catholic concern: "Side by side with the cardinals, bishops, princes, and the learned professors there sat mechanics, carpenters, shoemakers" (Sweeney 1965, 53). Spalding observed that the assembly gathered together there "in active thought and cooperation for the furtherance of definite and religious social ends. The brotherhood of the race was there . . . and one felt the breathing of a divine Spirit" (Spalding 1877, 246). This was European Social Catholicism in practice and Spalding was getting an early dose of it. He saw in the Catholic congress at Aix-la-Chapelle an organizational model for the American Catholic Church, one allowing for the cooperation of all social groups. He wrote:

> If we wish to be true to the great mission which God has given us, the time has come when American Catholics must take up the works which do not specially concern any one diocese more than another, but whose significance will be as wide as the nation's life. (Spalding 1877, 247-48)

The stirrings of a vision of a national Church actively and publicly engaged in social issues excited the mind of John Lancaster Spalding as a young man studying for the priesthood in the climate of European Social Catholicism.

Spalding earned bachelor and master degrees in sacred theology and was ordained into the priesthood in 1863. Spalding was in Europe at the time of the issuance of Pius IX's *Syllabus of Errors* (1864). Spalding had little to say against it at the time but years later, in a somewhat dramatic shift, he came to see that there was little way to avoid the onset of modernity and so there should be "a *rapprochement* between American Catholicism and the spirit of the age (Sweeney 1965, 67).

After some travel in Germany and a brief period of studying canon law in Rome, Spalding was given a prophetic mission by Father De Néve of the American College of the Immaculate Conception at Louvain. Father De Néve proposed that the young priest consecrate his first years of service to African-Americans who suffered from enslavement and oppression in America. Upon returning to Louisville in 1865, Spalding realized that the growing population of newly emancipated slaves was in need of pastoral assistance. Insisting on the need for a separate parish of their own, Spalding believed that, with persistence, the funds might be found so that this increasing Catholic population might be kept within the fold. In 1870, St. Augustine's parish and school was dedicated and Spalding, its young pastor, lived happily and simply for a time among the parish members. The parish remains vibrant today (Sweeney 1965, 69).

Father Spalding's early years of priesthood signaled to his peers that he would be a force to be reckoned with in the American Catholic Church. His oratory and writing skills quickly gained him recognition. In 1866, at only twenty-six years of age, Spalding was chosen to accompany Bishop Blanchet of Oregon to the Second Plenary Council in Baltimore as his theologian (Schroll, *xvii*). Spalding's biographer, David Sweeney, writes that Spalding's address to the Council, entitled "The Visible Head of the Church," acknowledged Christ's choice of Peter to preserve and teach the faith, but that "it was the privilege of the Church, notwithstanding her immutable constitution, to adapt herself, without harm to her unity and catholicity, to the various modifications of human society" (1965, 79). The Church in the United States was not different from the Church of Europe, but the context in which it existed was different enough to warrant variances. As Sweeney notes, this predates any discussion of "Americanism," but foreshadows Spalding's reaction to the apostolic letter of Leo XIII, *Testem benevolentiae* in 1899.

After the death of his uncle, Archbishop Martin Spalding of Baltimore, in 1872, Spalding was invited by Isaac Hecker to the New York Paulist residence to write the archbishop's biography in his stead. In little over a year the work was completed and was hailed by Orestes Brownson as one of the finest American examples of the biographical literary genre ever written (Sweeney 1965, 95).

The years in New York afforded Spalding opportunities to develop his speaking skills as well as his knowledge of the Catholic educational system. He came to see that public schools were necessary for building up a responsible citizenship in a democratic setting, but that, lacking a religious component, they were destined to produce nothing more than "improved machines." Without compromise, he upheld religious education as indispensable for the development of virtue and for the realization of the only complete life–a life in God (Curti 1935, 356). While in New York, young Spalding became more involved in issues of school and education. The Depression of 1877 led to his involvement in the Irish Colonization Association, a group that sought to help Irish families leave the destitution of overcrowded cities to find land to farm in rural areas. That same year, when Father Michael Hurley, pastor of

St. Patrick's Parish in Peoria, declined to accept appointment as first bishop of the new diocese of Peoria, John Lancaster Spalding was nominated. After some initial concern in the Vatican about his orthodoxy, Spalding was appointed and he accepted "in spite of an apparent reluctance to shoulder the burdens of the episcopacy" (Sweeney 1965, 107).

Among the key issues that captured Spalding's energy and attention during the 1880s and 1890s were the development of the *Baltimore Catechism*, the founding of the Catholic University of America (1888), the Catholic school questions, the World's Columbian Exposition in Chicago (1893), and the Americanist controversy.

The Third Plenary Council of Baltimore (1884) gave major impetus to the eminent role Spalding came to play in Catholic education in the United States. The issue of a national catechism that would give unity to the presentation of the faith was of great concern to many bishops and Spalding was appointed to the Council committee to address the matter. The move to develop a national catechism was quickly approved and a draft prepared by Monsignor Janarius De Concilio of St. Michael's in Newark, New Jersey, was presented to the Council just eight days later (Mongoven 2000, 40-42). The Council closed on December 7, 1884, and Spalding was left with the task of collecting suggested revisions from the archbishops in order to expedite the publication of the catechism. He was anxious to complete the work and did so in less than a year. Sweeney described the outcome:

> While it is a tribute to the bishops of the commission, and especially Bishop Spalding, that within six months after the end of the Council there appeared the first edition of the *Baltimore Catechism*, the bishop of Peoria was undoubtedly relieved, as he said, to get the work off his hands so that he might devote his time and energies to what would be a more difficult task, namely the making of a Catholic university a reality. (Sweeney 1965, 175-76)

There is some evidence that the revised catechism was prematurely submitted for publication before all the archbishops had time to respond. Anne Marie Mongoven wrote: "Spalding, a dynamic and self-confident man, did not follow the recommended procedures" (41).

Foreseeing long discussion and argument among the archbishops, Spalding submitted the catechism to John Cardinal McClosky for his imprimatur and shortly thereafter James Cardinal Gibbons gave the text his approval. Mongoven described the results:

> The *Baltimore Catechism* was a small book, seventy-two pages, with 421 questions in thirty-seven chapters. It was not universally well received when it was first published. An anonymous critic writing in *Pastoral Blatt*, a monthly periodical from St. Louis, found the work to be pedagogically unsuitable and theologically inadequate. . . . While the *Baltimore Catechism* was endorsed in some dioceses, from its beginning it encountered serious resistance from both instructors and bishops. (Mongoven 2000, 41-42)

Whether or not Bishop Spalding can be blamed for the inadequacies of the catechism remains unclear. Monsignor De Concilio, another author to which the writing has been attributed, was a respected scholar and a former professor of theology at Seton Hall's Immaculate Conception Seminary (Mahwah, NJ). Spalding made what he thought were the necessary changes. To many minds, the text was theologically flawed. Nevertheless, the *Baltimore Catechism* would be the primary sourcebook for Catholic religious instruction for decades to come with little or no revision occurring until 1941. As noted, one possible, and most likely the primary reason for Spalding's haste in getting the catechism published was his desire to begin work on the task closest to his heart: the development of a Catholic university on American soil. Years before, Spalding and his uncle Martin had discussed the possibility of establishing in this country a national university along the lines of the American College of the Immaculate Conception in Louvain, Belgium. The younger Spalding thought seminary training of the time narrow and limited to preparation for professional practice. He held that

> priests who are zealous, earnest, self-sacrificing, who to piety join discretion and good sense, rarely possess the intellectual culture of which I am speaking, for the simple reason that a university and not a seminary is the school in which this kind

of education is received. That the absence of such trained intellects is a most serious obstacle of the progress of the Catholic faith, no thoughtful man will doubt or deny. . . . (Spalding 1895, 214-16)

At the time of the Third Plenary Council, James Cardinal Gibbons invited Spalding to speak on the need for higher education of the clergy and the need for an American Catholic university. Oddly, Spalding asked to be excused, only to later change his mind. Mary Gwendolen Caldwell declared her intention to donate a large amount of a personal inheritance for such a university project, thus bringing hope to a long held dream. Much debate ensued over issues of financing, where to locate such a university, and how much control the twenty-one years old Miss Caldwell might exercise. Approval for a "higher seminary" came just as the Council was coming to a close, "but the seed that was planted in 1884 is today the university of which Spalding had dreamed (Sweeney 1965, 170). While Miss Caldwell stipulated that she be named foundress, Spalding is widely credited for his zealous efforts in establishing the Catholic University of America. James Cardinal Gibbons stated:

All great works have their inception in the brain of some great thinker. God gave such a brain, such a man, in Bishop Spalding. With his wonderful intuitionary power, he took in all the meaning of the present and the future Church in America. If the Catholic University is today an accomplished fact, we are indebted for its existence in our generation, in no small measure, to the persuasive eloquence and convincing arguments of the Bishop of Peoria. (Gibbons 1916, 195)

Years later, John Tracy Ellis heralded Spalding's accomplishments:

The Catholic University of America will, indeed, always remain the principal monument to Spalding's memory as an educator. . . . Both by the spoken and written word, employed over a period of forty years, John Lancaster Spalding earned the distinction of having made the most significant contribution to education of any single member of the

American Catholic community, as well as having won an honored place in the general educational picture of the United States of his time. (Ellis 1961, 50)

In 1892 Spalding was appointed to oversee the Catholic educational exhibit at the World's Columbian Exposition in Chicago, which was ultimately successful in making public the practical and philosophical contributions of the nation's Catholic school system and its zealous pursuit of Christian education. In an article written for the *Catholic World* about the upcoming Catholic exhibit, Spalding stated that there could be no compromise: "The Catholic Church is irrevocably committed to the doctrine that education is essentially religious, that purely secular schools give instruction, but do not properly educate" (Spalding 1892a, 4). The article proposed a religious education congress of Catholic schoolteachers to stimulate learning and discussion in the science of pedagogy. Spalding also hoped the educationally-based exhibition would lead to the development of a journal of Catholic education. He asked:

> What more interesting subject is there than education? It is a question of life, of religion of country; it is a question of science and art; it is a question of politics, of progress, of civilization; it is a question even of commerce, of production of wealth. What could be more instructive than a series of articles on the history of education, on the great teachers and educational reformers, on pedagogics as a science and as an art; on educational methods; on the bearing of psychology upon questions of education; on hygiene in its relation to the health of teachers and pupils; on the educational values of the various branches of knowledge; on personal influence as a factor in education; on the best means of forming true religious character? (1892a, 8)

Spalding's work in bringing about this exhibit cannot be stressed enough. Speaking at Spalding's Golden Jubilee ceremonies, Archbishop Glennon of St. Louis remarked that the "exposition gave an opportunity for his genius with the result that America was made to realize that there were millions who believed in and were prepared to defend the platform of Christian education" (*Ceremonies*, 16).

The 1890s were years of major educational controversies between public and parochial school systems and Spalding never shied away from stating his views. While state schools had their place, any school that excluded religion, being less than holistic in its approach to the students, was inferior. Spalding, whose rhetoric was less inflammatory than some of the other Catholic voices, recognized both school systems would inevitably have to exist side by side. American Catholics should, he believed, recognize the freedom inherent in this great country's founding and acknowledge the universal right of all people to a religion and an education of their choice. The focus and energy should be on improving methodologies and teacher training, not in arguing over what seemed to him the inevitable problems (Sweeney 1965, 203). In addition to the suspicions of the general American public concerning the rising numbers of Catholics and Catholic schools, the Holy See's plan to send a permanent apostolic delegate to the United States fanned the flames of anti-Catholicism. Spalding strongly opposed Leo XIII's proposal:

> This opposition arises from the fixed and strongly-rooted desire, which exists throughout the whole English-speaking world to manage as far as possible one's own affairs. . . . Catholics who live here, and who, wherever they were born, are true American citizens, feel the impulse of this desire and wish to manage as far as possible their own affairs. They are devoted to the Church; they recognize in the Pope Christ's Vicar, and gladly receive from him the doctrines of faith and morals; but for the rest, they ask him to interfere as little as may be. (1892b)

Spalding made significant contributions to the development of Catholic social thought during the years of his service. Involved deeply in causes of anti-racism, anti-sexism, immigration, and labor disputes, Spalding served as a role model to others, including a young priest named John Ryan, who later became the premier writer and spokesperson on social justice for the Catholic Church. Ryan considered Spalding "undoubtedly the greatest literary artist in the entire history of the American hierarchy" and acknowledged that the Bishop of Peoria had "a greater influence upon my general philosophy of life, my ideals, my sense of comparative values than any other contemporary writer" (Ryan 1941, 28).

Keenly aware of the plight of all immigrants, Spalding was chosen to preside over the Board of Directors of the Irish Catholic Colonization Association in 1879, a position he held until the dissolution of the agency (Sweeney 1965, 120-21). In 1880, Spalding wrote *The Religious Mission of the Irish People and Catholic Colonization.*

Spalding became embroiled in the tense debate concerning Americanism, which cautioned against making concessions with regard to faith, doctrine, and ways of living with other religions or governments, especially the American democracy experiment. In March of 1900, just nine-months following Leo XIII's condemnation of the ideas tabbed as the "heresy of Americanism," Spalding gave a sermon in Rome that came to be called the Gesú discourse on the topic of "Education and the Future of Religion." Spalding pleaded for intellectual freedom and made his case for the necessity of addressing the science and culture of the times. John Tracy Ellis wrote that this sermon was

> his most notable pulpit performance. Delivered at a time when the memory of all informed men was still alive with the subject of Americanism, it constituted a bold challenge to those who seemed determined to find doctrinal errancy among American Catholics. . . . The leading Protestant weekly of the United States made it the subject of an enthusiastic editorial in which it was said, "For the intelligence, courage and sound Americanism of this admirable sermon Catholics and Protestants may be equally grateful. Such a leader, who is scholar, theologian and poet, is an honor to his Church. (1961, 79)

European modernists and liberal bishops in the United States hailed Spalding for his firm stance against any who would claim as heresy any of the actual practices of the American Catholic Church.

The twentieth century marked a decline in the Bishop of Peoria's health. Shifts in episcopal assignments in major U.S. dioceses meant political maneuvering for Spalding. Considered for the dioceses of Milwaukee, San Francisco, and Chicago, he preferred to remain in

Peoria. What energy Spalding did have went into the building of The Spalding Institute, a secondary school for young men of his diocese and serving at the request of Theodore Roosevelt on the Strike Council for the anthracite coal crisis of 1902. He remained active in speaking and fund-raising on behalf of the Catholic University of America. His ideas would encourage Father Thomas E. Shields to establish the Sisters College of the Catholic University of America (Ellis 1961, 81-82).

Spalding said in 1905 of the stroke that left him partially paralyzed and considerably weakened, "I was intoxicated with work and God saw it and struck me down" (Sweeney 1965, 343). His remaining years were spent in such a state of ill health that in 1908 he was forced to resign as bishop of Peoria. Old rumors about his support of the heresy of Americanism threatened to be exposed and those who knew and respected Spalding sought to protect him from "further harassment and humiliation" (Sweeney 1965, 351). He was elevated to the rank of titular Archbishop of Scythopolis and moved into a home overlooking Peoria built for him by the priests of the diocese. In 1913, Spalding managed with some assistance to preside over his golden sacerdotal jubilee mass where he was addressed as "the prophet of Catholic higher education" (Sweeney 1965, 368). He died shortly thereafter on August 25, 1916, at the age of 76.

Spalding's biographer, David Sweeney, O.F.M., wrote:

> Because of Spalding, education in the United States, and particularly higher education, was changed forever, and for the best. He was, by determination, if not explicitly, a champion of the religious and political pluralism so cherished in our day, and a staunch advocate of intellectual freedom. (1965, 373)

Archbishop John J. Glennon spoke these words at Spalding's funeral:

> I need not recount for you what Archbishop Spalding has done for the cause of Christian education. How he has sought to unify and strengthen the parochial school system, to bring it from the narrow confines of race or language to the broad platform of Christian teaching; how a national exposition gave an opportunity for his genius, with the result that America

was made to realize that there were millions who believed in, and were prepared to defend the platform of Christian education. (Cosgrove 1960, 107)

The philosophy underpinning Spalding's understanding of education is neither comprehensive nor is it systematic. It may be pieced together from his writings and public addresses. As time went on, education became increasingly pervasive in his thought. The next section addresses key elements of Spalding's philosophy of education.

The Divine Impulse and
the Human Pursuit of Truth

The philosophy of education put forth by John Lancaster Spalding has been characterized as a unique combination of German idealism and American progressivism (Barger 1976, 37) with some discernable influences of the dominant philosophy of education of his early school years, scholasticism. The ultimate end of all humankind's educational pursuits was an eternal life lived out with the divine. This life, however, was to be lived in this world through engagement with all of creation, including cultural development and scientific discoveries. In 1863, as a young man studying in Louvain, Spalding wrote to his uncle, Bishop Martin Spalding: "You would almost say that I am German, I am so mysteriously and deeply philosophical" (Cosgrove 1960, 41).

The eclectic nature of the young priest's views did not go unnoticed and there is evidence that he earned a reputation "at the Roman Curia for being a man of 'liberal' views" (Ellis 1961, 45). Robert Barger wrote that "although [Spalding] was educated in the Neo-Scholastic tradition at he University of Louvain, he did not share the emphasis on truth and the intellect that is the heritage of Aristotle and Aquinas" (1976, 38). Spalding's oft-spoken views on progress included comments on Aquinas as part of a "vague and incomplete . . . medieval scheme of education" (Spalding 1890, 196). Yet, paradoxically Spalding also identified with Aquinas as one who was, like himself, willing to speak against the conventions of his time. Though Spalding was an accomplished historian of education, he was

not inclined to glorify the Middle Ages as a golden era for the
Church. Rather he saw it as a "privilege to live at a time when
knowledge is increasing more rapidly even than population and
wealth" and that scholars should endeavor to "keep pace with the
onward movement of the mind" (Spalding 1890, 196). He
continued, "To turn away from this outburst of splendor and power;
to look back to pagan civilization or Christian barbarism—is to love
darkness more than light" (196).

Spalding's strong belief in progress and the ascent of the mind
toward the divine were hallmarks of a philosophy of education that
predated the progressive educational thought of John Dewey by some
twelve years. In "Progressive Education and Bishop Spalding," Edward
J. Power compares Spalding's educational perspectives with those of
Dewey and the progressives and finds that on points of progress, life
and growth, nature, self-activity, and sociality Spalding anticipated all
that would be said (Powers 1953, 673). The primary distinction that
Spalding made was the idea that the human person was more than a
social animal (the naturalist position). For Spalding, the human person
was the jewel of God's created universe and moral character, love, and
will were as important, if not more so, than the pursuit of truth and
intellectual activity (Barger 1976, 38). Reason and the intellect, God's
great gifts to humankind, must be used in the service of living the
moral life. Spalding reflected:

> We get nearer to the heart of being when we act rightly than
> when we speculate acutely. The chief value of the study of
> philosophy lies in the exercise it gives the mind, which, when
> made strong and luminous, is best put to use, not in
> metaphysical inquiry, but in directing life to moral ends.
> (1901a, 65)

Wisdom is in the service of the will, which is oriented by it to the
practice of virtue and moral rectitude. But for the scholar, Spalding
held education and the things of the mind as the sublime and most
delightful of pursuits. "All things have an educational value" (1901b,
173) and Bishop Spalding believed one of the greatest values of
education is that it is the corrector of inequality in human beings. In
education, the end is the "idea of human perfection" (1901b, 89).

The following sections address three salient characteristics of Spalding's philosophy of education as culled from lectures, essays, and articles. The end of education is to prepare oneself "to bow before the sovereignty of God, to seek His paternal guidance, to acknowledge His supreme authority, to humble oneself in His presence as becometh a creature, to become a little child" (Hovre 1934, 192.)

The Supremacy of the Gift of Life in Religion and Education

Life alone has absolute value: the rest, as religion, philosophy, art, science, wealth and position, have worth only in so far as they are related to life, proceed from it, express its meaning, and increase its power and beauty.

–John Lancaster Spalding (1901a, 284)

Spalding's emphasis on life as the Creator's greatest gift led to his understanding of the abundant life as the ultimate goal of all religion and education: "Religion is life in and with God through Jesus Christ; and the stronger, the purer, the more loving the life, the higher and holier is one's religion" (Spalding 1902b, 147). The Catholic religion is more a way of life to be lived than a doctrinal body to which one would adhere. The bishop wrote:

Since education is furtherance of life, its value is manifest. Life is the only good, and the supreme good is the highest life. At the heart of all things, giving them reality, endurance, splendor, and serviceableness, there reigns not death, but life. Nothing has worth except for living. . . .

What can give us wealth and power and goodness and freedom and joy? Education and education alone. . . .

Religion is judged by its influence on faith and conduct, on hope and love, on righteousness and life, by the education it gives. (Spalding 1905, 1969, 127-29)

Religious education leads to a higher and richer life. It is "a kind of celestial education, which trains the soul to godlike life" (Spalding 1895, 185). Education and religion act together in bringing about the blessings of "a larger liberty, wider life, purer delights, and a juster sense of the relative values of the means and ends which lie within or reach. . . . Wisdom and religion converge, as love and knowledge meet in God" (Spalding 1895, 191). For Spalding, a religious education is essential to the attainment of the highest qualities of human life.

Ironically, it was Spalding's passion for living the higher life of religion and education that connected his thought to the American spirit of progressivism. He wrote of this alignment of Catholic and American thought,

> If we are to act along an inner line upon the life of America, we must bring to the task a divine confidence that our Catholic faith is akin to whatever is good and true or fair . . . so it is prepared to welcome whatever progress mankind may make. . . and to cooperate without misgivings or afterthought, in whatever promises to make for higher and holier life. (Spalding 1900, 76)

Indeed, Spalding's exalted view of life as the supreme reality would place him within the parameters of progressivism. De Hovre pointed to the foundational element of Spalding's pedagogy: "Real life is a process of education and education is a life-process" (1934, 171). Humans cooperate with God in the ongoing creation and progress of life to the extent that they participate in life-enhancing religious education of self and others.

Spalding's philosophy of education is grounded in his elevation of the value of human life above all else. Life as the end and means of religious education gives coherence and consistency to this philosophy. This sort of education for life and life-process does not end. Spalding believed that

> education is not merely or chiefly a scholastic affair; it is a life-work, to be carried on with unwearying patience, until death bids us cease or introduces us to a world of diviner opportunities. The wise and good are they who grow old still learning many things, entering day by day into more vital communion with truth, beauty, and righteousness, gaining

more and more complete initiation into the life of the wisest, noblest, and strongest who have thought, loved and accomplished. (Spalding 1905, 92)

Addressing the 1901 gathering of the National Education Association, Bishop Spalding gave his views on the close relationship between the Christian understanding of the sacredness of life and the ultimate goal of education:

Faith in the goodness of life, issuing in ceaseless efforts to develop it to higher and higher potencies, has determined our world-view and brought us to understand that the universe is a system of forces whose end is the education of souls; that the drama enacted throughout the whole earth and all the ages has for its central idea and guiding motive the progressive spiritual culture of mankind, which is the will of God as revealed in the conduct and teaching of Christ. (Spalding 1902b, 209)

The Pursuit of Truth as a Religious Endeavor

All truth is orthodox, whether it come to us through revelation, reaffirmed by the voice of the Church, or whether it come in the form of certain scientific knowledge. Both the Church and the men of science must accept the validity of reason, and must therefore hold that reason cannot contradict itself. Knowledge and faith both do God's work.

–John Lancaster Spalding (1902b, 156)

Spalding believed there was no higher purpose in life than the pursuit of truth. This is part of the human struggle toward perfection in all areas of life, but the nature of the pursuit is, for Spalding, religious. Likewise, Spalding held that truth is housed in discoveries of all kinds–intellectual and affective, scientific and theological, natural and supernatural. A firm supporter of liberal education, he believed strongly in a broad curriculum that included the arts, science, literature, theology, music, and history. All knowledge is related and all truth is orthodox. Spalding wrote:

All facts are sacred, since the truth is sacred. . . . Our Catholic
faith is akin to whatever is true or good or fair; that as it allied
itself with the philosophy, the literature, the art, and the forms
of government of Greece and Rome, so it is prepared to
welcome whatever progress mankind may make, whether it be
material or moral or intellectual; nay, that it is prepared to
cooperate, without misgivings or afterthought, in whatever
promises to make for higher and holier life. (1900, 74, 79)

The deep pursuit of self-knowledge, insight into life's mysteries, and
comprehension of things natural and supernatural are the most human of all
efforts. For Spalding, "We are human because God is present in the soul; we
have reason because the divine light shines with us" (1902b, 155). Therefore,
humanity need not fear the consequences of the discovery truth. He asked:

Does the religion of Christ, the absolute and abiding faith,
need the defense of concealment, or of sophistical apology, or
of lies? Truth is the supreme good of the mind, as holiness of
the heart; and truthfulness is the foundation of righteousness.
. . . If only we go deep enough, we never fail to find God and
the soul. . . . What God has permitted to happen, man may
be permitted to know. . . .
    The fundamental principle of the Catholic theologian and
apologist is that there is harmony between revelation rightly
understood, and the facts of the universe rightly known; and
since this is so, the deepest thought and the most certain
knowledge must furnish the irrefragable proof of the truth of
our faith. (1902b, 159-60)

    From the point of view of the first bishop of Peoria, education, and more
specifically a religious education, is a lifelong, humanizing endeavor which has
the potential to elevate humanity to a higher level, closer to the divine that
transcends all reality. He was not naïve enough to believe that all would spend
their life's energy in this pursuit, but for those who are able to,

The unseen world ceases to be a future world; and is
recognized as the very world in which we now think and love,
and so intellectual and moral life passes into the sphere of

religion. We no longer pursue ideals which forever elude us, but we become partakers in the divine life; for in giving ourselves to the Eternal and Infinite we find God in our souls. (Spalding 1890, 171)

Religious Education and Moral Development

The aim and end of education is to bring out and strengthen man's faculties, physical, intellectual and moral; to call into healthful play his manifold capacities; and to promote also with due subordination their harmonious exercise; and this to fit him to fulfill his high and heaven-given mission, and to attain his true destiny.

–John Lancaster Spalding (1894, 128)

Humanity's perfection in Christ is the ideal of all education, but in particular, Christian religious education. Without such a vision, the Christian identity is blurred or lost. Spalding's philosophy of education was that it be essentially religious because he saw religion as "enveloping and diffusing itself through the whole life of man. It must therefore be a fundamental part of his education. To exclude religion is equivalent to denying its truth and efficacy" (Grollmes 1969, 242-43). All truth, all things, are to be seen in light of their relation to the divine. All education then must be directed toward this sort of growth. Spalding believed that

growth is development, and the universal means God has given us to unfold and strengthen our being is education. . . . Religion itself, the worship of God in spirit and in truth, can be maintained only by education. . . . To educate rightly, we must touch the depths of man's being; we must speak to him in the innermost recesses where faith, hope, and love are born where God is present and appealing. (1902b, 149-50)

The enlightened human spirit sees all things and all truth as "bound together in harmony around the feet of the eternal Father" (Spalding 1902b, 166). Morality serves to strengthen religion and schools, and therefore we should strive to become centers of moral influence. For

Spalding this is the essence of the Catholic view of education. He queried, "Do we not all recognize that to quicken the wits and leave the conscience untouched is not education?" (Spalding 1900, 99). Any hope of a moral transformation of humanity and society is seated in right education and a right education is religious by nature.

Education for moral growth and development does not have to exclude the intellectual aspects of a proper education. Spalding's holistic understanding of the human person gave impetus to a balanced philosophy of education where reason and intellect were as important as the affective and moral dimensions. He wrote, "Man exists that he may grow; and human growth is increase in the power to know and love and help, and to promote this is the purpose of education" (1905, 137).

Essentially, character development, the primary aim and end of all education, demands the environment of a religious and liberal education:

> Information is, of course, indispensable; . . . but the end is a cultivated mind. . . .
>
> In a rightly educated mind intellectual culture is inseparable from moral culture. . . . Moral character is the only foundation on which the temple of life can stand symmetrical and secure; and hence there is a general agreement among serious thinkers that the primary aim and end of education is to form character. (1902b, 234)

Religious education is best suited to this task, in Spalding's view, because "conduct springs from what we believe, cling to, love, and yearn for, vastly more than from what we know" (1895, 170). For Spalding, "Religion is the profoundest and most quickening educational influence. . . . It has been and is the chief school in which mankind have learned to understand the worth and sacredness of human life" (Spalding 1905, 117). Religion, Spalding believed, was to be judged by the education it gives and "the deeper tendency" of his time was not "to exclude religion from any vital process, but rather to widen the content of the idea of religion until it embrace the whole life of man" (Spalding 1895, 181).

Spalding gave remarkable philosophical creditability to Catholic education in general but it was Catholic higher education that most captured his interest. The following section addresses some of Spalding's most significant contributions to education in the United States of the early twentieth century.

Contributions to the Catholic Intellectual Tradition

Perhaps more than any other U.S. bishop in history, John Lancaster Spalding took seriously the teaching office of his episcopacy. At Spalding's silver jubilee (1903), Cardinal Gibbons remarked that he had enlightened people throughout the land, and at Spalding's golden jubilee, E.L. Rivard remarked:

> For all time he has linked his name with the greatest Catholic educational enterprise of our country and when his splendid dream is realized . . . we shall know the extent of our indebtedness to the Father of the Catholic University. (*Ceremonies* 1913, 7)

It is difficult to judge whether it was his educational philosophy or his actual endeavors on behalf of education that most significantly influenced Catholic education in his time. His great zeal for both is evident in his efforts to develop Catholic educational institutions and in his call for the best of preparation for those who would teach in them. As the biographical portrait in this chapter has pointed out, Spalding made many significant concrete contributions to Catholic education in the United States. However, Spalding's greatest contributions fall in the realm of ideas and perspectives on education, many of which are still operative today. The following themes are key to the bishop's thought.

The Role of the Teacher

> The truest patriots are not party leaders nor captains of industry, nor inventors, but teachers–all the men and women who live and labor to make themselves and all who are brought under their influence wiser, holier, and happier. This is the noblest work. This is honor, worth, and blessedness.
>
> –John Lancaster Spalding (1905, 140)

Bishop Spalding spared no accolades for teachers. A right education depended on the quality of the teacher and a school was only as good as its teachers: "The teacher makes the school; and when high, pure, devout, and enlightened men and women educate, the conditions favorable to mental and moral growth will be found" (Spalding, 1895, 179). Perhaps harboring his great love and respect for his mother who home-schooled him, Spalding exalted the role of the educator: "O fathers and mothers, O teachers and ministers of God, be mindful that in your hands lie the issues of life and death, that you are committed to the highest and holiest hopes of the race" (1901a, 120). In "The Meaning and Worth of Education," he wrote:

> The mother-heart is indispensable in whoever would teach, for nothing is so persuasive as love, and nothing inspires such patience and such desire to help. It makes workers unmindful of disappointment and fatigue, holding their thoughts to one supreme end. (Spalding, 1905, 125)

All persons have a responsibility for self-education, but the fortunate student has the teacher who will

> inspire the love of mental exercise and a living faith in the power of labor to develop faculty, and to open worlds of use and delight which are infinite. . . . It is the educator's business to cherish the aspirations of the young, to inspire them with confidence in themselves, and to make them feel and understand that no labor is too great or too long, if its result be cultivation and enlightenment of the mind. (Spalding 1890, 75)

Well-acquainted with ancient pedagogies, Spalding, like Socrates, thought teaching is best accomplished as a labor of love: "We can teach what we know and love to those who know and love us. The rest is drill." The bishop continued:

> Nothing has such power to draw forth human strength and goodness as love. The teacher's first business is to win the heart and through the heart the will of his pupils; and to this end a generous faith in them is the most effective means. (Spalding 1900, 116)

Only those of a gentle and loving nature can educate souls: "The teacher accomplishes more by making strong impressions than by constructing lucid arguments" (Spalding 1900, 122). For Bishop Spalding, students should be able to observe and grow to love the virtues exhibited by the example of their teachers (1902a, 131).

The true educator strives to possess what he or she would pass on to students: "Educableness is man's true characteristic; and the teacher who loves his calling and understands his business will give his chief thought and labor to education, whether it is his own, or that of a few, or of the whole race" (Spalding 1900, 124). Spalding went as far as to say that the effectiveness of any school is dependent on the character of its teachers. Character is contagious and, conversely, disinterested, uncultivated teachers will produce only more of the same. Teachers should model the joyful pursuit of truth, goodness, and beauty, inspiring students toward the highest ideals of human personhood: "Little depends of what is taught; everything on who teaches" (Spalding, 1905,127).

In an address entitled "The University and the Teacher," delivered at the 1899 Convocation of the University of Chicago, Spalding said:

> The whole question of educational reform and progress is simply a question of employing good and removing incompetent teachers. And those who have experience best know how extremely difficult this is. In a university, at least, it should be possible; for a university is a home of great teachers or it is not a university at all. (Spalding 1900, 140)

Spalding knew how difficult it was to find and keep good teachers. He recognized the lack of respect held for what he considered the noblest profession. Addressing educators assembled at the 1901 NEA convention in Detroit, Bishop Spalding expounded on the challenges of teaching:

> The wise take an exalted view of the teacher's office, and they know the difficulties by which he is beset. He is made to bear the sins of parents and the corruption of society. His merit is little recognized and his work is poorly paid. The ignorant take the liberty to instruct him and they who care nothing for

education become interested when he is to be found fault with. The results of his labors are uncertain and remote, and those he has helped most rarely think it necessary to be thankful. But if he knows how to do his work and loves it, he cannot be discouraged. (Spalding 1902b, 230-31)

Spalding believed that if education as a whole was to be fostered, first and foremost educational leaders must encourage and inspire the brightest of young teachers in their work. He held that teachers and scholars should be granted intellectual freedom in study and research and that diversity in interpreting the Christian perspective should be expected and encouraged. He feared that censorship would drive the brightest Catholic scholars into disciplines where their work would be better appreciated (Grollmes, 1969, 72-75). Spalding stated:

The number of born teachers, however is not great; and nothing is left to us but to train, as best we may, those who lack power to interest, to command attention, and to create enthusiasm. (1897, 72)

He wrote: "Whatever else the incapable be permitted to do, let them not become teachers" (Spalding, 1901a, 232). Spalding called for serious thought on the question of how to make the profession of teaching more attractive, respected, and well salaried. Better conditions in schools, smaller classes, and shorter hours would lead to more pleasant working conditions for teachers and give them more hope for advancement in their vocation. Spalding hoped

to persuade the best men and women to devote themselves to teaching; for we shall make them feel that the teacher does not take up a trade, but the highest of art–the art of fashioning immortal souls in the light of the ideals of truth, goodness and beauty. (1902b, 232)

Educating Women

We must give to woman the best education it is possible for her to receive. She has the same right as man to become all that she may be, to know whatever may be known, to do whatever is fair and just and good.

–John Lancaster Spalding (1902b, 152)

Sister Agnes Claire Schroll, O.S.B., observed that Bishop Spalding changed his thinking about women's education over the course of time. In 1879 Spalding said, "When I hear a woman use intellectual arguments I am dismayed" ("The Blessed Virgin Mary," *The Ave Maria,* 1879, ix). By 1884, Spalding was professing that women should receive the best of education if humankind was to achieve genuine progress. In the home, school, church, and workplace, women should be equal to men. Where society does not educate women it lacks the hope of progress and its young, male and female alike, remain callous and uncultivated. As noted earlier, Spalding's mother was a highly educated woman, rare for her time. He valued the early education she gave him and the love of learning she imparted. While sometimes seemingly motivated by the benefits women's education would have for men, Spalding nevertheless was well ahead of his time in his thinking on all aspects of women's equality. In a lecture entitled "Women and Education," Spalding expressed his resolve to promote the equality of women in all arenas of life:

There is not a religion, a philosophy, a science, an art for man and another for woman. Consequently there is not, in its essential elements at least, an education for man and another for woman. In souls, in minds, in consciences, in hearts, there is no sex. What is the best education for woman? That which will best help her to become a perfect human being, wise, loving and strong. What is her work? Whatever may help her to become herself. What is forbidden her? Nothing but what degrades or narrows or warps. What has she the right to do? Any good and beautiful and useful thing she is able to do without hurt to her dignity and worth as a human being. (1895, 101)

Spalding lamented that women were excluded from many professions and "rarely get the same pay as men for the same work" (1897, 227). That women had been treated unequally for so long was for him "an indelible stain on the page of history" (1900, 49), one that was completely out of line with the notion of democracy. Spalding observed:

> The domination of the animal in man had kept woman in subjection, had made of her a slave, a drudge, or a plaything; but faith in education as a human need and right revealed to the nineteenth century the duty of providing for the education of women as of men. (1905, 84)

Spalding genuinely endorsed women's participation in higher institutions of learning and all professions. He observed that women were superior students and read more books than men (1895, 111). In Spalding's view, education for women is not toward motherhood or being a good wife but toward human perfection as the ideal. In a lecture given on behalf of Trinity College, a Catholic women's college to be established in Washington, D.C., Spalding made his stance for women's equality perfectly clear. Historian and Spalding biographer, David Francis Sweeney, O.F.M., described the speech as eloquent, inciting an enthusiastic response from the listeners for both the future women's college and the higher education of women (1965, 329). Spalding's classic talk was entitled "Women and the Higher Education." In it he noted:

> Woman's sphere lies where she can live nobly and do useful work. The career open to ability applies to her not less than man. It is good to have a strong and enlightened mind; therefore it is good for a woman to have such a mind. . . . To be a human being, many sided and well-rounded, is to be like God; therefore it is good that woman be developed on many sides in harmony and completeness. (Spalding 1900, 58)

Without question, the Bishop of Peoria met with opposition to this line of thinking concerning women's equality in the late nineteenth and early twentieth century. This did not deter him. In her dissertation, Sister Agnes Claire Schroll wrote that, for Spalding, the end of education is the same for girls and boys—"to develop power, faculty, self-control, sanity, breadth of view, wide sympathies, and an abiding sense of justice" (1944, 257). De Hovre called Spalding "a champion of the higher education of women" (1934, 190).

The Importance of Freedom in Academic Research

> If the Church is to live and prosper in the world, Catholics must not only have the freedom to learn, but also freedom to teach.
> –John Lancaster Spalding (1902b, 158)

Spalding was ahead of his time in stressing the need for open scholarship in order for the Church to become an intellectual force in a nation founded on principles of human freedom. He looked upon his generation of Catholic thinkers and writers as sadly behind in their contributions to the body of American intellectual tradition. For the scholarly Bishop of Peoria, education and the free pursuit of new ideas about the relationship between religion and culture were the only remedies for the dearth of Catholic scholarship and the university was the place to best prepare such future scholars, men and women alike.

The nature of Church teachings was not static and therefore it was the role of theology to reflect on and express these truths as rethought by each generation. This required freedom: "If the Church prohibits this self-criticism–one which draws its power from contemporary thought–then a decay of doctrine rather than a healthy development will be the result" (Killen 1973, 428). For Spalding, the Church must be open to the "spirit of the age" and this includes both natural and the supernatural truths, both scientific and religious. In his view:

> A truly catholic spirit deems nothing that may be of service to man foreign to the will of God as revealed in Christ. We hold fast to the principle of authority: and at the same time we believe that a man's mind is free, and that he has the right to inquire into and learn whatever may be investigated and known. If the Church is to live and prosper in the modern world, Catholics must have not only freedom to learn, but also freedom to teach. (1902b, 157-58)

Whether clergy or lay, Catholics were encouraged by Spalding to study, read widely, and put their intellectual talents to use on behalf of both the Church and the country. John Tracy Ellis noted that Spalding's real fear was that "if Catholics isolated themselves and withdrew from the circles where the thought of the modern world was being shaped, . . . they would drift into a position of inferiority and lose whatever chance they might have to make themselves heard and understood" (1961, 74-75). Thus, in Spalding's view, "If mistrust of ablest minds be permitted to exist, the inevitable result will be a lowering of the whole intellectual life of Catholics." (1902b, 163-64).

The Importance of Improving the Education of Clergy

Professional men are united by indissoluble bonds. They all alike find their reason for being, in the needs and miseries of man; they all minister to his ills, and to all, science, culture, and religion supply the means which render them capable to help.
–John Lancaster Spalding (1894, 122)

That Spalding was exceptionally concerned with the role of priest as educator is confirmed by his repeated references to the necessity of improving their education so that they may become adequate to the task of pastoring the most active and progressive people of their churches. The task of teaching and preaching God's word, so central to the priestly vocation, should be performed by the most cultivated and eloquently expressive bishops and priests. Only a higher education given to such excellence could help effect such a standard of quality in the priesthood. To Spalding, "so long as no step is taken to give to the Church in the United States men of the best cultivation of mind, each year seems like a decade, and each decade a century" (1882, 157).

Such an education is an education in the preparation for knowledge. It is a liberal education, bestowing freedom, courage, and confidence. The clergy should not only be mindful of their initial preparation but should understand themselves as life-long students (1894, 102-03). Freeing themselves from any narrowness of mind, the bishops and priests may execute the charge of teaching God's word in openness and freedom. The Church and its people are deserving of no less.

Spalding's dedication to the establishment of an American Catholic university is indicative of his great resolve that priests be afforded opportunities for the best of educations, "For what is the pulpit but the holiest teacher's chair that has been placed upon the earth?" (Spalding 1895, 186) The urgency in his plea makes evident his desire for Catholics to take their place among the cultivated and intellectual minds of the new world. When priests are able to bring scholarly advancements into the realm of religion, Catholic theology "will again come forth from its isolation in the modern world" (Spalding 1895, 216).

Conclusion

John Tracy Ellis noted that Spalding's "Lifelong crusade on behalf of higher educational standards for all Americans . . . was, perhaps, the characteristic by which he was most frequently identified in the minds of his contemporaries" (1-2). Spalding's work displays a wide knowledge and deep understanding of the history and impact of Christian education. There is very little of his work that does not allude to some aspect of teaching, education or school. Historian Nathan Mitchell records that the early church defined the responsibilities of bishops as "overseeing and regulating the community's life, administering its fiscal resources and teaching sound doctrine" (1982, 156). Clearly, Spalding saw the latter as the central focus of his vocation.

John Tracy Ellis and David Sweeney agree that the best of the Spalding's energies were probably "on behalf of religious education and social betterment" (Sweeney 1965, 14). His understanding of the importance of Catholic education in helping an immigrant Church find its place in the United States and his unrelenting belief in the educational power of the Christian religion are true legacies for religious educators everywhere and for all times. His writings on educational philosophy are unmatched by any U.S. prelate to date. John Lancaster Spalding was without precedent or successor as an American Catholic philosopher of education. Widely acknowledged as a true Catholic intellectual himself, Spalding knew that if "we permit ourselves to fall out of the intellectual movement of the age, we shall lose influence over the minds that create opinion and shape the future" (1902b, 161). The visionary Bishop of Peoria was a giant upon whose shoulders the Catholic intellectual tradition in education stands.

Edward Pace:
Pioneer Psychologist, Philosopher, and Religious Educator

JOHN L. ELIAS

In his book *American Catholic Intellectuals During the Progressive Era, 1900-1920*, Thomas Woods argues that many Catholic intellectuals at the beginning of the twentieth century strongly resisted the chief tenets of progressivism while adopting only minor elements of the progressive agenda. In his interpretation these intellectuals staunchly held out for absolute truths of Catholic faith against the pragmatism of the progressives. In philosophy, sociology, education, and economics the so-called progressive Catholic intellectuals maintained the purity of Catholic truths against the relativism and pluralism of the progressive spirit. They did, however, make use of those aspects of pragmatism and progressive thought that served their purposes of defending the true faith.

Prominent among the so-called Catholic progressives Woods names are Edward Pace and Thomas Shields, both educators at Catholic University. In Woods's view, while in proposing changes in Catholic education these two men adapted some of the methods of the progressives in psychology and education, they simultaneously held out against the radical teachings of progressive educators such as John Dewey and William Kilpatrick that would be harmful to the teaching of the Catholic faith. (Other Catholic intellectuals treated in the book are the sociologist William J. Kerby and the economist John A. Ryan, both professors at Catholic University.)

Woods's historical thesis is a clearly expressed present-day polemic. In holding up the Catholic progressives of the early part of the century he contrasts them rather unfavorably with the Catholic reformers at Vatican II. In his comparison Woods contends the latter largely abandoned the absolutes of faith and philosophy for a relativism and pluralism that has led to widespread losses to the church and the disarray of American Catholicism. The heroes in his book are past and present-day Catholic intellectuals, together with Popes Pius IX and Pius X, who were stalwarts in defending the Catholic faith against dangerous teachings of modern culture such as liberalism, relativism, and pluralism.

While this is not the place to argue with Woods's broader thesis and agenda, I would like to argue a contrary thesis about the early twentieth-century Catholic progressives, at least in the case of the Catholic educator, Edward Pace. He, along with his colleague Thomas Shields, began an American Catholic educational endeavor that eventually led to noteworthy changes in Catholic education and especially in Catholic religious education. Though there is little direct link between their work and the emergence of the catechetical movement in Roman Catholicism in the 1960s, they began the trend of taking secular developments in science, psychology, and education so seriously that future scholars, beginning at Catholic University and later extending to other universities, introduced considerable changes in the theory and practice of Catholic education. It is no accident that the department of Religious Education at Catholic University, under the leadership of Gerard Sloyan, Berard Marthaler, and Mary Charles Bryce and their many graduates, most especially Gabriel Moran and Michael Warren, were highly influential in the Catholic educational renaissance in the 1960s and 1970s. It is Bryce's view that while European scholars in the 1950s on "gave the movement a vocabulary, new insights, a kind of cohesion and an element of fresh excitement, they were able to do so because of the foundations laid" (1978, S-57) by men like Pace, Shields, and others.

One needs to recall the situation in Catholicism around the turn of the century to put in perspective the world of Pace and other Catholic intellectuals. The *Syllabus of Errors* of Pius IX issued in 1864 condemned all elements of modern liberal and progressive thought. Furthermore, American Catholics in the papal condemnation of Americanism by Pius X in 1899 were charged with an exaggerated adaptation of the Catholic faith to American culture. Pius X's 1907 encyclical against modernism led to some outstanding intellectuals leaving the church and the suppression of serious intellectual work by many Catholic scholars (McCool, 1989; Appleby, 2004).

It should be noted that in the early years of Catholic University a number of its professors were perceived by some Catholics as dangerous liberals and even materialists. Pace was almost barred from speaking in Green Bay, Wisconsin, by Bishop Sebastian Messmer. The bishop wrote to him that he would allow him to speak "only on the clear understanding that you will not treat or bring up any matter or questions in connection with your subject that might give rise to dispute and unpleasant objections. We cannot allow any opinion or theory on our platform of the C.C.S.S. [Columbia Catholic Summer School] which would not be in full harmony with the commonly accepted Catholic Science" (Messmer, 1896). Pace was also one of the three professors at Catholic University whom the Apostolic Delegate Cardinal Satolli was said to have recommended to be dismissed for their progressive and liberal views (McAvoy 1957, 143).

The purpose of this chapter is to examine the contribution made by Edward Pace to the development of Catholic education, especially as it relates to the teaching of religion in schools. It is my contention that he was in many ways a progressive educator and helped to pave the way for the catechetical renewal of the 1960s.

This chapter describes and evaluates Edward Pace's contribution to religious education utilizing his many articles and talks found in such journals as the *Catholic Educational Review*, *The Catholic World*, and the *Catholic University Bulletin*. One of the main thrusts of Pace's academic work was to bring the findings of psychology to the field of religious education. Pace was also a strong advocate for the inclusion of religion in the public school curriculum, which he made clear in an address to the National Council of the National Education Association in 1903. In this address he observed that "the child comes very quickly to look on the school as the place in which everything is taught that is worth knowing. The absence of religious instruction has for one of its effects ignorance of certain important truths" (Ryan 1932, 7).

Biographical Sketch

Edward Pace was born in Starke, Florida, in 1861. He received his early education at public schools in Starke and nearby Jacksonville. After studying for the priesthood at St. Charles College, Elliot City, Maryland, and at the North American College in Rome, Pace was ordained to the priesthood in 1885, receiving a doctorate in theology in 1886. For two years he served as a pastor in Florida and then returned to Europe at the request of Cardinal Gibbons and Bishop Keane, the rector of Catholic University of America (CUA), to take on a teaching position at the newly established institution in Washington, D.C. Pace studied biology and psychology at the University of Louvain, the Sorbonne in Paris, and the University of Leipzig, where in 1891 he received a Doctor of Philosophy degree in experimental psychology, studying under the renowned psychologist Wilhelm Wundt. Pace was the first Catholic priest and third American to study under this pioneer German psychologist. His competence in psychology is attested by the fact that in 1892 he was one of the first five men elected to membership by the charter members and founders of the American Psychological Association. Later, Pace was one of the founders of the American Philosophical Association (Braun 1969, 4-5).

Pace became professor of psychology at Catholic University in 1891 and remained there until his retirement in 1935. Among the first American priests on the faculty, he joined a distinguished group of European scholars (Neusse 1990, 92, 93). A professor of psychology from 1891 and of philosophy from 1893 until 1935, he held over the years many administrative positions at the University: dean of the School of Philosophy, director of studies, general secretary, and vice rector for eleven years. In his position as vice-rector, Pace was deeply involved in the academic administration of the university. As dean of philosophy, he argued for the expansion of the curriculum to include all branches of learning, including the natural sciences, pointing out that

> The lack of instruction in Biology is a serious drawback to the investigation of fundamental problems in Philosophy, and without a department of History the efficiency both of the Divinity School and the School of Social Sciences is seriously impaired. (Pace 1896-97, 32)

Pace's first three years at the university were dedicated to teaching courses in psychology and establishing a laboratory for psychological experiments (Murray 1979). Sexton's (1980) study highlighted the significance of this laboratory:

This department became the model for most of the early departments of psychology at Catholic colleges and universities as well as the training center of many teachers who staffed the new departments at these Catholic colleges and universities. From Catholic University of America in Washington, DC, the experimental psychology of Wundt radiated to Catholic circles throughout the United States. (47)

While some of Pace's early articles are reports of experimental work in the laboratory, most of his articles from this period were a defense of experimental psychology as a discipline at a Catholic university. Many religious persons viewed experimental psychology as necessarily committed to a philosophy of materialism that rejected spiritual realities. Pace argued, however, that religious believers could employ the methods of experimental psychology without committing themselves to an atheistic or agnostic philosophy. Through membership in psychological associations, acting as editor of several psychological journals, and developing the department of psychology at Catholic University, Pace paved the way for establishing among Catholics throughout the world the legitimacy for the study of psychology (Gillespie 2001, 32-36).

An active scholar in many fields, Pace helped to establish several academic journals: the *Catholic University Bulletin*, the *Catholic Educational Review*, *New Scholasticism*, as well as *Studies in Psychology and Psychological Monographs*. He was president of the American Council of Education in 1924, where he was instrumental in establishing academic standards for schools and colleges, including Catholic schools (Gleason 1995, 70, 72). Pace also worked with the Catholic Education Association, later the National Catholic Educational Association (NCEA), and the Department of Education of the National Catholic Welfare Conference (NCWC). Furthermore, as the first president of the American Catholic Philosophical Association (ACPA), he addressed its initial meeting to welcome "a new era in the Catholic life of our country" (Gleason 1995, 136).

From the very beginning of his academic career Pace took an active interest in education. With Shields he was a co-founder of Trinity College and deeply involved in the Catholic Sisters College at Catholic University. In many of his activities he worked with Shields, professor of psychology and education at the same university. Shields's biographer described the differences between the two men: "Temperamentally, the two men were at opposite poles. Pace, though intelligent and thorough, was slow, ingrowing, plodding, as diffident in action, as hesitant in decision as Shields was rapid" (Ward 1947, 111). Pace was instrumental in bringing Shields to the university and in helping him establish a Department of Education (Ward, 120). With Shields he wrote religion textbooks for children, with Shields doing most of the work, according to Ward. Though their relationship became strained (Ward 1947, 136, 164, 165), they worked together in establishing the Sisters College at CUA, since both thought that Catholic school teachers should be taught in a Catholic Normal school (Ward 1947, 186-87).

Pace was a leader in the effort to educate teachers for Catholic schools. With Shields he lobbied the board of CUA for a department of education. Before this he helped in establishing the Institute for Pedagogy in New York City, which began in 1902 but ended in 1904 when Pace was not able to find in the city adequate instructors for the institute. In 1907 the board of CUA gave approval for a department of education, which was headed by Shields until his death in 1921 (Nuesse 1989, 130).

Pace's corpus of writings comprises four areas: psychology, philosophy, theology, and education. Trained in experimental psychology, he published numerous articles in scientific journals. His philosophical contributions won him the reputation as one of the leading Thomistic philosophers of his time.

Pace made a significant contribution to the education of American Catholics by his work on the *Catholic Encyclopedia*. This was a major undertaking for the group of scholars of which Pace was a prominent leader. Fifteen hundred scholars were involved in this enterprise to present church teachings and history in a highly accessible manner. Articles were translated from languages other than English. Pace translated many articles on philosophy and theology. Pace's articles were on a wide range of subjects. Besides the lengthy article on education, to be discussed later in this chapter, he wrote on Absolutism, Quietism, Spiritism, and Pantheism. He authored articles on many philosophical figures and was responsible for theological articles on Dulia, Beatific Vision, and Ex Cathedra (Ryan 1932, 3, 4).

After briefly reviewing his work in psychology and philosophy, this chapter will focus mainly the educational writings of Edward Pace. In the view of a prominent scholar of his day, Pace was "a consistent and authoritative spokesman for Catholic education. He has spoken and written on such diverse aspects of our educational problems as: Religion and Education, The Seminary and the Educational Problem, The Present State of Education, The Place of the University in National Life, American Ideals and Catholic Education" (Ryan, 1932, 5).

Pace was regarded as an outstanding classroom teacher and doctoral mentor. Many of his students went on to teach psychology or philosophy in Catholic colleges and universities. Leo Ward, a philosopher at Notre Dame University, recounted Pace's influence on him. After finishing his studies at Catholic University, Ward had difficulty choosing a topic for his dissertation. He recalls that Pace told him to read through philosophical journals and make a list of ten top topics. Ward returned to report that the issue of values was at the top of the list. He speaks of Pace in this manner:

> He [Pace] was generous with his time and talents and did me immeasurable good. . . . Dr. Pace, though worn out with the year's work, said to come and we would look the dissertation over. Each hot, D.C. morning when I went to his study he had a chapter on his lap. "This chapter, I was going over it again last night. Exactly what did you mean to say in the first two pages?" I had to speak my piece. "Now let's see if you said it. So far, but I was wondering here: is this exactly what you mean?" He rarely pushed me to say what he wanted said. (Ward n.d., 1)

Ward summarized the things that he learned from Pace: learn to say what you mean; get students to find out for themselves both the questions and the answers, so far as this can be done; let students enjoy a wide and ample freedom in philosophy; be patient. *Nova et vetera*: This was a favorite Dr. Pace aphorism, the old truth and the new full of life (Ward n.d., 2).

Defense of Science: Experimental Psychology

Pace began his work at Catholic University defending experimental science, which was greatly indebted to philosophical pragmatism. One of the chief tenets of progressivism and pragmatism was a commitment to the scientific and experimental method. The use of this method in the natural sciences carried over into psychology and the social sciences. Many religious persons were threatened by this new approach to gaining knowledge. Darwin's theory of evolution triggered a negative reaction by many theologians and church leaders who considered the findings of the theory in contradiction to long-held religious truths about the creation of the world and especially of humans. At the turn of the nineteenth century the new sciences of psychology and sociology engendered widespread distrust because of their perceived commitment to materialist and determinist worldviews.

At this time experimental psychology was especially suspect in the eyes of the Catholic Church. A number of adherents of the new psychology, notably the former priest Franz Brentano, had left the church. Experimental psychology seemed to go counter to the accepted rational psychology of Thomas Aquinas and his neo-scholastic followers. The new psychology also seemed to deny the existence of a spiritual soul. The implied materialism and acceptance of evolution by the new psychology appeared contrary to accepted teachings of the Catholic Church (Misiak and Staudt 1954; Ross, 1994). The suspicion about experimental psychology found expression in an article by the Jesuit historian Thomas Hughes, who argued that the soul could not be subjected to experimental testing:

> If those authorities mean by their psychometry to measure physical motion or vibration in the nerves we wish them well. But, if they or any one else shall pretend to measure physiological functions, as though sensation consisted of motions running up to the brain and down again, we beg to submit that the notion is a philosophical absurdity. And if they really mean to subject psychological activity to laboratory investigation, as though the soul could in any way be measured or weighed, we do not scruple to call the whole enterprise a theological impiety. (1894, 790)

One of Pace's first intellectual tasks upon returning to Catholic University after completing a doctorate in experimental science was to defend this new discipline from attacks by Catholic theologians and philosophers. In various articles he defended the new discipline, contending that there was no logical connection between experimental psychology and materialism, even though some psychologists were in fact materialists. In his view experimental psychology was not committed to any system of philosophy but is neutral in its theoretical assumptions. Pace also justified the use of psychometrics to understand human behavior, contending that such phenomena as sensation and perception lend themselves to statistical examination.

Pace answered the main charge against the new psychology, that it entailed the denial of existence of a spiritual soul. He rejected this conclusion by arguing that the existence of the soul is a metaphysical and not an experimental or scientific issue. Pace, however, stressed the importance of introspection for gathering psychological data all the while maintaining that even this method of gaining knowledge did not lead directly to truths beyond the physical.

Pace recognized that in his time there was hostility between scientists and philosophers. As one trained in both disciplines he tried valiantly to combat the prejudices and to point out the value of each discipline for the other. It was his view that the data supplied by psychologists could be valuable for the philosopher and theologian. It provided findings about which both philosophers and theologians could speculate. According to Pace, psychology provided data for addressing major philosophical problems:

> There are sizable philosophical problems concerning man; what precisely is his nature, what are the reasons for his acting in such a manner, how culpable is he for a particular action, and so forth. The discoveries of experimental psychology offer not only an aid to the solution of these problems but also provide indispensable knowledge for a better philosophical understanding of man. The more we know about the operations of man, the better we are prepared to speculate about his nature. (1906, 542)

Pace asserted that "no one today can pretend to an apprenticeship–to say nothing of a mastery–in philosophy, who has neglected his scientific training" (Pace 1898, 349). He also insisted that philosophy has much to offer science by providing indispensable ideas and concepts, including the important principle of causality. For him the findings of psychology cannot be in opposition to those of philosophy and theology. In fact, psychology fostered a better understanding of human nature, especially human freedom and personality. For Pace, psychology supported the scholastic axiom that all knowledge begins in the senses. He included in his work this strong suggestion to his fellow Catholics:

> Either get hold of this instrument and use it for proper purposes, or leave it to the materialists and after they have heaped up facts, established laws and forced their conclusions upon psychology, go about tardily to unravel, with clumsy fingers, this tangle of error. (1894, 535)

Though Pace was not a modernist in the theological sense of the word, his scientific training led him to wonder why for religious people being "modern" was considered synonymous with being "evil" (1895b, 8). Negative attitudes towards science in the academic world were not restricted to religious institutions but permeated many liberal arts faculties that viewed themselves as preservers of ancient traditions which they felt the new natural and social sciences threatened (Rudolph 1962, 411, 413).

Pace's defense of the scientific method as a legitimate but limited method of attaining knowledge stressed the inductive methods of science in contrast to the deductive methods of the philosophies and theologies of his time. He made clear that the realm of ethical, moral, and religious values lies beyond the reach of the scientific method. Science deals with what can be observed, measured, and quantified and "leaves untouched those deeper problems which can be approached only by metaphysical reasoning" (Pace 1895a, 148). Throughout his scientific work Pace always recognized the important role that philosophy held with regard to the new field of psychology (Gillespie 2001, 35). Additionally, he recognized the value of psychology and its potential for growth:

> Further results will doubtless prove that the experimental study of mind may be turned, indirectly, at least to the profit of all the sciences, and that whatever psychology allows them may, in time, be amply repaid. In rendering this practical service, based upon exact and painstaking research, the new

psychology not only helps us to know the mind but also helps the mind to know. In both respects it has progressed, in neither can it be blamed for being modern. (Pace 1894, 544)

While Pace made important contributions to the acceptance of psychology among Catholics, he did not remain in the field of psychology. In 1894 he was named professor and dean of the school of philosophy, which at first included psychology until the latter was given its own department. Pace, however, continued to foster the field of psychology through his doctoral students, mainly Father Thomas Verner Moore, who led the department for twenty-five years and contributed a number of important books to the field of psychology. As an administrator Pace made sure that psychology remained an important part of the curriculum. His interest in psychology continued to the last decade of his life, when he edited *Studies in Psychology and Psychiatry and the Psychological Monographs of the Catholic University* (Hart, 1932, 3).

Pace the Scholastic Philosopher

Pace started to teach philosophy in 1894 and continued to do so until his retirement. Publishing extensively in this field of study he was considered one of the leading figures in the neo-scholastic movement in the United States. He was judged by his colleagues as "having done more than any living exponent of Thomism to bring before the American university world the strong points of medieval Scholasticism" (Ryan 1932, 2). As a student in Rome he had shone in a disputation in the presence of Leo XIII, who led the Thomistic revival. In 1925 he was elected the first president of the American Catholic Philosophical Association. Pace's work has been characterized as the principal impetus to an open and progressive form of Neo-Scholasticism at the Catholic University which contended "that Thomism could meet modern problems only if it was in touch with the findings of natural science" (Gleason 1995, 110-11). In Gleason's view, Pace was both progressive and liberal, not a usual alignment among Catholic philosophers at this time (111).

In his work on the undergraduate curriculum, Pace directed students to study all branches of philosophy as well as take courses in the sciences. Philosophy for him meant dealing with "the principal problems of the day, such as: the idea of God, the meaning of life, the building of character, evolution, agnosticism, and so on (Pace, n.d., 1-12).

For Pace as for other Catholic educators of his time, philosophy was the main unifying discipline in undergraduate education, since it dealt with the basic principles of reality that were studied through other disciplines, including the natural and psychological sciences. Philosophy provided the tools by which students were able to think critically about what they learned in other disciplines. In his view, scholastic philosophy could determine the true or false assumptions found in other disciplines. It also could counter the agnosticism that might be engendered by the sciences. Scientist that he was, Pace insisted that science be taught properly, especially when it came to evolution, concerning which he thought science could safeguard the distinctive nature of the human and human freedom as well as avoid the pitfalls of materialistic determinism. An additional advantage of philosophy was that it could aid students to understand divine revelation and thus "obtain a deeper insight into the divine teaching" (Pace 1911c, 590).

Pace judged philosophy to be an extremely important subject in the college curriculum, since it provided students with the wisdom of the past as well as developed their ability to think and criticize. He pondered whether logic should come first or after other subjects to which logic might be applied. For him a major value of philosophy was its ability to provide students with a perspective in which they "shall see the relations that bind in one whole the facts of science, of history, of economic and social life, along with the products of literature and art–and see them from the viewpoint of philosophic principle" (Pace 1913b, 111). As expected, Pace gave attention to the method of instruction, discussing the advantages and disadvantages of lecture, recitation, disputations, single textbook or series of readings. For him teachers of philosophy should have knowledge of history and the physical sciences as well as the science and art of education.

Pace's contribution to scholastic philosophy was highlighted in a festschrift presented in his honor on the occasion of his seventieth birthday (Hart 1932). Written by colleagues and former students, the collection was a testament to his status as one of the outstanding interpreters of Thomistic philosophy in his day. In many articles he addressed such issues as teleology, order, arguments for immortality, application of Thomas to modern thought, and the soul. Paced related Thomistic philosophy to the issues raised by philosophers who wrote after Thomas as well as to issues raised by contemporary philosophers. Of course issues in philosophy of religion such as the nature and actions of God received extensive attention from him (Pace 1899; 1900; 1928).

One example of Pace's effort to apply scholastic philosophy to modern philosophical issues were his arguments for human freedom, which he directed against the behaviorist school of psychology, a dominant theory in his time. In an article in *New Scholasticism* (1936), Pace argued against the view that behavior is determined, doing so by pointing out the weaknesses in the behaviorist position: their failure to account for ethical values in society and people's consciousness of the possession of human freedom. One of his chief arguments against behaviorism was the sense of responsibility that people possess. He contended that,

> A moment's reflection will lead those of us who have learned the lesson to acknowledge or rather to emphasize that life, so far as it has meaning or value, means responsibility and is of worth according to the measure in which that responsibility is realized, borne and discharged. For him who would live, there is no option in this matter. Society is there where he comes upon the scene; and to be a member of society in any worthy sense is to be responsible. (1927, 515)

Pace the Educator

When it comes to educational writings, there appears to be two Paces. There is the dogmatic Pace, the author of the article on "Education" for *The Catholic Encyclopedia*, published in 1903. There is also the rather progressive or liberal Pace who wrote on education in 1915 for the ecumenical Christian publication, *The Constructive Quarterly* and other periodicals. The Pace of the *Catholic Encyclopedia* takes the stance of the expositor of church teachings. The latter Pace enunciates many of the tenets of progressive education that dealt with issues relating to the teaching and administration of schools. This section will treat his theory of education, teaching religion in Catholic schools, and teaching religion in public schools.

In the *Catholic Encyclopedia* article, Pace gave an outline of the Catholic position on education at the end of what is a rather comprehensive statement on the history of education among the ancients and the history Christian education. Pace defined education in the general sense as "that form of social activity whereby, under the direction of mature minds and by the use of adequate means, the physical, intellectual, and moral powers of the immature human being are so developed as to prepare him for the accomplishment of his lifework here and for the attainment of his eternal destiny" (1913a, 1-2). The constants in education include human nature and destiny as well as relationship to God. The variables are all the changes in the theory and conduct of education thorough various agencies including the home, school, and churches.

In Pace's perspective, the education that took place in the East among the Greeks, Romans, and Jews prepared the way for the high point in education that was realized in Christianity. In turn, Christianity offered new knowledge and principles of action as well as effective means for realizing these. Jesus was the teacher *par excellence* both in what he taught and in how he taught. His teachings have universal and perpetual significance, hold out the highest ideals of human personality and perfection, raise the dignity of women, and present truths through a revelation not available to reason alone (Pace 1913a, 11-14).

Almost half of the article on education is devoted to the educational mission of the Catholic Church, the organization to which Jesus committed the task of carrying on his work through the teaching of doctrine and training persons how to live. This mission was initiated through preparation of persons for baptism and the defense of the church. The church advanced its educational mission through the celebrations of the liturgical year and the establishment of schools attached to monasteries and eventually in universities, seminaries, and parish schools. The style of Pace's writing is standard for the time in which the article was written. The efforts of other Christian churches receive a negative assessment for their efforts in carrying out the work of Christ in the modern period. Pace does mention the recognition that non-Catholics gave to the need for moral and religious education in the establishment of the Religious Education Association in 1903.

Pace boldly outlined what he considered to be the Catholic position on education. First, intellectual education should be connected with moral and religious education. Attention to the intellectual without attention to moral and religious is dangerous for the individual and society. Second, religion should be an essential part of education, the center around which all subjects are taught. The failure to do this leads to an incomplete education in school and lessens the importance of religion in the mind of students. Third, sound moral instruction must be connected with religious education. Religion provides the best motives for good conduct, being not merely doctrinal instruction but also practical training of the will through religious practices. Fourth, such an integrated education strengthens the home and family and prepares students for civic duties. Thus, the welfare of the state benefits in having members who respect its laws through the practice of virtue. Fifth, advances in educational method increase the need for such an education. The church welcomes advances in the sciences that make the work of the school more efficient. Sixth, Catholic parents are obligated to provide for the education of children either at home or in schools. They should do this through their example and through direct instruction (Pace 1913a, 20-23).

On the other hand, Pace's many articles on education in educational journals present a less dogmatic view of education. He had a number of overriding purposes in his enormous output of articles on education. Always the teacher, he wanted to find ways to help students learn. He did this by appealing largely to the psychological theories and research he knew so well. Furthermore, as an administrator, he advocated flexibility in the curriculum, including openness to new advances in knowledge, which were considerable in his time. As a philosopher and theologian, Pace was concerned with combating what he perceived to be erroneous views emanating from the philosophical systems of naturalism, pragmatism, and positivism—that were in his day influencing educational theory and practice. In many articles he opposed their rejection of a transcendent God and ultimate values as well as exclusive dependence on the empirical method as the only sure way to arrive at truth (Baum 1969, 90).

Theory of Education

As one would expect, Pace's theory of education is based on his Thomistic philosophical orientation. As early as 1902 he was critical of the materialistic and highly mechanical view of education that had gripped some educationists who depended on many aspects of the new psychology. He stressed that education is fundamentally a spiritualistic enterprise whose essence is self-activity and freedom. Drawing on Thomas Aquinas' *De Magistro* (1256-58), he proposed a theory of education that was a *via media* between education as the implanting of knowledge from external sources and education as dependent upon innate knowledge in the mind. This approach balanced "internal activity, whether physical and moral, and changes that are brought about by environment" (Pace 1902, 293). From an initial endowment of "qualities, active and passive, from which production and action originate," individuals learn from experiencing the environment through the direction of teachers. Education is compared to the development and growth of seeds which contain in a potential manner particular items of knowledge. Reminiscent of Augustine's theory of *rationes seminales*, Pace explains how these seeds develop through self activity directed by God and the human teacher.

Pace followed Thomas Aquinas in giving both human experience and the teacher important roles in education. Teachers are significant because they possess the instructional knowledge in an explicit and perfect manner. The teacher's task is to lead students along well-marked paths. What students possess innately has to be drawn out or activated by a teacher. He utilizes the Thomist comparison between teacher and physician by pointing out that both do their work by helping and serving. The teacher

> supplies the mind with assistance it needs and the means it requires for its orderly and healthy action. Mere instruction avails about as much as the dose, however powerful, which is given to a depleted system. In neither case is there any vital response. (1902, 297)

For Pace, the role of teachers is to lead students through the same stages of reasoning and learning that they themselves passed through, with the result that that student's learning would be similar to that which the teacher possesses, to be acquired however with the student taking the principal role in the process.

Pace's description of human learning, based on St. Thomas, is similar to that espoused by John Dewey and later by Jean Piaget. It is in opposition to the behaviorist theory that explains human learning as responses to external stimuli as well as to the innate learning theories of romantic educational philosophers like Jean Jacques Rousseau who describe education as simply drawing out what already exists potentially in the learner. Pace drew attention to such psychological functions as sense, imagination, memory, and attention. Following Thomas again, he stressed that in a very real sense the teacher cooperates with God in the educational process. Teaching is no less than cooperation in a divine work (1902, 302-03).

The Teaching of Religion

Ever interested in the teaching of religion in the schools, Pace began to carve out his own distinctive approach at the 1907 meeting of the Catholic Educational Association in Milwaukee. In his summary of a number of talks given by members, he emphasized that their attention should be given not only to the content of teaching or the personality of the teacher but also to the method by which teachers taught. Method for him meant the accommodation of teaching to the growing mind of the child. He urged the members of the association to devote more attention to methods of instruction. At a meeting of the association the following year in Cincinnati, Pace defended the religion series which he and Thomas Shields, his colleague at Catholic University, wrote by pointing out that the texts made use of the teaching methods of Jesus and the Church in its liturgy. Some members of the association objected to the fact that the books did not stress memorization of answers from the catechism (Ward 1947, 137, 143, 144).

In the first issue of the *Catholic Educational Review* (1911a), which he edited with Thomas Shields, Pace contributed an essay on the papacy and education in which he neither mentioned a particular pope nor quoted a papal document. Rather he described the Church under papal leadership as a teaching and educational institution whose task is to teach a definite body of religious truths designed to achieve practical effects. He also explained how the church has always followed the best principles of applied psychology. In reality, the teaching of religion makes use of the same methods that are employed in other subjects. Pace rejected the opinion held by some:

That religion must be kept apart from the teaching of other subjects on the ground that its methods are incompatible with those that are employed in the "regular" work of the school; and it is worth while inquiring whether the Church in her long experience has not made use of methods that are free from any such objection. (3)

For Pace, education was a process of adjusting the mind to objective truth or reality, which is actually the scholastic explanation of knowledge. He stressed that religion is not merely a subjective attitude, since the full life of faith demands works and the spirit of obedience to laws. It was Pace's view that the Catholic school aims at the training of the will no less than cultivating the intelligence. Pace, however, rejected the idea that religion is all of life and consists only in doing: "Religion accordingly includes more than an attitude or a creed or a group of feelings; it means the observance of law" (5). In his view while belief in a body of truths is essential, religion also needs the concreteness that the liturgy and ritual gives it. One sound psychological principle that the church advocates is the need for imitation "which should be emphasized rather than reduced to a mere recital of deeds" (8). The highest ideal is to follow the moral teachings of Jesus.

In the first volume of *Catholic Educational Review* Pace also contributed two articles on the educational value of the liturgy. It was his contention that "the Church has shown a profound insight into the needs of human beings and anticipated in her practice the formulation of some important psychological laws which are now generally accepted" (1911b, 239). These principles include an appeal to the senses and imagination, adaptation to the developing mind, and the value of imitation. In these articles Pace anticipated some of the insights of later psychologists about children's development from a concrete stage to a critical and abstract stage as well as how the teaching of religion can be adjusted to these changes. He also recommended what has come to be called the spiral curriculum, according to which in educating the child "at each stage of development a new presentation of the same truths should enable him to find that meaning ever richer and deeper" (1911b, 243). In adapting teaching about the liturgy to the developing mind, Pace warned against two extremes: not to give "the complete explanation of liturgical practice . . . at the outset, nor should that explanation be reserved until the pupil is able to seize its full historical and theological import" (242). He recommended that teachers should give children some idea of what the liturgy is about and then increase their knowledge as children develop.

In an address to the Catholic Educational Association (1911d), Pace criticized the reformulation of religion as a general subject area in the curriculum. He seemed to be countering the liberal Protestant view of religion and the ideas of the prominent educator William T. Harris, whom he does not name. Pace contended that "education must be religious and religion must be educational" (770). In this article religion clearly refers to the Catholic Religion, the religion of revelation. Pace also criticized the view of natural morality and proposed the morality prescribed in divine revelation. He stressed the relationship with God as the basis of all religion and morality. He also contended that if religion is understood in the general sense, then he "does not stand for that kind of religious education nor any alliance between the school and religion or between the Church and the school" (776). This is a position which he softened in a later article.

In a noteworthy article in the *Constructive Quarterly*, Pace made the case, which few Catholics of his time were doing, for the teaching of religion in the public schools. For Pace, the construction of a better society entails extensive attention to the teaching of religion in the schools. Education is valuable for making Christian unity permanent and also for the transmission of the spiritual inheritance of Christianity. Pace takes it for granted that there will be courses in religion at colleges and universities. But he also calls for "a primer of religion" to be prepared "in strictly scientific form and adopted as the final enrichment of the curriculum. It would do no more harm, certainly, than Aesop or Homer" (Pace 1915, 588). Pace also gives a reason for including psychology in the curriculum, arguing that for religion to exert any influence on conduct it must be correlated with other subjects, lifted up into the mental structure, and properly assimilated.

Pace recognized that the religion to be taught in public schools must be more than merely knowing the things that are to be believed or holding fast to articles of faith. His description of religion in this article approximates what liberal Protestant religious educators were proposing in the pages of *Religious Education*:

Religion is a life, not merely an assent to set forms of belief; but it is a human life and it therefore involves man's entire being. It needs the guidance of the intellect and the effort of the will. It does not spend itself in feelings nor does it seek to strangle the emotions, but to purify them and make them allies of the reasoning powers. Its center is within the soul, but it radiates through word and work, through the outward forms of worship and the fulfillment of the duties that are owed to God, the fellowman, society and country. (1915, 590)

After this description of religion, Pace goes on to describe religious education as

The imparting of religious truth, but it is something more: it is a training of sense and feeling and will to such purpose that action in conformity with the Divine Law will result. Of necessity it is at once intellectual and moral, ideal and practical. Its truths are sacred and for them it demands reverence; but their sanctity permeates all other knowledge and their value is great in proportion as they quicken everyday thought and deed, the commonplaces of existence. (590-91)

Pace does not think that the weekly instruction in Sunday school is enough to provide the kind of religious education children need, though it is "an indispensable adjunct of the church and a necessary supplement to the instruction given in the everyday school" (591). Not all Catholic educators were as positive about the Sunday school movement. Perhaps it was his own public school education in Florida that influenced his thinking on this matter. Pace's problem with the Sunday school was its isolation from the rest of schooling. He was insistent that religion be taught in conjunction or in correlation with other school subjects.

Pace identified method as the central question when it comes to the teaching of religion. Teachers of religion should have the same degree of preparation as teachers of other subjects. He decried the fact that improvements in methods of teaching had not sufficiently influenced the teaching of religion. Pace identified a vicious circle:

"Religion is kept away from general education; it is not taught by proper methods; it fails of its promise to form upright men and women; therefore, it is a superfluous sort of knowledge for which the school has neither time nor place" (593). The proper methods for teaching religion and other subjects come from a psychological study of the mind and its development.

Like Thomas Shields, whose work is treated in the next chapter, Pace contended that the principles of method of modern education are essentially the teaching methods that Jesus employed and that are used in the liturgy of the churches. Jesus was a great teacher not only because of what he taught but also because of how he taught. He drew from the common experiences of his listeners. His use of parables manifested profound psychological and educational principles, for example "the law of association, which serves both to get the doctrine assimilated and to secure its recall whenever the scene of the parable and its homely items recur in later experiences" (596).

The value of method in education was a recurring theme in his educational writings. In an early article (1910), Pace connected method in education with the truths of psychology and philosophy. Taking issue with the philosophy of materialism, which Pace often did in his educational articles, he stressed that education progresses by developing the mental capacities of the mind and soul. Teachers need to know about the mental life and the processes through which teachers can come to grasp the ends and means of education. Proper training enables a teacher to know not only that a method is good but also why it is good. A principle of method that he recommended was apperception—connecting what is now being learned with what is already known, which can best be accomplished through the process of self-activity. Pace was insistent that proper method entailed that education be adapted to each of the stages of development through which learners pass, a knowledge of which is essential for the educator. Pace concluded this article by pointing out the importance of the teacher's philosophy of education:

> The teacher is not called on to philosophize at every step, or to have a dictionary of philosophical terms constantly open on his desk. None the less, education is the working out in practice of some one's ideals, and therefore of some one's philosophy. It lies within the teacher to decide whether he shall serve as an

instrument for the application of principles which, perhaps, he could not accept–or, by shifting the true from the false, become the master of his method and the owner of himself. (1910, 825)

Pace offered an illustration of the progressive principle of learning-by-doing in liturgical rituals where participants are influenced more by actions and things than words. Jesus and his followers stressed that doing the word was equally as important as preaching and teaching the word. The liturgy also appeals to the dramatic and imitative instinct which is a feature of children.

Pace also focused on moral education, recognizing the growing call for some sort of moral training in the public schools. While he contended that moral training is best done on a religious basis, in contrast to many Catholic educators, he accepted the value of a broad moral education not connected to religion. For him religion has a place not only in individual conduct but also in the life of society.

For Pace, the mission of the school was "to shape the development of the individual with a view both to his personal growth in virtue and to the discharge of his social obligation . . . to retain what is of value in individualism and yet avoid its narrowness by emphasizing the social element" (1915, 601). In words reminiscent of John Dewey, Pace contended that the progressives' stress on the social importance of the school was a hopeful symptom and a guide for constructive effort in society. He ended this essay on the optimistic note that

> Education is returning to the deepest of all the questions that concern human life and destiny; and it only remains to be seen whether with our advance in knowledge and our psychological research we have gained a deeper insight into man's spiritual needs or a more thorough understanding of his social relations than was shown by Christ and the Church which he founded. (1915, 602)

University Education

Pace spent his entire career at Catholic University, which was during those years the only Catholic University in the country, modeled after the Catholic University in Louvain, Belgium. The university had its origins in the initiative of Pope Leo XIII, who made it a pontifical university, under the authority of the Vatican. On a number of occasions He addressed the unique role that Catholic University was expected to play in the work of Catholic education in the United States. As the only graduate school under Catholic auspices, the university was designed "to be the center and source of vitality for all our institutions" (Pace 1912b, 107). Pace viewed the structure of Catholic education as a pyramid, with Catholic University at the top, coordinating and completing all the other educational institutions established in parishes and dioceses.

For Pace, the task of Catholic education in the broad sense was the "union of culture with religion and moral training." Students would pass from parochial school through high school and college to the university. The same doctrines were to be taught at every level, beginning with simple statements and then moving to language increasingly more technical and complex (Pace 1912b, 108). The importance of the university in this vision is that it develops the knowledge that will find its way into the colleges and schools. Thus all other Catholic educational institutions were to be affiliated with Catholic University, which was viewed as the center and source of vitality for all Catholic educational institutions.

Pace had a special interest in the university's work in preparing teachers for Catholic schools. For him, real progress in Catholic schools would take place only if teachers were properly prepared, preferably in a Catholic institution. Pace outlined what the Catholic University was to do in this regard in an article on "The University: Its Growth and its Needs" (Pace 1912c, 352-58). He deplored the situation where many received graduate degrees without "even an elementary course in the principles and methods of educationûas though the possession of knowledge in any department gave assurance that the possessor could impart it to good effect" (357).

Seminary Education

Given that so many priests were in his classes at Catholic University and that priests were increasingly important in the sphere of Catholic education, Pace gave special attention to seminary education. In an article "The Seminary and the Educational Problem" (1911c),

Pace presented a rather full exposition of his views on education. He argued that seminaries should take account of modern education, which includes new theories, methods, and ideas. Continued vitality in seminary education entailed adjustment to new developments. Pace *pointed out* that much could be learned from modern education about how to improve education. Education for him was the "development of intellectual and volitional power or the training of the mind or the imparting and acquiring of culture" (580). For Pace, those persons are educated who have acquired a certain amount of knowledge, the ability to think, and the power to express thought through at least the essential means, such as the languages to pursue studies of a higher sort. While he exhibited some dissatisfaction with the current vocational educational movement, Pace noted some value in the elective system in colleges.

Pace described modern education as a certain way of looking at things, perceiving their relationships, connecting new ideas with old, stimulating and sustaining interest, translating thought into action, and consolidating action into habit. Education was a particular way of working or functioning that characterizes the mind's development and makes other modes of thinking either difficult or impossible. It was not so much a content that has been acquired as a form into which all later acquisition is cast. Education entailed not primarily a settled and definite store of information but rather a power to grasp and put to use such knowledge as later experience may offer. Though Pace was not totally convinced by this rather Deweyan view on education, he advised seminary educators to be aware that students in schools, including Catholic schools, were being taught in this way. Thus in teaching religion, educators should adapt to these modes of thought by shaping their message to the needs of students. He described Jesus' teaching method as one of adaptation to the needs and modes of people. He believed that teaching religion demands using the same methods that are used in other subjects.

Pace offered the view that those priests being trained to be superintendents of schools should know all about modern education for the sake of the schools and in order to take part in public discussions with educators. In what was originally a talk given to the seminary department of the Catholic Educational Association, he advised that a course on education should be given in all seminaries.

In another article, "The Seminary and Education," Pace (1912a) cautioned against materialistic evolution. He stressed the value of education in philosophy. While he saw some value in self-activity as a method of education, Pace placed scholastic rational psychology before experimental psychology. Pace assigned value to laws of mental development, adjustment, or adaptation as long as they are not interpreted in a materialistic or determinist sense. In this vein, he criticized recent books in philosophy of education "in which the definition of education is drawn after a study of its various aspects, the biological, physiological and sociological aspects being presented before the psychological and the philosophical" (74). This example of putting the cart before the horse illustrates where he saw the dangers of materialistic evolution. For him the human mind was not simply a later development of the brute's consciousness. In this article, as in all his work, he adhered to the traditional faculty psychology of rational psychology. It was the task of philosophy to decide on the value of the findings of experimental psychology. However, he gives few examples or illustrations.

Conclusion

We return to the Woods thesis, presented at the beginning of this chapter, that Pace and his colleague were not true progressives in that they staunchly defended the truths of the Catholic faith while merely adopting some of the methods of the progressives in their educational program, including the teaching of religion.

It is true that Pace was no modernist who attempted to formulate a progressive or liberal approach to Catholicism. He was thus not a religious educator in the mode of the liberal Protestant educators Clayton Brower, Sophia Fahs, and George Coe. While he knew of the Religious Education movement and its association, he did not participate in it. In his article on "Education" in the *Catholic Encyclopedia*, he applauded the association's advocacy of moral education in the public schools. His colleague at Catholic University, Thomas Shahan, did address the Religious Education Association at an early convention. But what Pace advocated in stating the aims and methods of religious education was truly progressive and liberal. Negative reactions to his work and that of Shields were indicative of this as well as the judgment of historians like Mary Charles Bryce and Philip Gleason, cited in this essay.

What made him progressive was his emphasis on the fostering of critical thinking and self-activity and his advocacy of methods that fostered questioning on the part of students. He was opposed to purely rote catechetical training. In his view, teaching religion would logically and practically foster a more questioning attitude towards religious doctrines and dogmas. While his opponents seemed to sense this, he himself does not appear to have done so. His commitment to the scientific method from his studies in experimental psychology and his attempt to reconcile scholasticism with modern science implied an approach to knowledge, learning, and education that questioned the rigidity of established dogmas. The time would come in the 1960s when Catholic religious educators, following the lead of theologians and philosophers, would develop a truly progressive and liberal form of religious education, which has been at the center of controversy for the past few decades. For conservative writers like Woods, Pace and his colleagues at Catholic University represent bulwarks against the secularization of Catholic education. For many religious educators, they should be recognized as adventurous pioneers who laid the foundation for a more enlightened approach to Catholic religious education.

Thomas E. Shields:
Progressive Catholic Religious Educator

JOHN L. ELIAS

In the process of writing a research paper on Catholics in the Religious Education Association, I came across the name of Father Thomas Edward Shields, professor of education at the Catholic University of America in the early part of the twentieth century. A number of Catholic contributors to the journal *Religious Education* referred to the Shields Method of teaching religion in Catholic schools and noted that though the textbooks were widely used, they were considered controversial (Elias 2004). Father Shields was not a member of the Religious Education Association, nor did he ever publish in its journal. His influence was restricted to Catholic education, journals, and associations.

Historical reviews of the catechetical movement in the United States Catholic Church give scant attention to the work of Shields, the first American Catholic catechetical writer of the twentieth century, and his collaborators at Catholic University of America. The origins of the modern catechetical movement are usually traced to the introduction of European scholars of the 1950s and 1960s into this country, especially the work of Josef Jungmann, Johannes Hofinger, and educators at Lumen Vitae, Belgium. Shields and his collaborators get a brief mention in Gerard Sloyan's article on catechetics in the *Catholic Encyclopedia* (1967). Sloyan gave Shields more credit in an earlier piece included in Joseph Jungmann's *The Good News Yesterday and Today:*

> In the first place there comes to mind the Right Reverend Thomas Edward Shields. . . . Shields knew what the

Europeans had done in fostering learning-by-doing,
discovering the laws of apperception, encouraging the use of
"steps" in learning, from orientation to culmination. . . .
Shields made Americans aware of the European stress on a
new catechetical methodology, the merits of which Jungmann
later absorbed. (Jungmann 1962, 214-15)

Harold Buetow described him as "the great Catholic educational
psychologist . . . the first who, while giving religion a central place,
successfully utilized in his primary school readers the best to be taken
from the new psychologies prevalent in is time" (1970, 196). Mary
Charles Bryce (1978) presented a brief treatment of his work as one of
the progressive pioneers in Catholic religious education.

The purpose of this chapter is to retrieve Thomas Shields's
philosophy of education, especially as it relates to religious education
and catechetics. Knowledge of his successes and failures might provide
some important perspectives on religious education today. Though
none of his works are in print today, the work of this early pioneer
contains the earliest attempt by United States Catholic educator to
deal with the influential ideas of psychologists and progressive
educators that were prevalent in the latter part of the nineteenth
century and the early part of the twentieth century. Steeped in the
knowledge of the biology and psychology of his times, Shields
developed an approach to Catholic education that was educationally
progressive, yet theologically orthodox or conservative. Though little
known today, his scholarly and administrative achievements were
considerable. In his time he was the Catholic educator closest in spirit
to John Dewey.

Shields began his scholarly career at a significant time in the
history of Catholic education in the United States. The Catholic
University of America had recently opened as a graduate school to
educate clergy and laymen for the work of the Church and the
professions. The efforts of Archbishop John Lancaster Spalding had
born fruit. While many of the first professors at the university were
recruited from European Catholic institutions, there was a great desire
to have more scholars from the United States. Shields was among the
first to teach at the University to which he made a lasting contribution.
Professor Edward Pace, already on the faculty, wanted to have his

services at the university as early as 1895. Coming in 1904 he made a significant impact on the university and Catholic schools in the country (Nuesse 1990, 129-30).

Biography

There are various sources for biographical information about Thomas Edward Shields, professor at Catholic University of America from 1904 to 1921. In 1909 he published *The Making and Unmaking of a Dullard* (1909e), describing his early childhood experiences as a backward child and his strenuous effort to educate himself. Justine Ward, a collaborator, used this book and her own acquaintance with Shields to write a rather personal and laudatory account of his life, *Thomas Edward Shields: Biologist, Psychologist, Educator* (1947). The most critical biography of Shields is John Francis Murphy's unpublished dissertation, *Thomas Edward Shields: Religious Educator* (1971). Other dissertations on Shields are by O'Connor (1941), Kilcawley (1942), Cantwell (1949), and Wohlwend (1968).

Thomas Edward Shields, "perhaps the leading Catholic educator in the U.S. during the first quarter of the twentieth century" (Evans, 2003, 86), was born on May 9, 1862 to John and Bridget Broderick Shields, Irish immigrants, in Mendota, Minnesota, about six miles from St. Paul. The sixth of eight children, he was educated in his parish school by Sisters of St. Joseph from St. Paul's. Removed from school as a dullard at the age of nine to work on his family farm, he busied himself with farm work and developed a machine for grubbing. From 1879 to 1882 Shields engaged in private study with his parish priest in preparation for entrance into a seminary to prepare for the priesthood. In 1882 he entered St. Francis College in Milwaukee, Wisconsin, as a third year high school student, though he was already twenty years of age. He excelled in his studies and was accepted as a candidate for the priesthood by Archbishop John Ireland, who sent him to St. Thomas Seminary in St. Paul, Minnesota. While in the seminary Shields published his first book, *Index Omnium* (1888), a reference book to correlate information from his wide reading, a book that was read avidly by his fellow students. Father Shields offered his first Mass at St. Peter's Church,

Mendota on March 15, 1891, at the age of twenty-nine. The next year and a half he spent as an assistant pastor at the Cathedral of St. Paul.

Archbishop Ireland sent Father Shields to Johns Hopkins University to study natural science in preparation for a teaching post at the archdiocesan seminary. While residing in Baltimore at St. Mary's Seminary he gained a Master of Arts degree in 1892 in preparation for his studies at Johns Hopkins. At the same time he was enrolled in the newly established Catholic University of America in Washington, D. C., where he came into contact with Professor Edward Pace, who was keenly interested in experimental psychology. Shields did studies in biology, physiology, and zoology at Hopkins from 1892 to 1895. His Ph.D. dissertation on *The Effects of Odours, Irritant Vapours, and Mental Work upon the Blood Flow* (1895) was based on experiments he conducted. Although Catholic University was interested at the time in his joining the faculty, he returned to St. Paul at the bidding of Archbishop Ireland to teach in the new diocesan seminary where he remained from 1895 to 1898. From 1898 to 1902 he worked as an assistant pastor in churches in St. Paul until he moved to Catholic University in 1902, where he stayed until his death in 1921.

At Catholic University Shields joined the Faculty of Philosophy lecturing on biology and physiology. However, in the words of his biographer Justine Ward, "His own heart was elsewhere…his mind was turning more and more toward education as the great need of the day. . . . He bided his time, however" (1947, 127-28). In 1908 the trustees of the university gave approval to a Department of Education in which Shields functioned until his death. This enabled him to realize his dream of establishing a Catholic teacher training institution which would combine high professional standards with a commitment to Catholic doctrine.

With his colleague Edward Pace, Shields became committed to the professional education of Catholic school teachers, which he thought should take place under Catholic auspices. Responding to this need, Shields had already traveled around the country conducting institutes and courses for Catholic teachers (Neusse 1990, 172). By 1904 he had also begun teaching at the newly established Trinity College, a higher education institution for women located close to Catholic University. In 1905 he also launched the Catholic Correspondence School, which was conducted by professors of the university for the benefit of teaching sisters. In 1906 Shields founded the Catholic Associated Press, later to be known as The Catholic Education Press, through which he published a number of his books. Shields also established a Sisters College at Catholic University in 1914.

Shields's first writings on education were in *The Catholic University Bulletin*. In 1911 with Professor Edward Pace he established the *Catholic Educational Review*, which he and Pace initially financed. The review published ten issues a year in such areas as curriculum, methodology, history, administration, philosophy, psychology, teacher training, and federal relations (Murphy 1971, 134). Between 1911 and 1921 Shields authored one hundred signed articles plus book reviews. Notable were his surveys of the fields of both secular and Catholic education. The teaching of religion, however, became the main focus of many of his articles. The review continued after his death but ceased to exist in 1970. It has been noted that his pattern of control and his dedication to the review led to "a severe drain on his resources of time and energy which could have been directed to his textbook plans" (Murphy, 1971, 136).

Shields established a Program of Affiliation, whereby schools became connected to Catholic University through a type of accreditation. Pope Leo XII had urged Catholic University to enter into such arrangements to oversee Catholic education. High schools were affiliated with the university in 1912. Together with Professor Pace, Shields worked for the improvement of the Catholic school system throughout the country. The affiliated program included reports, inspections, and examinations, most of which were conducted by religious orders of sisters.

Shields devoted a great deal of his energy to the establishment of a Sisters College, a teachers training institution. Before establishing the college he invited women religious to study at Catholic University in the summers when the male population was on vacation. He worked for the establishment of this institution for four years, purchasing the land, designing the building, and raising the money. Finally, on April 1913, the Board of Trustees approved the government of the college, calling it "The Catholic Sisters College." In 1914 it was constituted as a separate corporation and affiliated to the University so that it could grant degrees. A separate building was put up in 1915. Later in 1929-30 the Sisters College became a residence when the university was opened to women students.

Shields's later years were marked by serious health problems. Though he suffered a heart attack in 1918, he still continued his strenuous schedule of teaching and writing. His teaching load in the fall of 1919 was three hundred and fifty students in three institutions: his teachers college, Trinity College, and Catholic University (Murphy 1971, 183). By December he suffered another heart attack but continued his administrative and teaching work until February 2. 1921. He died on the fifteenth of February, three months before his sixtieth birthday (Murphy 1971, 183-84). Dr. Pace spoke these words at his funeral:

> The final tribute remains to be paid not by one but by all, not in words but in deeds. The work which he began must be continued. The noble aims which he pursued must be completely fulfilled. . . . Thus shall we build the only monument that is worthy of him. None other would he have desired. (Ward 1947, 281)

In 1921 an entire issue of *The Catholic Educational Review* was dedicated to an assessment of his achievements.

Shields's Philosophy of Education

Shields's *Philosophy of Education* (1917) treats the entire curriculum of the school, not just the teaching of religion. As will be seen in the next section, religion was for him the integrating principle of the entire curriculum, since he viewed all subjects as related to religion through the important principle of correlation or integration.

Shields's *Philosophy of Education* was based on lectures that he gave at various colleges and teachers institutes between the years 1895 and 1910. Several chapters in the book were published in the *Catholic Educational Review* in 1916. Thus there is little direct engagement with John Dewey, whose classic *Democracy of Education* was published in 1916. Only one direct quote from *Democracy and Education* is found, a favorable comment on Dewey's assessment that school curriculum and practices have not sufficiently been influenced by the advance of pedagogical science (1917, 408). (References in this section, unless otherwise noted are from Shields's *Philosophy of Education*.)

There are many similarities with Dewey's thought, since both were drawing in large part on the new biology and psychology and both did their doctorates at Johns Hopkins, Shields in biology and Dewey in philosophy. Shields's main criticism of Dewey was in the latter's perceived atheism and his view that religion should be removed from the public school curriculum. Shields noted that "Professor Dewey assures us that the public schools are developing a new and higher form of religion that is devoid of all denominational content" (1911), a view that Shields contended would undermine all religion. In an earlier article, Shields explained that

> John Dewey speaks of a common religion being developed as a sort of a residual calx [*sic*] after the elimination of all divergent elements, and sundry efforts have been made to find a substitute for religion in the culture epoch theory, while a large and influential element in our midst is seeking to find a non-dogmatic morality to give strength and cohesiveness to the child's character. (1909e, 402)

Shields divided his philosophy of education into three sections: the nature of educational processes, educational aims, and educative agencies such as the home, school, and church. For him philosophy of education is a branch of applied science whose "business is to apply the truths and principles established by pure philosophy to the practical conduct of the educative process" (23). True philosophy for Shields stems from the principles of Catholic philosophy recognizing "the existence of God and the continuance of personal consciousness beyond the grave" (24). His treatise is directly opposed to those naturalistic and materialistic philosophies of education which reject religious principles and have no place for religion in education. He sets himself especially in opposition to educators who reduce religious truths to psychological processes. Shields's philosophy of education, however, draws on many principles of biology and psychology. He contends that those

Who have learned to think in terms of biology, no matter how widely they may differ in their religious beliefs or in their fundamental philosophy of life, have learned to look upon education as a process by which society seeks to perpetuate its institutions and its life and to adjust each generation of children to the environments which they must enter at the close of the school period. (31-32)

Shields thus draws extensively on the sciences of his time but always complements them with the religious truths of his Catholic faith.

Educational Processes

Part One of *Philosophy of Education* is a treatise on educative processes drawn largely from the biology and psychology of the time. Incorporated into his treatment are important elements of Christian thought. In enunciating pedagogical principles for Catholic educators Shields often uses the examples of Jesus' teaching and the liturgical rites of the church.

An important educative process is the transmission to the child of the physical and social heredity of the human race. This inheritance includes literature, science, art, institutions, and religion. Education's aim is primarily a social one, since this heritage is transmitted so that "the individual may become a more efficient member of society. To benefit the individual is secondary, as far as society is concerned, and it must always remain so" (39). For Shields, education completes individuals by preparing them to live a life in service for others as well as for themselves. Religion provides not only the belief that individuals are children of God but also affords the strongest motivation for individuals to seek the common good above their own individual interests. He also notes that the church is the institution that throughout the centuries has made this heritage available through its teachings and liturgy:

Her liturgical functions themselves have a teaching power of a high order. The very edifice in which Catholic worship is constructed points heavenward and tends to gather up the successive generations of the Church's children into solidarity;

it carries the mind back to the days of the basilica in ancient Rome and to the ages of faith. . . . The music from her organ and from her chanters stirs the feelings and the emotions of worshippers and directs them heavenward that they may harmonize with the uplift that is being experienced by all of man's consciences life. (Shields 1917, 307-08)

Shields's philosophy of education is committed to an organic and evolutionary view of the world, which he believes demands a reformulation of the functions of all educational agencies. His view is that "didactic methods are yielding to organic methods in the structure of textbooks no less than in the work of the teacher" (49). This evolutionary view affects all branches of science, linguistics, humanities, and even religion and philosophy, leading to a fundamental change from a static to a dynamic world view. The evolutionary view is especially valuable in understanding the developmental stages through which individuals pass. Embracing an evolutionary view in his *Psychology of Education,* Shields commented that,

The attitude of man's mind towards the problems of nature has undergone many important changes in modern times, one of the most remarkable of which is the shifting of his center of interest from the static to the dynamic. Formerly man studied all objects in nature as if they had come to him unchanged from the hands of the Creator; today the processes through which these objects have come to be what they are hold the chief interest of all students of nature. (1906, 41)

An understanding of the developing child and the choice of methods of instruction benefits from this dynamic view of nature, human institutions, and education.

The evolutionary view of human nature contends that humans, especially in the years of childhood, have a plasticity that educators can use to adjust individuals to a changing environment. This plasticity is necessary for the survival both of the race and the individual. On first reading one gets the impression that Shields sees education as merely adjusting individual to their environment since he argues that children's plasticity enables the teacher to educate children "to deal effectively with the new and rapidly changing social and economic conditions under which they must live" (66). But Shields goes further to assert that plasticity includes "the ability to change environment in many ways so as to make it meet the needs of self" (66). For Shields:

> It is the business of education to help the child so to modify himself and so to modify his environment that the one may be properly adjusted to the other. It is the business of education so to strengthen the will, so to clarify the intelligence, and so to preserve the plasticity of the individual, that he may conquer his environment and permanently conquer himself. (67)

Shields further states that Christianity has historically been involved in the process of conquering the environment and controlling the self. The church has adjusted itself to live in many environments and many forms of government. Thus, human plasticity enables the Christian educator to help individuals to transform the inner person through a redeeming process. Education's spiritual task is both to conserve what is good in the past and "to help individuals meet new conditions and new environments with new adjustments" (77).

Mental growth and development get special attention from Shields. He distinguishes between mental growth, which is a quantitative increase and mental development, which implies qualitative increase. His interest is primarily in mental development, that is, "in changes from simplicity to complexity, from homogeneity to heterogeneity, from latency to epiphany" (99). Since Shields recognizes the importance that environment, both physical and social, plays in both growth and development, he stresses that educators should provide an environment "which will permit of the fullest realization of each individual life" (108). A mindless memorization of facts, even if they are the truths of the catechism, does not constitute real mental development for Shields. A healthy pedagogy recognizes that growth and development come from within the person, not through accretion of information. It is for this reason that Shields favored organic methods over didactic ones. Committed to methods that stress process, he asserts that the quantity of truth given to the child in the beginning of the educative process is a supremely negligible factor.

Shields recognized stages of mental development, though he does not clearly differentiate them. In later stage theories, stages are linked together in a rigid causal sequence in which each previous stage is an adequate preparation for the next stage as well as its cause. Thus each stage is reached through a reconstruction of the previous stage in which that which was latent is brought forth and made functional. Each stage is connected with an adjustment to the environment. Shields, however, describes the stages of development in rather general terms: "Human consciousness passes from the instinctive phase of infancy through the imitative phase of childhood and youth to freedom and self-determination in adult life" (124). Some connections with the cognitive development theory of Jean Piaget are apparent. It is Shields's view that knowledge of stages of mental development is important for educators. For him, as for Piaget and other stage theorists, mental development precedes mental growth and thus "the pupil's growth in knowledge should not be advanced beyond the point where such growth is necessary or helpful to mental development" (131).

The upshot of Shields's discussion of educative processes according to the new scientific understanding of the person is that the role of the teacher should change greatly. Teachers are no longer mere purveyors of facts but rather must "minister to the growing mind . . . [and] guide the complex processes of development that are taking place in the minds and hearts of pupils" (145). This is so because since education is a process that takes place in the mind of the student and is governed by the laws of the mind, teachers can influence education only if they know the laws of life and mind that govern these processes.

Like the educational progressives of his era, Shields assigned great importance to the function of experience in the educative process. For him, experience is the most important factor in education. New experiences serve "to modify inherited or previously acquired adjustment since education is far more extensively occupied with modifying previous habits than with modifying the meager inheritance of the child's instincts" (143). Thus Shields assigns two roles to personal experience: modifying and improving adjustments to the environment, and perfecting children's use of the experiences of others and the wisdom and experience of the race. He was also realistic about the limitation of experience in education, for while it may be the best teacher it is at the same time "the slowest of teachers and the most

expensive" (152). For him the task of teachers is to guide children in
the acquisition of personal experiences by selecting those experiences
that will enable students to learn from present conditions and keep
themselves open to future developments and prevent exposure to
experiences that might arrest or be harmful to mental development.
Like Dewey in his *Experience and Education* (1938), Shields recognized
that experience could function efficiently in the wrong direction.
Disagreeable experiences might build up inhibitions towards future
activities or even arrest mental development. He warned against poor
experiences in the learning of religion, such as "the practice of
compelling children, under threats of punishment, to memorize
catechetical formulas which are unintelligible to them" (153). Shields
adds that the power of experience is so strong that it would be highly
imprudent to expose the child to haphazard experiences until such time
as their mental development allowed them to prudently select
experiences from which they might learn.

Educational Aims

A large part of Shields's treatise on philosophy of education is
devoted to the aims and purposes of education. As other progressives,
Shields broadened the discussion of aims to go beyond the transmission
of liberal culture to include political, economic, and social aims. His
discussion of aims seems to be in line with the progressive Cardinal
Principles of Education, which dominated educational debate in the
United States for a number of years (Spring 1986, 202-04).

Shields made it clear where his educational priorities were. He
began his discussion of aims with a chapter entitled "The Ultimate Aim
of Christian Education," which for him must deal with the individual's
intellectual, spiritual, and ethical nature and to which all other
considerations, though important, are subordinate. For determining
the ultimate aim of Christian education, Shields turns to the Gospels
and the guidance of the church to arrive at this formulation:

> The unchanging aim of Christian education is, and always has
> been, to put the pupil into possession of a body of truth
> derived from nature and from divine revelation, from the
> concrete world of man's hand, and from the content of human

speech, in order to bring his conduct into conformity with Christian ideals and with the standards of the civilization of his day. (171)

This definition raises a number of questions. One is struck with the apparent contradictions it manifests when compared to previous and subsequent discussions in the book. In this definition Shields reverts to a transmissive and didactic approach that he otherwise rejects. Though a progressive in many ways, he is not only far distant in this definition from John Dewey, but also from liberal Protestant religious educators such as George Coe and Sophia Fahs. None of these could have said as Shields did that "dogmas must be accepted without change or modification by all those who enter into her [the church's] fold" (300). Shields's religious views remain dogmatic though his understanding of persons and the educational process are scientific and progressive. He, however, did not view revelation as hampering human freedom but as imparting "security, greater keenness and a wider range to human vision" (172). Revelation does not supplant human intelligence but presupposes it, removing limitations as well as defects from human understanding. For Shields, knowledge in itself was not the ultimate aim of Christian education, but rather knowledge that leads to an adjustment of the pupil to Christian ideals of life and the standards of civilization. For the reasons given above, Woods (2004) hesitates to call Shields a progressive. This matter was treated in the chapter on Shields's colleague, Edward Pace.

It is clear that Shields considers the issue of authority as very important in Christian education. He invokes the axiom of Augustine and Anselm, *credo ut intelligam*, in contending that faith and authority are necessary at the beginning of learning. He believes, however, that truths should eventually be accepted by the intellect for their own sake. Thus dependence comes before independence in both the physical and intellectual sphere. For Shields, the task of the teacher of religion is "to establish vital continuity between the powers of the natural man and the supernatural virtues which he [the teacher] would inculcate through divine authority" (177). It is the teacher's task to channel the child's natural instincts into higher values for the conduct of adult life. In concluding his chapter on the ultimate aims of Christian education, Shields describes education as a process of transforming natural instincts while preserving and enlarging their power, bringing the flesh under the control of the spirit by drawing on the experience of the human race, divine revelation, and grace to bring the individual into conformity with Christian ideas and the standards of civilization of the day. The overall aim is to transform egoism into altruism, a social development that would lead to a regard for all persons.

Philosophy of Education treats a number of secondary aims of education that Shields considers as means for attaining the ultimate aim and which give direction to the efforts of the teacher. Physical education, concerned with the preservation of health and the development of the organism, entails an understanding of the laws of health. Both home and school are involved in this education, which proceeds through the formation of good health habits and includes outdoor play for children. He warns that children should not be permitted to follow their own impulses without restraint and without any guidance from authority. Physical health is important because it is the basis for mental development. This Catholic progressive concludes this section with these wise words:

> In all that is done for the child, consideration must be given both to his mental and moral nature as well as to his physical life. The preserving of the proper balance is not the least difficult tasks which are so lightly assigned to the teacher. (193)

A healthy balance between physical and mental development is a dominant theme in Shields's philosophy. Accepting the teaching of Thomas Aquinas on the unity of body and soul, Shields bids teachers to respect the growing development of the child. His axiom is that teachers should give children "only that which is necessary and helpful to the phase of development" (202) through which they are passing. Limitations of the children's minds demand that truths and ideas be cast in an appropriate manner, a principle that Shields applied in his religion textbook series. Teachers are directed to avoid giving the child an adult point of view, since teaching should proceed by awakening children's interests and developing their powers to internalize their social inheritance. Specialized learning should be introduced only in secondary and higher education.

Education for economic efficiency is an additional secondary aim, which for Shields means to train the eye and hand so that they may in due time be able to achieve the means of support: food, shelter, physical comfort, and well being (213). This aim is important, for it will engender in children self-respect and an integrated personality. The school should build on this form of education, which begins in the home. Economic efficiency serves not only individual needs but is also greatly desirable for societal growth. Like Dewey, Shields points out that people do not live in isolation and that the growing complexity of economic systems demands an education comparable to the demands of the marketplace. Many forms of cooperation are needed in the new industrial society of the turn of the century. For Shields,

> The more complex our civilization becomes and the more completely we pass from a tool to a machine civilization, the more necessary does it become for man to learn to cooperate efficiently with his fellow-man in order to sustain life and to attain to the well-being and happiness that his nature demands. (221-22)

Like progressive educators but unlike other Catholic educators who favored a strictly liberal and non-utilitarian curriculum, Shields was a strong advocate of industrial education in the schools as well as separate industrial schools. While considering industrial education a public and governmental matter, he did not advocate this education primarily for the benefit of employers. Though he rejected the rigid educational system in Germany, where at an early age certain students were channeled into industrial schools, he may have come closer than he wanted to this system when he contended that "it is the business of education to fit the children of each generation to take their places effectively under the conditions of the economic world which they will meet on reaching adult years" (227).

The aim of economic efficiency, however, must be balanced by education for individual culture, which serves both individuals and society. Shields is consistent in making it clear that education for individual culture does not consist primarily in the transmission of a culture, though a wide range of knowledge is required of the cultured person, but in "the development of the student's powers and faculties and his mastery of the art of study and of the utilization of knowledge" (243). Content is valued not in itself but as food and direction for a growing and developing life. For Shields, culture

> consists not in the knowledge of any one subject nor in the ability to do any one thing, however valuable such knowledge and ability may be, but in the power to understand the thought and to sympathize with the work of all who labor for the upbuilding of mankind. (246)

Culture also demands development of the aesthetic faculty as well as normal development and control of the emotions. However, for Shields, culture is not a mere addition to life or an embellishment but rather a quality affecting the whole of life, permeating the depths of character and leading to the completion of persons by inspiring them to the service of God and humankind. In summary, culture for Shields includes a reasonably wide knowledge, a thoroughly coordinated knowledge, a ready and easy control of the knowledge possessed, the habitual use of knowledge and mental power to meet the demands of an ever-changing world, an aesthetic sensibility, and control over emotions.

The final secondary aim of education in Shields's philosophy is education for citizenship. After reviewing various political philosophies of the state and education from Plato to Bismarck, Shields proposes an education for democracy that would prepare citizens for the discharge of their duties towards the state. He holds the Jeffersonian view that a democratic state demands some kind of inequality in the education of its members. While some persons are to be educated for leadership, others should be trained for the ordinary tasks of dedicated citizens and judicious voters. Democracy demands universal education of a general nature so that children may be able to determine their vocation in life and thus the state will benefit from talent wherever it is found.

Citizenship education should strive to inculcate six chief moral qualities. First, citizens need faith in their fellow citizens and in their leaders, courts of justice, merchants, and teachers. Citizens require the moral quality of hope for a stable social order. A healthy democracy requires love towards one's fellow citizens, which manifests itself in respect, cooperation, and solidarity, and should extend beyond the boundaries of national interest to include other nations. This spirit of love, based on Christian principles, must combat excessive competition, selfishness, and greed as well as inspire citizens to work for the common good. The good citizen should consider the public good before any private advantage and be willing to sacrifice for others even on the battle front. Education should inculcate respect for the law, which entails involvement in enacting just and wise legislation, cooperating with the legal and judicial system, and obeying the law. The final quality in citizenship education is self-government over one's desires and passions. It is Shield's view that while public schools inculcate these virtues, religious schools can offer stronger basis for motivating students for education for citizenship, which is essentially moral education.

Educational Agencies

Education in one sense consists in adjusting children to various environments in which they will spend their adult years. The chief environments that children need to be adjusted to are the institutions of home, state, and the church.

For Shields, the family is the chief environment for shaping the life of individuals. Within families parents have "complete control over the rearing and the education of the children, subject only to such state supervision as is needed to prevent neglect of the children's welfare" (281). Shields recognized that in industrialized society the school, state, and church took over some of the educational responsibilities that families exercised in the past. Freed from some of its industrial tasks, the family can more effectively seek a higher development of mental and moral life. However, children's attendance at school does not remove all educational responsibility from parents, since the family is still the most formative institution in the education of children. In Shields's view, both the state and the church should seek ways to help families in their educational mission. What is needed is a new type of family life in which families can adjust to the new economic and social conditions of the world. For Shields, the home of the future should develop high ideals in children; become a gathering place of love in the evening, a sanctuary of life, and a dwelling place of love where the mind can grow in truth and beauty.

Shields's view of the family is what we might expect from a man of his time: father at work, mother in the home. He repeats many ideas from his *The Education of Our Girls* (1907) about how the girls of the then new age were to be educated. As women are freed from many home chores, they should spend time "in the adornment of the home, in the pursuit of literature and art, and in the wider intellectual and moral interests that are shaping the course of advancing civilization" (290). Since women's principal function rests in procreation and education, they need to possess a keen knowledge of the society in which their children will eventually live as adults. Women who work before marriage have the advantage of first-hand experiences of these conditions. The education given to women should be directed first of all towards her role as mother and educator of children and secondarily toward preparing them for work in the world. Shields was very much in favor of the then contemporary movement for preparing parents to be effective educators in the home, especially for children that need special care. He also urged the Catholic public to become involved in the progressive movement for "improving the conditions of home life, by proper housing, adequate measures for sanitation, proper diet and artistic embellishment of the home" (297).

Shields described the role the Catholic Church has played through the centuries in providing surety through exercising an infallible teaching office. The Church, unlike the school, teaches all persons and adapts its message to all people in all situations. The Catholic Church exercises a teaching function through Councils, definition of dogmas, the example of its members, and through liturgical expressions.

The distinctive feature that Shields adds to an understanding of the teaching role of the Church is his psychological analysis of how this role operates. He finds in the teaching Church the embodiment of all the psychological principles that had been recently been discovered. The Church reaches the entire person, intellect, will, emotions, senses, imagination, aesthetic sensibilities, muscles, and powers of expression. The very structure of Church buildings and the liturgical rites touch many aspects of peoples' lives. While Shields finds in these structures and rites sensory motor training, appeals to emotions and to individual and group memory, it is especially the emotional nature of this teaching method that is attractive to Shields. Liturgical expressions appeal to the emotions, which psychologists consider most important in learning. In his analysis of the sacraments of the Church, he shows how emotional elements are paramount in liturgical celebrations. Thus, in his view the Church manifests the organic methods of teaching that schools are asked to use:

> The Church, through all the forms of her organic teaching, aims at cultivating feeling, but she does not allow her teaching activity to culminate in feeling, which she values as a means to an end; she employs it to move to action and to form character and she never leaves it without the stamp and the guidance of intellect. As the feelings glow to incandescence, she imparts to them definite direction and animates them with a purpose which, after the emotions and the feelings subside, remains as a guiding principle of conduct. (314)

The Church appeals not only to basic instincts but also to the desire of its members, especially children, to imitate powerful models. She stresses the following of Christ and holds before members the example of many holy men and women.

Because of changes in society and its needs the school originated as an institution to supplement the work of the home, the church, and the state. Schools came into existence to prepare children to take their place in society and its various institutions, though they remain subordinate to the institutions–home, church, and state–that established them. Though Shields deplored the emergence of the secular school in the United States where religious teaching was not permitted, he did applaud efforts to introduce moral teaching into the school. He did not think, however, that such teaching would be effective, disconnected as it was from religious moorings. For him,

> When religion is properly taught, it fixed in the mind certain beliefs that steady it in the midst of doubt and certain principles of conduct which guide and protect it in the midst of temptation. The adaptation to environment which religion inculcates is not a weak yielding to every influence, but rather the power of discriminating good from evil and holding fast to that which is good. (346)

Shields recognized changes in the purposes of schools once they came under the control of the state and moved away from the moral and affective control of church and home. Character building, the formation of social habits, and instilling of patriotism became more important than the development of intellectual culture. The purpose of state schools became the preparation of children for enlightened citizenship and proper adjustment of the individuals to institutional life. The curriculum shifted from an emphasis on formal knowledge to technical skills, history, economics, and literature. The emerging social sciences also influenced changes in schools with their recognition that feelings are powerful motivations for knowledge and action, that education should develop moral qualities that enable individuals to control social actions, that education has as its task the assimilation of each generation to social life, and that it is through the school that society achieves its progress by implementing necessary changes in curriculum.

Shields was not totally satisfied with these educational developments since they included the removal of religion from the schools and came close to minimizing the role of the home and the church in the sphere of education. Deploring German influence on United States schools with the introduction of vocational schools, Shields appeared to be in favor of efforts to reinstate the aim of developing the culture of individuals. He was also uneasy with vocational schools "whose explicit aim is the increase of individual efficiency and increased power of the individual to enlarge his learning capacity" (370).

Because of their stress on religion and moral education and the integration of all subjects around religion, Catholic schools remained the main focus of Shield's concern, though he did advise Catholics to work for better public schools. His philosophy of education is for the most part a philosophy of Catholic schools. The religion which Catholic schools were to teach was not something apart from life.

Shields and Religious Education

It is clear that Shields's main educational concern was religious education. His first educational writings were on the teaching of religion. In this section his views on teaching religion will get greater attention, even though some of these ideas have already been touched upon in treating his general philosophy of education.

Shields first addressed the teaching of religion in *The Psychology of Education* (1906), in which he tried to close the gap between pedagogical science and the principles of Catholic education. In this book he drew on the work of progressive educators such as William James, William Kilpatrick, and others in enunciating important principles designed to move school teaching from a subject-centered curriculum to a child-centered one. Shields saw a consonance between the methods of Jesus and the methods of the new pedagogical science. He did not, however, ignore the content of education, as many progressive educators were charged with doing. For him, children were entitled to be taught the scientific, literary, aesthetic, institutional, and religious inheritance, without which they could not be educated persons. For him the purpose of religious education was

> to put the pupil into possession of a body of truth derived from those four sources [revelation, nature, human thought and action, language] and to bring his conduct into conformity with Christian ideals and with the standards of the civilization of his day. (Shields 1906, 38)

Shields gave even more explicit emphasis to religion in *The Teaching of Religion* (1908a), where he centered teaching on the child's experiences, feelings, needs, and potential. The teaching of religion was also to be correlated with all subjects in the curriculum:

> To teach religion effectively it must, of course, be taught in connection with history and philosophy, with the growth of languages, the development of human institutions, and the works of God which meet us at every turn along the pathways of natural science. (1908a, 18)

Shields devoted special consideration in his work to the teacher of religion, distinguishing between the role of theologian who propounded theology and the teacher of religion who was concerned primarily with the formation of character and not with conveying theological knowledge, not with increasing "the store of theological knowledge about God, about man or about subjects deemed important in the world of adults" but with shedding "light on every truth that claims admittance to the mind" (1908a, 34). Shields concern for children and teachers of religion inspired him to develop texts for teaching religion that abandoned the methods of the catechism.

Attack on the *Baltimore Catechism*

Though Shields had already written on the teaching of religion, his ideas received greater notice when he addressed the Catholic Educational Association at their annual meeting in 1908. At this meeting he made use of progressive educational principles to attack the question-and-answer approach to teaching religion used in the time-honored catechisms of the Church, notably the *Baltimore Catechism*, which was almost exclusively in use in Catholic elementary schools. The *Baltimore Catechism* was the most widely used tool for teaching religion from 1885 to the 1960s. It has been noted that

> The large majority of religion teachers and textbook writers almost totally ignored advances made by professions in the sector of public school education. Perhaps the question-answer mold of the catechism genre had become so set that any departures from it, if accepted at all, were tolerated as a kind of fad that, if sufficiently disregarded, would surely go away. (Bryce 1970, 143)

An exception to this was the work of Shields. In his 1908 talk he presented theories of learning, the need to adapt religion to the child's psychological development, the necessity of a new method to replace the question-and-answer method of the catechism, and the need for new textbooks that would incorporate modern psychological findings.

Shields's ideas were challenged by Father Peter Yorke, a respected social activist and Catholic educator who had published religion textbooks and was an officer of the Catholic Educational Association. Yorke did not directly address Shields's dependence on psychological principles but drew upon his own pastoral experience in arguing that there was no danger in overloading the child's memory but rather a danger in not cultivating the power of memory. Calling Shields's system of teaching religion no less than revolutionary, he saw no need to go outside the Catholic system "to give scientific justification for the principles and methods which are the noblest gifts your holy founders gave you brothers and sisters of the Catholic schools" (Shields, 1908b, 235-36). An unsigned editorial *Catechetics* in the *American Ecclesiastical Review* (1908) called for a thorough review of catechetical methods in light of Shields's criticism. The review also praised the religion textbooks authored by Shields. Though called for by Shields, this revision did not happen until the 1960s. Shields efforts to replace the *Baltimore Catechism* did not succeed, but he stands at the beginning of an approach to teaching religion that would eventually undermine its approach and dominance. His pedagogical approach would eventually win the day, except among traditionalist Catholics. Yet Shields receives little credit among historians of Catholic religious education, perhaps because of his early death, lack of colleagues to continue his work, and his manner of going it alone (Murphy 1971, 128).

The Teaching of Religion

Shields further explained his theory of teaching religion in the *Catholic University Bulletin* in 1909. This bulletin was founded in 1895 by Thomas Joseph Shahan, rector of the University, to bring the newest educational ideas to professors and students at the university. In one article, Shields sought to bring "the teaching of religion into conformity with the fundamental principles of education which have been firmly established through the advance of pedagogical science" (1909a, 65). Decrying ultra-conservatism in methods of teaching religion, he appealed for organic methods based on the principles of genetic or developmental psychology and on modern psychological studies of memory, mental assimilation, the role of feelings in learning, imitation, and the principle of correlation or integration of all learning.

It was Shields's contention that these principles are all found in the way that Jesus taught and the way in which the Church has taught its members throughout the centuries, principally through its liturgy. Jesus taught in a direct and simple manner. He taught people not "truths to be accepted in set phrases and stored in the memory, but as the bread of life that was to enter into the depths of their being and transform all their thinking and their acting" (1909a, 69). He taught truths that were to take root in intelligence and bear fruit in conduct. Thus teachers of religion should not rest content with the students' verbal memorization of truths but attempt to make sublime truths intelligible to learners.

According to Shields, there were four phases in Jesus' method of teaching. First, he appealed to listeners' observations of familiar phenomena in the vegetable and animal world, such as birds, trees, and sowing of seed. Second, he appealed to human feelings and emotions, such as a shepherd's love for his sheep, a father's forgiveness of a wayward son, and the anger of a king. Third, he encouraged listeners to contemplate the state of children of the kingdom in comparison to dwellers in lower stages. Finally, he pointed out the obligation for children of the kingdom to "bring their conduct into conformity with their high estate as children of God" (1909a, 71). Jesus taught by proceeding "from the known to the unknown; from the tangible and concrete to the abstract and spiritual, from the natural to the supernatural. (72). At times Jesus made use of object lessons, as when he cursed the fig tree or commended the one leper who returned to give him thanks. He used his miracles to drive home truths about the Eucharist by multiplying bread and fishes. Through all of these ways Jesus led listeners to understanding sublime spiritual truths.

It is noted by Shields that Jesus' method of teaching was continued by his followers. His apostles instructed the first Christians in spirituals truths. Gradually, the fundamental truths of Christianity made up the Christian Scriptures and eventually found their way into clear definitions in creeds and later catechisms. But in a special way these truths were kept alive before the people through the sacraments of the Church and the liturgy. The liturgy with its poetry and music lent beauty and eloquence, while paintings, sculpture, and architecture in the great churches and cathedrals spoke eloquently to the hearts and minds of believers. To be faithful to Jesus' model of teaching, the teacher of religion

> must take into account natural phenomena, human emotions and passions, the figures and prophecies of the Old Testament and their fulfillment in the New. He must seek to make the Saviour live in the imagination and in the heart and he must call to his assistance every resource of art. (1909a, 75)

This is the method of teaching that influenced the series of religion texts that Shields published for children.

In a second article on the teaching of religion, Shields (1909b) described the philosophy behind his religion textbooks and readers. He noted how improvements had been made in arithmetic and science textbooks for elementary schools according to psychological and pedagogical principles. He then launched into a criticism of the catechism of Christian doctrine which was widely used in Catholic schools. He considered it for the most part

> cast in the dryest of didactic forms and completely isolated from all the other subjects of the curriculum. The thought is abstract in the extreme and it is couched in language for which the child had no preparation either proximate or remote. There is no attempt made to build up in the child-mind vigorous masses capable of aiding in the assimilation of religious truth. The book seems designed solely for production of a verbal memory product as if there were a consciousness somewhere that this was the only end possible of attainment. The whole stress is laid on the form of question and answer which will facilitate a test of the capacity of the pupils' memory. . . . Back of this method there seems to be an incredible belief in the power of memorized formulae to translate themselves at a later period into vital elements in the conduct of the adult. (Shields 1909b, 159)

The philosophy behind his textbook series, which included textbooks for the first four grades plus readers, was based on a correlated or integrated curriculum utilizing the most recent developments in genetic psychology and cognate branches. This philosophy can be illustrated by an examination of *Religion, First Book* (Shields 1908c). The book presents the Lord's Prayer, a large portion of the Apostles Creed, and the birth of Jesus. At the same time the book is the child's first reader, first nature study book, and a description of institutions that affect the child. It lays the foundation for aesthetic development along the three distinct lines of form, color, and rhythm. Religion is thus integrated into a book containing nature studies, domestic scenes, and songs all adapted to the child's mental capacity. It speaks not of doctrinal definitions but of the child's home, and familiar objects of the environments. Use is made of songs and pictures. The book contains the five essential elements of Catholic education: *Science*, an exploration of the child's physical environment; *Letters*, human achievements transmitted though oral and written language; *Aesthetics*, recognizing beauty in all its forms; *Institutions*, knowledge of the home, church, and state; and *Religion*, a basic knowledge of Christian truths. Each part of the book begins with nature study and ends with two songs. The five parts of the book deal with fundamental instincts that determine the child's attitude towards parents, namely love of parents. A story about a family of robins presents all the elements of healthy family living.

Shields gave his own summary of what he attempted to accomplish in *Religion, First Book*, the initial book in the child's formal religious instruction:

> It contains five parables in each of which a scene from bird life is used to develop a corresponding scene in human life and to teach the child his duties in relation to the truth presented. The two scenes are often used as the natural basis of the corresponding supernatural truth and supernatural virtue. The movement in each case is the same as that in Our Lord's parables. The truths are thus presented to the child in such a way that they fill his senses and lay hold of his imagination; they are lifted into the structure of his conscious life and find expression in his thoughts, words and deeds. In other words, the truths are not carried by the child as a memory load, they have become a joyous part of this life. (1909c, 287)

An important principle of learning for Shields, as for many other psychologically-oriented educators of his time, was the principle of correlation. As a principle of learning it meant that each new thought element be related to the previous content of the mind not along structural lines alone, but in a relationship of reciprocal activity (Shields 1911). Correlation was also a curricular principle according to which subjects are organized in such a way that they are related to one another. For Shields and many Catholic educators, this entailed that religion be part of general education, since without it such subjects as history and literature could not be adequately understood and religion itself would suffer its isolation from the rest of the curriculum. For him, "religion, to be effectively taught, must be interwoven with every item of knowledge presented to the child and it must be the animating principle of every precept which he is taught to obey" (1911, 425).

Conclusion

When one examines the career and writings of Thomas E. Shields, one wonders why he has not found a more prominent place in the history of Catholic education in the United States. He was the first person to bring a scholarly approach to the teaching of religion by introducing principles from biology, psychology, and pedagogy into the teaching of religion. He attended not only to the content of religious education but also to sound methods. His passion for the education of teachers for Catholic schools has few peers. His works on psychology of education and philosophy of education provided a basis for the entire enterprise of Catholic education. He initiated a journal dedicated to Catholic education which lasted for almost seventy years.

Besides his scholarly contributions, Shields contributed to Catholic education in many other ways. The School of Education at the Catholic University of America which he lobbied for still thrives. The enterprise of catechetics and religious education within that university owes much to his initiatives. His tireless efforts in behalf of preparation of teachers for Catholic schools through institutes, a summer school, and a separate college should receive greater recognition.

Possible reasons for Shields's lack of recognition are discussed in Murphy's dissertation (1971). An early death from heart failure left a number of his tasks uncompleted. Shields's style of work did not include close collaboration with others at Catholic University, nor did he leave disciples at Catholic University to continue his work. Perhaps he tried to do too many things while carrying a heavy teaching schedule both at Catholic University and Trinity College, Washington. Also, most of his books were published by a press which he established, thus limiting their circulation. Murphy also speculates about limitations in his personality development, especially an ability to work collaboratively with others and to delegate to others responsibility.

The times in which Shields lived were not right for a full appreciation of his abilities. He was a progressive at a time when the Church was in combat with modern thought, loosely called modernism. Shields would have benefited greatly from association with members of the then newly established Religious Education Association. There is no evidence that he participated at any of its meetings nor was he ever published in its journal, though his work receives a number of favorable comments by both Catholics and Protestants.

George Johnson:
Policy Maker for Catholic Education

JOHN L. ELIAS

Social and Cultural Context

The context of George Johnson's contribution to Catholic education was United States Catholicism in the years from 1920 to 1950. The Catholic Church had been committed to establish Catholic schools since the Plenary Council of Baltimore in 1888. These schools were to protect the faith of Catholic immigrants in a predominantly Protestant culture that Catholic leaders viewed as inimical to the faith of the immigrants. The formation of Catholic identity was entrusted largely to these schools, which also were to preserve a distinctive Catholic culture. The efforts of leaders were consumed with finding support for these schools as well as training people to lead and teach in them (Veverka 1988, 1993).

Opposition to Catholic schools increased after World War I. Anti-Catholic nativism focused on attacking Catholic schools for promoting values that were perceived as counter to the national democratic tradition. In response state legislatures designed measures to control Catholic schools through the regulation of the curriculum of the schools as well as teacher training and certification. The state of Oregon in 1923 passed a law banning all non-public schools in the early grades. Catholic educational leaders went on the defensive and attempted to meet the challenge by showing that their schools were educationally the same as public schools, except for the teaching of religion.

Catholic leaders breathed a sigh of relief when the Supreme Court in 1925 overturned the Oregon school law and asserted the rights of non-public schools to exist. After this decision Catholic educational leaders doubled their efforts to foster the opening of schools and attended to making these schools competitive educational institutions. They also grappled with issues such as the distinctive identity of Catholic schools, how much of progressive education Catholic schools could accommodate, how teachers and administrators might best be educated, and how these schools could make the teaching of religion a controlling factor in Catholic life. These educators were interested not only in Catholic schools but in the education of the Catholic community.

Among the leaders in this effort between the 1920s and the 1950s was Monsignor George Johnson of Catholic University and the National Catholic Welfare Conference (NCWC). Johnson labored tirelessly to improve Catholic schools. By the time of his death in 1944 the Catholic school system was a strong and vibrant force not only in the Catholic community but also in the nation. While Johnson began his career as a philosopher of Catholic education, once be became the United States Bishops' spokesperson and policy maker he became deeply embroiled in the politics of education at the federal level. He toiled strenuously to make the schools educationally sound, distinctively Catholic, and sufficiently American. He answered charges that these schools had lost their religious identity or were socially divisive. Johnson did this at a time of general suspicion about Catholic schools and at the time when the immigrant Catholic Church was in a "ghetto period."

George Johnson: A Short Biography

George Johnson was born in Toledo, Ohio, on February 22, 1889, and died in Washington, D.C. on June 5, 1944. He was the son of Henry and Kathryn (McCarthy) Johnson. After studying at St. John's University, Toledo, (M.A., 1912), and St. Bernard's Seminary, Rochester, N.Y., he was sent to the North American College, Rome, Italy, where he was ordained a priest in 1914. Following his return from Rome, Johnson served for two years as secretary to the bishop of Toledo. He then left the diocese to obtain his doctorate in education (1919) at the Catholic University of America, Washington, D.C., under Dr. Thomas E. Shields, at this time an outstanding scholar of Catholic education. Upon his return to the diocese, Johnson served as diocesan superintendent of schools in Toledo until 1921.

The trajectory of Johnson's career is shown in his writings and the various positions he held during his career. He wrote a dissertation in 1919 on the philosophy of Catholic elementary school. In a work of great erudition, Johnson reviewed the history and philosophy of the curriculum of schooling with special attention to Catholic schools. He manifested a thorough and sympathetic knowledge of scholarly developments in Europe and the United States. Like his mentor Thomas Shields, Johnson embraced many of the principles of the new psychology and pedagogy of the time. His entire dissertation was published over a period of two years in the *Catholic Educational Review* (1919-20), edited by Shields and Edward Pace at Catholic University.

Johnson succeeded Shields at Catholic University after the latter's sudden death in 1921. Upon taking this teaching position in the Department of Education he began to address many of the curricular, administrative, and policy issues facing Catholic education, especially those concerning Catholic schools. Johnson was often asked to address gatherings of Catholic educators on such topics as curriculum reform, preparation of teachers and administrators, the teaching of religion, parent teachers groups, the role of pastors in education, and teacher shortages. Most of these talks as well as articles on other subjects were published in the *Catholic Educational Review*, of which he became editor. Johnson also continued the work of the Sisters College established by Shields.

In 1925 the hierarchy of the Catholic Church chose Johnson to be their major educational spokesperson as head of the Catholic Education Department of the National Catholic Welfare Conference (NCWC). He was also named secretary general of the National Catholic Educational his Association (NCEA). He held both of these positions until his death in 1944. The premature death of Johnson in 1944 marked the end of the formal relationship whereby a professor of education at Catholic University was also head the Catholic Education Department of the NCWC (Neusse 1900, 348).

In his national role Johnson addressed such federal issues as the debate over the United States Office of Education, federal aid to schools, the centralization of schools at the federal level, the Depression Era educational initiatives of President Franklin D. Roosevelt, the wartime educational initiatives of the same president, and the plan for recovery after the war. Johnson was also appointed to many federal commissions that dealt with these problems where he articulated the bishops' opposition to many of these initiatives.

While Johnson became the chief defender of Catholic education, his reputation was that of a conciliator. He made the case for Catholic education on many occasions, and in so doing he gradually distanced himself from his earlier enthusiasm for many of the reforms of progressive education. He still accepted much of the psychology and pedagogy of the progressives but rejected what he thought were their heretical philosophical views. His progressive stance favored supplementing traditional study and recitation assignments with group discussions, field trips and projects.

A strong supernationalist perspective permeated Johnson's approach to education, untouched as almost all Catholic educators were at the time by the currents of liberal theology that appealed to many Protestant religious educators. Much of his work can be understood as an attempt to make the case that Catholic schools offer a distinctive philosophy of life and an education that would better serve the interests of Catholic parents and their children. Catholics and their schools were often on the attack during these years for distancing themselves from the public school movement.

Johnson was well suited to be the foremost spokesperson for Catholic education in the first half of the twentieth century. He was also well prepared to be their educational leader during the time of the Second World War. In the words of a contemporary historian of Catholic education,

> Johnson was practical, pragmatic, and self-serving yet he also had strong convictions about the purposes of Catholic schooling in a free society. He combined native organizational and political skills with the intellectual drive and educational philosophy of Thomas Shields. (Walch 2003, 124)

While not the scholar that Shields was, Johnson strove to articulate a constructive policy for Catholic education. He argued for the setting of defined aims and criteria for Catholic education and for effective diocesan structures. He also endorsed "the use of objective tests and supported educational programs geared to the individual needs of the child" (McCluskey 1973, 393).

In his capacity as the Catholic Bishops' spokesperson, Johnson served on many federal commissions. He was appointed by President

Herbert Hoover to the National Committee on Education. President Roosevelt appointed him to the following committees or commissions: President's Advisory Committee on Education, American Youth Commission, the Advisory Committee of the National Youth Administration, the Wartime Commission of the United States Office of Education, the Advisory Committee on Welfare and Recreation, and the Committee on Problems and Plans of the American Council on Education. He has been called the organization man of Catholic education (Walch 2003, 125)

Politically astute as he was, Johnson developed close cooperation among the NCEA, the NCWC, and the educational department of the Catholic University. His work extended to establishing ties with secular organizations such as the United States Office of Education, whose establishment he had previously opposed, the National Educational Association, and the American Council of Education, on which he served as secretary. As the Bishops' spokesperson, Johnson opposed many New Deal initiatives of President Roosevelt, mentioned above. The bishops were very wary of federal intrusion into education because ultimately this might affect Catholic schools negatively.

When the Commission on American Citizenship was founded at Catholic University by the American hierarchy in 1938, Johnson was named to its executive committee. In 1943 he was made director of this commission. He wrote the commission's highly regarded statement of principles, *Better Men for Better Times* (1943), as well as a study of Catholic elementary school curricula, three textbooks on Bible and Church history, and many periodical articles. On this commission Johnson was responsible for the education and curricular work. He also aided in the preparation of all materials that the commission produced. From 1921 until his death he was one of the editors of the *Catholic Educational Review*. In November 1942 he was named domestic prelate by Pius XII.

One fact about Johnson not usually mentioned in accounts of his life is that he was an active member and a vice-president of the Religious Education Association. He published articles in *Religious Education*, the journal of the association, in which he made a spirited case for Catholic education. A notice of his untimely death appeared in the journal in 1944.

Johnson's writings on all aspects of education are contained in two books and 117 articles, mainly written for the *Catholic Educational*

Review. One thing that Johnson did not do and what Shields had hoped that he would do was to complete writing the religion textbooks that Shields had begun (Ward 1947, 274).

Johnson's contributions to education were recognized well beyond the Catholic community. An editorial in *The Evening Star* of Washington, D.C. on June 8, 1944 praised him for his dedication and commitment to education. It credited him with sponsoring a major revolution in the ideas and practices of Catholic education. Calling him a "progressive visionary," it commended him for his talents of organization, noting that he did the work of at least three persons. The editorial called his *Better Men* an outstanding contribution to some of the larger postwar problems. It concluding by stating that

> His vitality and energy were remarkable; his capacity for sustained work was unbelievable; his love for our democracy a deep and unquenchable fire, and his capacity for friendliness, loyalty and personal kindliness unlimited. His untimely and unnecessary death at 55 is a serious loss to American education. (*Evening Star* 1944, 404)

Johnson's Philosophy of Education

Johnson's first writings were on the psychological and social foundations of the curriculum of the Catholic elementary school in an attempt to discover the philosophy of American elementary school education that Catholic schools might embrace and adapt. These articles, appearing from 1919 to 1920 in the *Catholic Educational Review*, were actually his doctoral thesis at Catholic University (Johnson 1919a). Johnson exhibited a thorough knowledge of the history and philosophy of education, especially as this pertains to the curriculum of the school. He situated the philosophical basis of Catholic education in neo-scholastic philosophy, which was prominently taught by his mentor Thomas Shields, Edward Pace, and other members of the faculty of education at Catholic University. His thesis was set in the context of growing industrialization, his discontent with the present situation in the schools, and the fact that religion had been increasingly eased out of the curriculum of the public schools.

In his detailed historical survey, Johnson showed how educational ideals changed from age to age to meet new social conditions. He reviewed the structures of curriculum in educational history beginning with the earliest forms of education and then moved to education in Israel, Greece, and Rome. He then described the main features of early Christian education and the emergence of Christian schools in the Middle Ages. All of these developments were presented as occasioned by social and religious needs of the times. The impressive influence of the Renaissance, Protestant Reformation, Catholic Reform and the rise of religious orders, and the Enlightenment were clearly described. Johnson charged the individualism spawned by the eighteenth-century Enlightenment with lessening the influence of religion in education. His historical analysis also showed that the schools have not been totally successful in adjusting individuals to the social environment, even though he admits that social forces and institutions have exercised a considerable degree of social control for what was perceived to be good for society and individuals.

Johnson recounted the history of the elementary school curriculum in the United States. He showed how the curriculum developed in response to social changes. Criticizing the formalism of education, Johnson accepted the progressive viewpoint that "the history of education reveals how the schools changed from age to age to meet the needs of society. Education is preparation for life and it is but natural to expect that the conditions of life at any time should influence educational agencies" (1919b, 528). He also noted that Catholic schools generally followed the lead of public schools in adding subjects to the curriculum.

Like other progressive educators at the turn of the century, Johnson's analysis of education depended to a large extent on early studies in sociology and industrialization. In his view, industrialization ushered in a time when the religious character of the schools was seriously challenged and the Church's influence over education considerably lessened. The emerging philosophies of rationalism, empiricism, and pragmatism challenged the power of religious authority and tradition. In his view, they fostered the increased secularization of society and were instrumental in reducing religion to a department of life and challenged its claims to provide people with the sole interpretation of the meaning and purpose of life.

Also, like progressive educators of his time, Johnson grappled with the remarkable advances in the science of psychology. He entered the debate over the serious challenges to faculty psychology, which had for years buttressed the arguments for the formal discipline approach to education in which the curriculum was taught through separate subjects. Engaging Edward Thorndike, Johann Herbart, William James, and others, he sifted through the values in the new psychologies but in the end he still defended the faculty psychology as presented by the neo-scholastics. Furthermore, like his mentor, Dr. Shields, Johnson showed a fine appreciation of the psychological theories and experiments that were prevalent of his time.

While Johnson found much to admire in modern educational thought, he warned Catholic educators against totally embracing these new ideas. He did, however, accept the progressive broadening of the curriculum opposed by many Catholic educators, which now included science, vocational training, health education, democratic education, economic education, cultural education, and education for social efficiency. Not being satisfied with the progressives' indirect approach to moral education, Johnson called for an explicit moral and religious education. For him "the relationship between religion and social life, between the love of God and the love of neighbor, between divine service and social service, should be made explicit" (1920, 21). Johnson argued that "religion is not a mere department of life; it is the meaning and end of life. Modern society will avoid ruin and desolation only in proportion as it recognizes this fact and accepts it" (1920, 20-21). He went on to make the unexplained statement that religion must be interpreted in terms of social and political life (21).

Like John Dewey and other progressive educators, Johnson wrestled with the tension between the individual and society when it comes to the aims, content, and methods of education. Like them, he was sensitive to recent research in the social sciences and psychology. He presented his own summary of his position, which deserves to be quoted in full:

> We have criticized the current interpretation of the principle that education is adjustment to the environment, and postulated that adjustment, to be adequate and effective, must be an active, not a passive process. The individual is not to be fitted into society as a cog into a machine, but is to be given the power of self-adjustment, the power of individual choice based on character, which will enable him to fulfill the

requirements of society and at the same time cooperate in the raising of society to higher planes of truth and justice. This power is the cultural effect of education and can only be realized when education is dominated by broad and general, and not merely narrow, utilitarian ideals. (1920, 237)

In describing the curriculum for the Catholic elementary school, Johnson drew on the thought of John Dewey and other progressive educators, as well as Catholic educators who were influenced by the philosophy and methods of progressive education. He made the case that in order to provide a proper democratic education the Catholic school curriculum should be considerably expanded beyond the three Rs and the catechism. He stressed that elementary education was not the time for disciplinary specialization, which is in his view better introduced in adolescence. Johnson set the overall objective of elementary education as

General growth and development and the imparting of that fundamental information concerning God and man and the world which will later form the basis of mature development and reasoning, and which must be the heritage of every citizen of the United States, whether he be laborer or statesman, merchant or savant, soldier or man of peace. (1920, 242)

Johnson also included a lengthy quotation from John Dewey's *Democracy and Education*, which decried excessive dependence on mechanical drill in education and called for a broadened and progressive curriculum for elementary schools.

In his description of the subject matter of Catholic education, Johnson followed Thomas Shields in including the spheres of both divine and human truths. He described the content of elementary education as "man's Religious, Humanistic, broadly interpreted, Scientific and Industrial Inheritance" (1920, 281). For Johnson, revealed truths are the principal but not the sole source of knowledge of God, for humans also learn from the natural world through the power of reason. History in his view was extremely valuable in pointing out how people in various eras have dealt with temporal and eternal truths. Moreover, Johnson noted that valuable knowledge also comes from probing the human heart as well as from intensive engagement with literature and the fine arts. Truth also comes from exploration by means of science and the scientific method.

Johnson stressed that care should be taken to develop the various faculties of the child, such as feeling, emotion, imagination, memory, intellect, and will, through education. Genuine knowledge can also come through participation in plays and dramas. Another essential learning process is the development of habits in education and life. The use of memory should be cultivated. He emphasized that efforts should also be made to engage the interests of students, an essential tenet of educational progressivism. While not neglecting the formation of values and ideals through preaching, Johnson pointed out that the formation of good habits occurred more often by placing powerful models before children.

To the progressive discussion of ideals, interests, and values, Johnson added religion as the first place to look for high ideals to place before children. He defined the aim of Christian education, adapted from Shields, as "transmitting to the child knowledge of God, of man and of nature, and fostering the proper intellectual, habitual and emotional reactions to this knowledge" (1920, 301). Johnson proposed means of achieving this broad end. He set efficiency in religious knowledge and practices as the principal means. Moral training for all spheres of life is a second means of achieving the ultimate purpose of education, which is conformity with the will of God for the purpose of saving one's soul. Efficiency in one's care of the body through physical education, economic, or occupational efficiency, good citizenship, and preparation for leisure time are other important avenues of education. Here Johnson is referring to the Cardinal Principles of Education, which was an important statement embodying the aims of progressive education.

What Johnson actually did was adopt the progressive's philosophy of elementary schools to which he added the teaching of religion. Both he and his mentor Thomas Shields advocated progressive methods in teaching religion. This is treated in another section of this chapter. Not all educators in the Catholic community were in accord with what these two men proposed.

In Johnson's last word on progressive education, he came to an ambivalent conclusion (1940a). He felt that even though progressivism is a theological heresy in its denial of the supernatural, a philosophical heresy in denying the ultimate principles of truth and morality, and a pedagogical heresy in rejecting scientific evaluation and common sense, it has rightly drawn attention to weaknesses in educational practice and contains some essential truths. It is right in protesting

> Against the regimentation, the standardization, the routine and the artificiality that have been concomitants of our effort to provide and administer an education that would reach all the children of all the people. (1940a, 258)

Furthermore, he also praised progressive education for its emphasis on the principle of learning by doing, self-activity, a broadened curriculum, manual training, and physical education. In another article, Johnson contended that the activity method originated in classrooms and "was not the product of Dewey's pragmatism and instrumentalism and is not inextricably bound up with what he holds concerning the nature of truth and morality" (1941a, 71).

The Preparation of Educators for Catholic Schools

The preparation of educators, both teachers and administrators, was a recurrent theme for Johnson. In speaking to priest-superintendents of Catholic schools, he made the case for an extensive training, beyond what priests received in their seminary formation. He advocated their learning a practical philosophy of education, different from the seminary philosophy course, which would include knowledge of the laws of learning from psychology and familiarity with the burgeoning social sciences. Superintendents should be well grounded in the theory of education, which he defined as "the application of philosophic, social, and psychological principles to the problems of the school" (1920a, 131). Johnson advocated a pedagogical course in seminaries that would include knowledge of administrative and teaching methods as an essential part of seminary education.

Johnson (1922) was aware that teachers in Catholic schools needed supervision if they were to be properly prepared for their roles. In this article, he described the character of supervision. Supervisors should come from the ranks of the teachers, be properly prepared for this position, visit classrooms with regularity, offer suggestions, and oversee testing of students. Johnson urged pastors of parishes to involve themselves in overseeing the functioning of schools. Pastors should work with the superintendent of schools as well as the principals. He urged them to keep abreast of educational developments.

Johnson recognized that teachers needed proper preparation for their multiple tasks. They would have this if they possessed the requisite scholarship, teaching skills, and holiness of life (1924b). To hand on a culture, teachers have to be in possession of it. Teachers deal with the roots of all knowledge, especially with the fundamentals of academic disciplines. To hand on this human heritage and culture they must have the pedagogical skills that come through training and practice. Catholic school teachers also need something deeper than personality; they need holiness of life. For Johnson teachers are measured by their "approximation to Christian perfection" (389). He urged teachers to a life of prayer in which

> our fainting spirits are refreshed, our minds clarified, our charity enkindled, our patience fortified, and all in all we are made more worthy and ready for the sacred task of teaching little children. Better fewer degrees than fewer prayers. (389)

At the 1921 meeting of the Catholic Educational Association Johnson presented a plan for teacher certification (1920b). He advocated that Catholics establish a standard system of certification that would include everything that is required for teachers in the public schools. This necessary step would defend the Catholic school system from a growing number of critics who wanted to enforce state certification for Catholic school teachers. While Johnson recognized the rights of the state in certain areas, he thought that certification to teach in Catholic schools should be in the hands of church authorities in each state. He also made the suggestion that the different certification approaches for Catholic school teachers should be coordinated through the Catholic Educational Association or through Catholic University.

With the growth of Catholic schools in the 1920s, a teacher shortage in religious teachers developed. There was a movement for bringing more lay teachers into Catholic schools. Johnson discussed the pros and cons of such a situation, including finances, proper training, and religious presence, and was ambivalent about these new circumstances (1921).

Johnson's articles drawn from his dissertation have some criticisms of elements of progressive education. However, by 1922 when he had taken a position at Catholic University and was deeply involved in the preparation of Catholic school educators he expanded his criticisms of progressivism in education. What disturbed him most was that many Catholic teaching sisters were pursuing their teacher education in secular universities rather than in Catholic institutions. In "Trying to Serve Two Masters" (1922), Johnson decried the increasing secularization of public schools in the country as well as the absence of teaching of religion in these schools. For this he blamed the philosophy of pragmatism propounded by John Dewey. He also rejected Dewey's statement that faith in education is as good a religion so long as it does not become dogmatic and ritualistic. Johnson warned against the influence of such schools as Teachers College, Columbia, and the University of Chicago, which trained many public school educators. Admitting the legitimate right of the state in the area of education, he stressed that the ultimate purpose of Catholic education was "to teach the religion of Jesus Christ, to contribute to the sanctification of souls, and to prepare them for citizenship in the Kingdom of God" (1922, 462). He ended this strongly phrased article with a call for what was one of his principal tenets: the establishment of a Catholic standardizing body that would oversee and coordinate Catholic schools. For him the task ahead lay not in the attempt

> to conform to secular standards, derived from a secular philosophy of education but [in the attempt] to work out a system of standards that are inherently Catholic, and then present it to the state as evidence of what we are doing. Such a method would satisfy the rightful claims of the state and at the same time preserve the religious character of our schools. (463-64)

This article is the first of many that showed the ambivalence of Catholic progressives who adopted the methods of progressives but distanced themselves from its philosophical principles. Dewey and the progressives received more negative criticisms here than in Johnson's dissertation and in some later articles (1922, 457-64). In responding to criticism of elementary school teaching in the popular press, Johnson laid out a plan for the self-improvement of teachers through greater scholarship, familiarity with modern methodology, and attention to the spiritual lives of children (1924, 385-89); "Sanctity, scholarship, teaching skills-a triple goal worth striving for" (389).

Johnson (1924b) built the case for a philosophy of Catholic education that accepted many ideas of the progressives but gave greater attention to the role of religion in the curriculum. In reviewing the curriculum theories of leading progressives such as Boyd Bode, Franklin Bobbitt, and William Charters, he argued that their theories lacked the integrating factor of religion in the curriculum. He urged Catholic educators to highlight the importance of religion rather than follow progressive ideas blindly. Johnson concluded that Catholic schools exist

> for the purpose of developing in our children Christian character. Our schools exist for the same reason that the Church exists, to bring individuals unto the knowledge and the love and the service of God. Out of this all else flows. But we have to direct the application. A rather definite task, it would seem to be, if carried out in the light of the Truth unto which we are dedicated. (450)

Soon after becoming the U.S. Bishops' spokesperson on Catholic education, Johnson began to worry that Catholic education had lost its soul and distinctive spirit. He commented:

> The pressure of the moment has often led us into compromises which, though they may not have injured us fundamentally, have, nonetheless, impaired our destined effectiveness. We have been forced by circumstances to follow where we should have led, to imitate where we should have provided the model. We have accepted curricula, methods and devices born of a secular philosophy of education and trusted the atmosphere of our schools to "Catholicize" them. We have been a bit too prone to emphasize the points wherein we resemble secular education when we should have been proclaiming the elements of difference. Or, perhaps at a time when we have raised our voices in condemnation of educational trends, we have offered nothing positive and, as a consequence, have failed to wield an influence commensurate with our importance. (1929b, 4)

After the Oregon decision affirming the right of non-public schools to exist, Johnson gave a major talk at the meeting of the Catholic Educational Association charting the road ahead for Catholic educators. Johnson (1925b) saw a warning in this decision which also asserted the states' rights in education to supervise all schools to ensure that children in them receive the education to which they are entitled. For Johnson this called for a strengthening of Catholic schools. He proposed that all dioceses should have superintendents of education. Teacher training must be a high priority with the introduction of certification of teachers based on the principles of Catholic philosophy of education. The curriculum should be reformed in light of the best thinking on what educational should entail. Johnson called for constructive thinking in all areas and chided Catholic educators for being overly defensive. In this article he also advocated more research and experimentation for Catholic education. He highlighted

> The need for courageous and intelligent workers, thoroughly grounded in the principles of Catholic philosophy, trained in the methods of modern educational science . . . who will be free to conduct experiments of a research character either in individual schools or in individual school systems. (394)

Johnson and the Teaching of Religion

As would be expected, Johnson wrote a great deal about the teaching of religion in Catholic schools. Here he followed in the footsteps of the work of his mentor Thomas Shields as well as Edward Pace. Johnson began his treatment of teaching religion with a series of articles in the 1920s. These articles brought to a more popular audience ideas first presented in his dissertation.

Finding the basic principles of Catholic education in the supernatural teachings of Christ and his Church, Johnson advised that, "they should yield a fundamentally different education than that suggested by principles of education based on naturalism and materialistic philosophy" (1925a, a 267). However, this education should not minimize the importance of fundamental skills and knowledge needed throughout life. He gave this as the aim of the Catholic elementary school:

To provide the child with those experiences which are
calculated to develop in him such knowledge, appreciations,
and habits, as will yield a character equal to the contingencies
of fundamental Christian living in American democratic
society. (260)

Thus, the formation of moral character is central in the educational
task. Character is promoted through engagement in activities
demanded by religion or our fundamental relation to God. These
activities include knowledge and worship of God; respect for oneself by
growing in virtue, culture, health; earning a living; and respect for
others through affection, common interests, and humanity. Finally,
character includes a respect for nature by using it properly.

In an article for *Religious Education*, at the time almost exclusively
a journal for Protestant educators, Johnson (1929a) described the
Catholic Church's approach to character education, which was then a
burning concern among educators in the United States, given that
religion was no longer taught in the public schools. He argued that the
life of faith must include a life of action in accordance with belief. In
his view, Catholic education attempts to avoid the danger of Quietism,
which contends that human activity is useless and that all moral action
depends on God. It also tries to avoid Naturalism, according to which
human activity alone can achieve the formation of moral character.
Johnson wrote of character education that it should entail "a definite
and specific plan for translating truth into terms of daily conduct," but
he favored such education only if it is "rooted in faith and Jesus Christ"
and hopes to achieve its ends with his cooperation (55).

Johnson went on to describe some of the ways the Catholic
Church has promoted character education: frequent Communion for
the young, participation in the liturgical life of the Church, the
layman's retreat, and newer methods of teaching religion such as the
Sower Scheme of Canon Drinkwater in England, the Munich Method
of teaching, the Montessori Method, and the religious education
program and textbooks of Thomas Shields.

In an article in a Catholic educational journal Johnson made the
case for character education as fundamentally an ascetic element in
education, believing as he did that the Catholic outlook is
fundamentally ascetical. For him, adjustment to the environment

should take place only within this dimension of Catholic education. This included for him the teaching of practical asceticism in the classroom, which should find its expression in the discipline of the classroom. Further, it should center on the person of Jesus and the celebration of the Mass, an examination of one's life before God, and prayerful meditation. The child should be taught forms of asceticism that can be practiced in the home through the daily recitation of prayers. What Johnson presented here was the character formation found in seminaries and religious novitiates (Johnson 1928a). In other articles in the same volume he advocated education for humility (1928d), learning lessons from church architecture (1928c), and practical means for teaching children to meditate (1928b).

Johnson (1926a) asserted that the fundamental principles for the teaching of religion were derived from the scientific psychology and pedagogy of John Dewey and Maria Montessori as applied to teaching religion by Shields. For him the fundamental principle of all pedagogy in religion as in all other subjects as well is that "the learner must do his own learning" (Johnson 1926a, 458). While Johnson recognized that many religious educators resisted the application of scientific pedagogy to the teaching of religion, he contended that in teaching religion the law of self-activity must not be ignored. It was not enough to appeal to students' imagination and memory, which could easily result in passivity on the part of students. The teaching of religion was to be governed by "the first principle of general method, and the first principle of general method is that we learn by doing, by self-activity, by experience" (1926a, 459). To know religion it is not enough merely to know something about it. Children need ideas that will generate love that leads to the service of others and the acquisition of virtue. Learning is to proceed by way of students' assimilating knowledge within themselves. Furthermore, learning by experience needs to be adapted to the various stages of the child's mental development. For the young child this is accomplished through excursions, pictures, specimens, the sand table, clay modeling, and other means (460). Older children should use the catechism merely as an outline to be supplemented by collateral learning from books and activities. Children in the upper grades could be afforded opportunities for the independent study of religion. Johnson gave examples of these forms of learning from his experiences in the Thomas Edward Shields Memorial

School, which was attached to Catholic University. At this time he was the director of the school as well as a professor at the university.

Johnson recognized that teachers were generally more interested in learning methods of teaching than they were in discussion of aims. Yet he stressed the importance of both as well as content. He summarized aims in teaching religion as knowing, feeling, service, and practice. He faulted educational theorists who thought that knowledge automatically leads to virtue. The importance that he gave to the discussion of aims in education comes through in these words:

> Truth is best learned by experience: knowing and doing go hand in hand. Religious truth, prescinding of course from the operation of divine grace, is learned by the same law. Thus learned, it leaves its trace not merely in the intellect, but in the will, the emotions, the impulses, the desires, in a word, the whole person. It becomes permanent and dynamic in the habits of the individual, in his attitudes and appreciation, not merely in his memory. It identifies itself with him and becomes the differentiating element in his conduct and personality. It defines him. (Johnson 1927, 563)

In an article on liturgy, Johnson (1926b) anticipated the catechetical movement of the 1960s with his advocacy of the educational value of the liturgy. Liturgy for him was neither a subordinate element in the teaching of religion nor merely a means for teaching religion but rather the very basis upon which the teaching of religion should be founded. He coupled liturgical experience with natural experience as starting points of religious education. Johnson decried the passive way in which many participated in the liturgy, even quoting John Dewey's description of experience as both passive and active in which "when we experience something, we act upon it. We do something about it. Then we suffer or undergo the consequences. We do something to a thing and it does something to us in return" (Johnson 1926b, 529). Pointing out the educational value of living the liturgical year, he stressed the emotions and values that its celebration inculcated in participants. The sacraments of the church make the events of daily life holy. Johnson explained how as children aged their appreciation of liturgy could grow through age-related instruction. He even advocated special Masses for children in which the liturgy, especially the sermon, is accommodated to their understanding. All in all, Johnson pointed to the liturgy as providing excellent opportunities for the objective or object teaching of religion that many educators advocated.

In an article in *Religious Education*, Johnson defended the Catholic Church's religious education against the charge of indoctrination by contending that indoctrination in religion is as good a thing as indoctrination into patriotism or mathematics. For Johnson, since what the Church teaches is infallible,

> It makes no apology for indoctrinating the minds of children, nor does any other religious body that takes its religion seriously. Strange that it should be perfectly satisfactory to indoctrinate children in patriotism, arithmetic, spelling, and any other human science, but unreasonable to indoctrinate them in religion. (1930, 567)

Johnson then decried the excessive freedom, self-expression, and experimentation in religion and countered that "if civilization is to perdure, there must be some measure of indoctrination" (57). He pointed to the fact that people in adult life change their religion as an indication that indoctrination does not impair human freedom.

Most religious educators today would not subscribe to Johnson's views about indoctrination. The Vatican II document on religious freedom makes it clear that faith is to be a free decision on the part of the believer. Philosophers of education have written extensively on this complex issue and call attention to various factors in their discussions of indoctrination: one's intention in teaching, the content of what one teaches, and the manner in which one teaches (Snook 1972). Indoctrination has become a pejorative word among most educators including religious educators.

Like many religious educators in his day, Johnson decried that religion was not taught in the public schools. For him, its omission was a primary reason for the social and moral ills of the nation. He pointed out that most countries in the world include religion as a subject in the school curriculum. For Johnson, that religion is not taught in schools leaves children with the impression that "religion . . . is something apart from life, something not vitally necessary; something that is more or less of an unnecessary burden" (1932, 516). Finally, Johnson argued that young people need the strength of religion to make their way through life's problems.

Johnson on Education and War

In a commencement address at Trinity College, Washington, D.C. on June 5, 1944, Monsignor George Johnson, the leading voice for Catholic education in his era, attacked the pragmatism that pervaded United States culture at that time, with the Second World War coming to a close. He decried that

> We are counseled to arrive at conclusions about things in general and the present state of human affairs in particular in a realistic manner, [that] we ought to be realistic about the war, realistic about the peace, realistic about matters social and economic, realistic in the sphere of domestic relations, realistic about the truth, realistic about morals. (Johnson 1944b, 407)

For Johnson this objectionable form of realism called for the sacrifice of principle for expediency; capitulation to circumstances; justification of means by their ends; minimizing the role of justice and right in the affairs of nations; neglecting the rights of small nations; and a denial of the hope that "out of all the horror, the waste, and the destruction of war there will emerge a world in which the weak will not be at the mercy of the strong" (1944b, 408). Johnson also challenged the doctrine of unconditional surrender as not squaring with the Christian canons of mercy. Many of these opinions were not popular in days replete with trumpet calls for loyalty and patriotism, especially in the midst of a war that the vast majority of the people judged to be just. In this speech Johnson no doubt had in mind the baneful consequences of the political realism and even the Christian realism of many defenders of the war.

Johnson countered this prevailing doctrine of realism with a philosophy of life and an educational philosophy that centered on the teaching of Jesus and supernatural truths, which emphasized the enduring value of Christian truths even in the time of a war generally viewed as a "good" and just war. Near the end of this talk Johnson was stricken by a heart attack, the cause of his death a day later. This premature death at the age of fifty-seven was lamented not only in the Catholic community but also among members of the Religious Education Association, which chose him as its first Catholic vice-president and called him "a great churchman, a man of scholarly mind and friendly spirit . . . [who] left a rich legacy of fruitful labors (1944a, 204). The last words he uttered were that "we still have a lot to learn about educating unto Christ in a world that knows not Christ" (1944b, 411).

Johnson came to his final judgments about certain policies concerning the war through his involvement in educational endeavors that were first initiated by Pope Pius XII and the United States Bishops.

In 1938 at the beginning of hostilities in Europe, Pope Pius XI asked the Catholic University of American to establish a Commission on American Citizenship. The Rector of the University organized such a commission, comprised of 141 members, both Catholics and non-Catholics. The Commission was headed by Johnson and Monsignor Frederick J. Haas, both on the faculty of the Catholic University of America. In time Johnson became executive director and the chief moving force in this endeavor (Johnson 1944a).

The purpose of the commission was to bring Catholic social and economic teachings to bear on Catholic educational endeavors, especially through the development of new curricula for schools and colleges. The context of the work of the commission was the emergence of totalitarian social theories such as Communism, Fascism, and National Socialism. With Robert J. Slavin, professor of philosophy at Catholic University, Johnson wrote the commission's statement of principles, *Better Men for Better Times* (1943) and directed the publication of textbooks.

What was happening in the world in the 1930s and 1940s finds expression in Johnson's writings as early as 1935. Addressing university graduates he reviewed the basic theological teachings of the church, especially the doctrine of Original Sin, in calling their attention to the relationship between religion and daily life. He called into question the false individualism that resulted in class hatred, international anarchy, and the destruction of sacred freedoms. He pointed to the Catholic theological synthesis as necessary "if civilization is to survive, and no such stop-gaps as dictatorship, planned economies, or international leagues based on the trading interests of selfish interests against selfish interests can take its place" (Johnson 1935, 519). Confident of the truth of Catholic theology, he asked these educated Catholics to bring this teaching to bear on the political, social, economic, and cultural problems arising in the world.

As an educator, Johnson (1937b) stressed that religious education should always involve itself in political, social, and economic realities without losing sight of its spiritual mission. Before a gathering of educators Johnson addressed the possibility of war in the midst of the social, political, and economic insecurity of the times. Economic ills in the country and the rise of dictatorships in the world caused him to observe that "all of us stand in constant dread lest sober thought yields places to bitter controversy and that before we realize it the whole matter will be proposed to the cruel and futile adjudication of war" (1937b, 258).

In a sermon at St. Patrick's Cathedral in New York City on September 15, 1940, Johnson addressed the duties of teachers in the defense of American democracy. In this sermon he contrasted the enterprise of education, which is a peaceful undertaking of noble and beautiful things, with the present atmosphere of the world in which war had already begun in Europe and in which defense preparations were being made in the United States. While he insisted that the school "could not, and should not, lose complete sight of the realities of the world in which it operates" (1940b), he went on to point out that

> As far as education is concerned, peace is the portion of its inheritance and apart from peace its aspirations are nugatory. It must hold fast hopes and refuse to admit that there can be nothing save wars and dissensions. It must learn from the present sad condition of the human family, the tragic consequences that result when the spirit of man loses its way, and must address itself to the heartbreaking task of finding that way anew. (450)

Johnson expressed concerns for the effects that defense buildup and the preparation for the drafting of young men would have on national endeavors, including education. Thinking only about war would affect college admissions, and the supply of skilled workers for the work force, and produce an attitude of thinking and talking only about war. He feared that defense was being defined too narrowly in military terms and called for defending America by "means of a dogged, untiring, uncompromising offensive against forces like selfishness, greed for power, and greed for wealth, love of pleasure and love of ease, refusal to admit the fact of our creaturehood and the deification of our whims and desires" (451).

For Johnson, education defended democracy by inculcating respect for human personality and recognition of basic human rights. He found the most satisfactory basis for these beliefs in the spiritual nature of human beings. Thus, for him the religious dimension of education should be an essential dimension of an education for democratic living that could ward off the threat of totalitarianism in many countries in the world. Education for democracy as he conceived it must also recognize the roots of human injustice that are in the hearts of humans and must also use the strength of religion to uproot these seeds. The education that can accomplish this is one that inspires learners through active methods to live the truth.

Johnson addressed the war again in 1941 before the National Catholic Educational Association (1941b). Speaking on "Our Task in the Present Crisis," he accepted the fact that entrance into the war was inevitable with the build up of armaments and shifts in the United States economy. For him, however, "something new, something different will have to go into the making of our future citizens if they are to meet what is ahead of them intelligently and bravely" (257). He also predicted that "our greatest problems will emerge only when the war is over, and it is then that educators will need to muster all the vision and all the adaptability of which they are capable" (257).

In this address Johnson discussed the upcoming draft of men, the role of women's colleges in the war effort, problems with the employment of youth in the defense industries, and the expansion of federal activities. Johnson also treated the touchy issue of teaching citizenship in schools. For the courses that had already been introduced, he argued that training of the will should go hand and hand with training of the mind, quoting Aristotle's dictum that "knowledge avails little, if anything, toward virtue." In his view democratic education is predicated on the fact that individual human personality is sacred and inviolable, a truth that must be rooted in affirming the existence of God. With what now might be regarded as infelicitous wording he asserted that individuals "must be made subject to restraint and regimentation in the name of the common good" (259).

During the month of October 1941 Johnson gave four radio addresses on the *Catholic Hour* on the practical aspects of patriotism. He called for a renewed patriotism in the face of attacks on United States democracy, which in his view had shown some weaknesses in economic and political life. He placed patriotism within the practice of the virtue of justice, which includes those duties we owe to our fellow humans by reason of the fact that we share with them the same homeland, cherish the same ideals, and live under a government that protects and fosters our common interests (Johnson 1941c).

In these talks Johnson discoursed on the role of patriotism in the home, the community, and in leisure activities. Civilian defense for him meant first of all that homes of the people were worth defending, citizens should contribute to the well being of their communities by aiding the needy and combating intolerance, communities should be socially controlled, and leisure activities should strengthen and re-create individuals. The guiding principle of patriotism for him is that citizens should work together for the common welfare. Nothing is found in these addresses on the role that criticism and constructive dialogue might contribute to a democratic way of life.

Johnson's loyalty to the war effort at that time was manifest in his 1942 report to the NCEA membership, in which he explained that

> Catholic education has a vital stake in the outcome of this war. The forces that are arrayed against our country are at the same time forces that in other lands are arrayed against the church. . . . Our schools and colleges do not live in a vacuum; they are part and parcel of life and living and were never intended to afford a cloistered refuge from reality. Though they thrive best in peace, they must now gird themselves for war. When freedom was imperiled their very reason for existence hangs in the balance. (1942, 75)

Johnson and *Better Men for Better Times*

When the Commission on American Citizenship was founded at Catholic University by the American hierarchy in 1938, Johnson was named to its executive committee and in 1943 he became director of this commission. Johnson was the principal author of the commission's highly regarded statement of principles, *Better Men for Better Times* (1943).

Better Men for Better Times formulated the principles of Catholic social teaching in a practical manner to be of benefit to teachers in the Catholic schools. It presented a vision of what responsible citizenship should be in a time of crisis. *Better Men* couched praise for American democracy with recognition that there are dark chapters in our history including slavery and civil war. It realistically pointed out that

> Oppressions have been wrought under the Stars and Stripes; they are being wrought today–which only proves that true democracy envisaged by the men who laid the foundations of our government and our nation, is not something that happens automatically. (4)

Despite these and other failures, including dislocations during World War I and corrupt politics, *Better Men* offered praise for American democracy for bringing about prosperity, a high standard of living, and good schools: "Often we have been stupid, frequently intolerant, and now and then vicious, but in the main we have been kind to one another (7). The authors made the case that the military defense build-up should not neglect the many ills that beset the nation: malnutrition, bad housing, unemployment, preventable physical illness, lack of security, starvation wages, sectionalism, discrimination, neglect of higher values, and irreligion (35).

The work called for broadening the social mission of the Catholic Church to embrace everything in life and urged Catholics to work as good citizens with all persons of good will. This went counter to the widespread practice of the time which often had the Catholic Church remaining within its own confines and refusing to cooperate with others, especially other religious groups, for fear of fostering religious indifferentism.

Better Men was sensitive to the danger of the state overreaching its powers in times of emergency in the name of national defense. It quoted the words of Pope Pius XII:

> No one of good will and vision will think of refusing the State, in the exceptional conditions of the world of today,

correspondingly wider and exceptional rights to meet the
popular needs. But even in such emergencies, the moral law,
established by God, demands that the lawfulness of each such
measure and its real necessity be scrutinized with the greatest
rigor according to the standards of the common good. (91)

Adherence to the moral law and the Constitution are thus considered
necessary to maintain freedom.

Education is presented in the book as playing an important role in
the making of a world fit for human living. Education is essential to
national welfare and the first arm of defense. Education provides the
experiences necessary for the development of ideas, attitudes, and
habits essential for democratic societies. It takes place in all areas of
human life where persons come together to influence one another.
Schooling is conscious of itself, since it is an intentional activity.

Better Men explains that education is the result of self activity,
learning by doing. Education is described as an active not a passive
process, which has experience as its basis. The authors make the case
that education takes place whenever we cooperate with the grace that is
in us and with the guidance and instruction to aid persons to exercise
their own "power into acquiring a fuller measure of the truth, a deeper
love of the good, and a finer appreciation of the beautiful" (14-15).
Education should include the training of the mind and will. The best
way to train the mind is to face it with real problems and to give it the
opportunity and the freedom to solve them.

With regard to his attitude toward the war, Johnson must be
understood within the context of the Catholic Church in the United
States, which had basically a defensive and apologetic stance *vis-à-vis*
Protestant America. At that time Catholics still had to prove that they
were not controlled by a foreign power and thus could be loyal citizens.
Also, Johnson was a member not of a peace church but of a church that
over the years honed a doctrine of just war that more often than not ended
up favoring whatever the nation's leaders decided. While within this
Church Johnson was an educational progressive, he was not a theological
liberal in the United States church at the time.

At the center of Johnson's writings about the war is the issue of
citizenship and patriotism. Though in some of his sermons and
addresses the patriotic citizen is loyal, obedient, and conforming, the

full corpus of his writings shows a more critical form of citizenship, which emerged as the war progressed and its moral ambiguities increased. While he admits the value of social control, he raised issues about what citizens and educators of citizens should do in times of national crisis.

Johnson makes us think about the nature of citizenship in the time of war, and about how educators deal with this complex issue. Religious education is equipped to deal with critical citizenship since it deals seriously with the tension of loyalty to a tradition and continuous questioning and critiquing of that tradition. At its best it "employs inquiry and debate, is sensitive to controversial issues and . . . is rooted in beliefs which motivate people to action" (Watson 2004, 263). Since religions transcend national borders, they are able to focus on responsibilities of global citizenship. Religious education has the potential of encouraging ethical indignation, respecting spiritual, moral, and ideological diversity, and encouraging dialogue.

George Johnson's Achievement

Of the three priests from Catholic University studied in the last three chapters George Johnson did the most to shape the direction of Catholic education in the United States. He began as a philosopher like Edward Pace and Thomas Shields, and Catholic philosophy of education always had a place in his many talks and articles. But once he became the national voice of Catholic education, he became embroiled in all the education debates within the church and indeed within the nation. It was he who made the argument for the distinctiveness of Catholic schools, walking a fine line between those who wanted to keep the schools segregated and removed from general education reforms and those who wanted to accommodate more of the progressive education agenda. He defended the schools against the charge that they were divisive and at the same time tried to make these schools distinctively Catholic.

Johnson also had to deal with the twofold social responsibilities of the schools at this time, as described by Veverka (1985, 75): to Christianize America and to Americanize Catholics. Since public schools had eliminated the teaching of religion, Catholic educators presented their schools as a religious and moral enterprise that kept the

United States close to their religious roots by presenting a curriculum that was permeated with religious and moral values. But other educators stressed the task of the schools to make the immigrant Catholics loyal and true citizens of the nation. This was important to offset the criticisms level against Catholics and their schools.

Johnson also found himself in a paradoxical situation with regard to the federal government. As the U.S. Bishops' spokesperson, he argued against centralization of the nation's schools through a federal office of education, standardization of curriculum and teacher certification, and various federal initiatives in education. At the same time he tried to convince Catholic educational leaders that educational should be centralized within dioceses and within the nation. While the Catholic bishops were fearful that federalization of schools would lead to a national system of education, they wanted to have centralized control over their own schools. While early in his career Johnson proposed a separate Catholic system of accreditation and standardization of education, he later had to accommodate the schools to increasing state supervision.

Veverka has aptly described the "mystified" and significant Catholic educational shifts during this period of Johnson's leadership

> from isolation to participation in social and civic life, from opposition to acceptance of the state's legitimate role in education, from local to diocesan levels of organization and control, and from schools functioning primarily as agencies of church education to schools as agencies of public education. (1985, 90)

George Johnson deserves much credit for shaping Catholic education during his lifetime. He left a legacy of Catholic schools with a distinctive religious identity and as an integral part of a democratic society. He won the respect of leaders in the field of education as well as politics at both national and state levels.

Virgil Michel:
Prophet of Liturgical
Education and Reform

Jacqueline Parascandola

Virgil Michel was a prophetic voice in the areas of education, liturgy, social justice, ecclesiology, and the role of the laity. In his brief lifetime he wrote numerous articles, book reviews, and pamphlets, translated texts, edited journals, and in collaboration with the Dominican Sisters developed a series of textbooks for catechetical use from the primary grades to the college level. Dom Virgil viewed the liturgy as the source of catechetical instruction for the faithful. For Michel, "every time the Church performs the liturgy [it] also instructs" (Marx 1957, 220). So intertwined was his thinking on liturgy, religious education, and social justice, it is difficult to isolate one area from another in his writings. One subject matter flows into the next with relative ease.

To understand Virgil Michel, one must envision the liturgy as the place where people not only worship God but also learn their faith. In addition, it is in the liturgy that one learns how "to be" in the world. Catholics are to take their sustenance from the liturgy and then go out into the world to make a difference. Thus, liturgy is both educational and inspirational for the faithful. It was to this end that Dom Virgil worked to instruct the laity in the Catholic faith. Before addressing his writings and work, this chapter examines the life of Virgil Michel. He was a man whose interests were broad in scope, yet fully grounded in his passion for the liturgy and its primacy for the instruction of the faithful.

Biographical Background

George Michel (1890-1938) was the second of fifteen children born into the fairly affluent German-American household of Fred and Mary Michel of St. Paul, Minnesota. By all accounts, he grew up in a happy, religious, and comfortable home. George excelled as a student at St. John's Preparatory School. An avid reader, he would read anything that came his way.

Entering the priesthood did not occur to Michel until his sophomore year at St. John's College in Collegeville, Minnesota. Then on July 4, 1909, George Michel took the name, Virgil, when he entered the novitiate of the Benedictine monks. Four years later on September 26, 1913, he professed his solemn vows to Abbot Peter Engel and was ordained a priest on June 14, 1916 (Whalen 1996, 4).

Michel later earned a bachelor's in Sacred Theology (STB) at Catholic University of America (CUA) and received excellent grades in his coursework: "Marks for class achievements at the University were given percentage-wise, and Michel's were nearly all "99" and "100" (Roach 1988, 203). While at Catholic University, Dom Virgil became interested in the field of education. In 1918 he earned his doctorate in English. Later that year he enrolled at Columbia University for advanced study. One year after earning his doctorate, Michel had an article published in *American Catholic Quarterly Review* (1919). The topic was the subject of his dissertation, Orestes Brownson, a free spirit who thought that Roman Catholicism was the fulfillment of the ideals of America. Brownson remained a source of inspiration for Michel: "From Brownson, Father Michel received his enormous interest in contemporary thought and modern philosophy" (Marx 1957, 12).

In his dissertation, Michael Whalen identifies four experiences in the life of Michel that provide a "hermeneutical key" to understanding his catechetical writings (1996, 6). I will highlight five major influences on the life of Virgil Michel that bear serious mention: 1) the Benedictine Order; 2) the European Liturgical Movement; 3) the journal, *Orate Fratres*; 4) the philosophy of personalism; and 5) the Chippewa Missions. Additionally, Whalen includes in his list of influences Michel's work with the Dominican Sisters of Grand Rapids Michigan, particularly Jane Marie Murray. This important collaboration is addressed in a later section of my chapter.

The Influence of the Benedictine Order

The influence of the Benedictine community on the life and work of Virgil Michel began when he was a young boy worshiping at his local parish, which was served by the Benedictine monks. At the time, the monastic community was in the midst of a liturgical renewal that lasted throughout the lifetime of Michel (Whalen 1996, 6). This early exposure to Benedictine liturgy inspired Dom Virgil to develop a deep appreciation for the role of worship in the religious formation of the faithful even as a youth.

His love for the liturgy developed further at St. John's Preparatory School, a Benedictine secondary school in Collegeville, Minnesota. Later in college at St. John's, Father Alcuin Deutsch, O.S.B., "won George's confidence" (Marx 1957, 6). Thanks to his example, "Virgil Michel was attracted to St. John's above all as a center of spirituality, learning and scholarship. Though he [later] joined an abbey in the Indianbush hidden in the woods, he did so in the faith that it possessed a power which could radiate and transform the society of his own time" (Franklin and Spaeth 1988, 49).

Michel spent some years teaching at St. John's College before he went to Europe in 1924-25. Michel studied philosophy under Joseph Gredt at the International Benedictine College of St. Anselm in Rome. There he came in direct contact with the already emerging European liturgical revival. Michel later met Dom Lambert Beauduin, who "fired Father Michel's interest in the liturgy and the doctrine of the Mystical Body" (Marx 1957, 27). Franklin and Spaeth write of Michel's reaction to Beauduin's activities:

> The success of these endeavors dazzled Father Virgil. . . . He became convinced that a similar popular liturgical movement was the great need for the revival of the Roman Catholic Church in America. More and more Virgil Michel began to copy Beauduin's personal style. (1988, 58)

The Benedictine spirituality and work ethic of Dom Lambert made a lasting impression on Father Michel. Tirelessly, Dom Lambert wrote books and developed media materials such as liturgical pamphlets, guides, and weekly and quarterly newspapers in order to promote and defend the new liturgical movement. These were widely disseminated at Mont César in Belgium and surrounding areas.

As much as Virgil Michel was committed to the Benedictines, it would be in his later separation from the monastery that he would find his greatest peace.

Michel and the European Liturgical Movement

According to Whalen (1996, 64-65), the influence of the liturgical movement on Dom Virgil was threefold. First, it inspired Michel to establish and explain many themes of the European Liturgical movement to American audiences. Michel's contribution therefore rested on his ability to tailor the themes of the European movement to appeal to the tempo and style of the American church. Chief among these areas of concern was the relationship between liturgy, catechesis, and social justice. These relationships were key factors in involving the laity in the liturgy and in the development of their personal and communal faith.

Second, Michel's European experience of the European liturgical movement made him critical of American individualism, a type of mindset that he considered as counter to the way Jesus would want us to live. He thought that individualism fostered a "privatized" form of religion on the part of the faithful. To Michel, this attitude led to a vertical relationship with God without any regard to the horizontal or communal relationship with others. Third, religious individualism is quite contrary to the conception of Catholicism (23). To counter this attitude, Michel used and adapted the ideas of notable European liturgists, such as Lambert Beauduin and Emmanuele Caronti. Whalen gives an analysis and comparison of Beauduin's *Liturgy the Life of the Church* and Caronti's *The Spirit of the Liturgy* as they influenced Michel's own *The Liturgy of the Church* (1996, 64-65). Beauduin wrote, "The Christian does not walk above on the path of his pilgrimage." He added that

> Between the Church of heaven and the Church of earth there exists an intimate union which shall one day become perfect. This union manifests, nourishes and develops itself by a common participation in spiritual goods, by communication

of merits and individual goods, by a continual exchange of prayers offered to God for the welfare and spiritual progress of each member and for the increasing prosperity of the entire body. (22-23)

Similar themes are expressed in Caronti's *The Spirit of the Liturgy*.

Finally, Michel learned from the European movement a multi-disciplinary approach to problems, understanding how all the parts could fit together. In other words, Dom Virgil learned that there was a connection among theology, life, education, and social justice. He saw how one could not be a fully participating member of the church if one did not understand their faith, liturgy, and justice. He also saw that an appreciation of the faith would lead to active participation in a faith community. Whalen explains that "Michel's works must be read in an integral and mutually interpretive fashion" (65-66) in order to understand his multidisciplinary approach to all issues.

Dom Michel was certain about what would result if religious educators neglected teaching the liturgy as vital to living a full Christian life. He cautioned:

> The neglect of the liturgy and the absence of liturgical inspiration in our teaching of religion may account for many of the characteristics that we find extant today in our Catholic life in its relation to the world about us: the lack of inner vitality of the faith that is in us, the absence of apostolic ardor, the lamentable confusion that mistakes regimentation and external *conformism* for the flourishing of spiritual life, and the spiritual inferiority complex which makes many Catholics hide their light under a basket only too often unto its own extinction. (1937b, 269)

Orate Fratres

Michel explored many ways to promote his ideas on liturgy and its close connection with religious education. In order to help educate the faithful, Michel founded the journal *Orate Fratres (OF)*, later renamed *Worship*. The first issue appeared during the Advent season of 1926 and was published by The Liturgical Press at St. John's Abbey in Collegeville,

Maryland. In publishing this journal, Dom Virgil promoted three of the traditional hallmarks of the Benedictine Order: reproducing texts, scholarship, and teaching. While Michel used this publication primarily to increase the appeal of the liturgy, he also saw the journal as a means to educate the faithful about the liturgy and social justice and their interconnection. To this end, he declared the mission of *Orate Fratres* to be: "The wider spread of the true understanding of and participation in the Church's worship by the general laity in order to foster the corporate life of the natural social units of the Church–the parishes" (1926, 29).

The Liturgical Press has remained faithful to its stated mission in producing pamphlets through its Popular Liturgical Library. At the time, under the direction of Virgil Michel, "The Library" sold 700,000 pamphlets at a cost of ten to thirty-five cents. According to R.W. Franklin, two of the most popular titles were, *Offeramus* and *Our Mass* (1988, 198-99). Because of these books, an informed laity could become active participants in liturgy, one of the goals of Dom Virgil. Above all, Michel believed that theology should be the domain of theologians and lay people. He wrote of the laity: "Theirs is a native right to share in this theological knowledge and understanding, in place of the relegation of theology to an abstract science for experts, such as it has been until recently" (1936, 485).

Building on its earlier successes, The Liturgical Press began to publish a hymnal, *The Parish Kyrie*. This publication made it possible for the laity to sing the Gregorian chants at Mass. The publishing house always kept its lay readership in mind. Their audience was not primarily academics but the faithful in the pews.

The Philosophy of Personalism

Personalism played a significant role in the life and work of Dom Virgil. Michel was attracted to the views of the French personalist Emmanuel Mounier and began a correspondence with him in 1936. By 1938, with the assistance of a confrere, Gerald McMahon, he translated Mounier's *Manifeste au service du personalism* as *A Personalist Manifesto*. Mounier's personalist perspective had its roots in the Catholic realism and Thomism. According to Mounier's personalism,

The human has an absolute value. In *A Personalist Manifesto,* Mounier writes, "A person is a spiritual being, constituted as such by its manner of existence and independence of being; it maintains this existence by its adhesion to a hierarchy of values that it has freely adopted, assimilated, and lived by its own responsible activity and by a constant interior development; thus it unifies all its activity in freedom and by means of creative acts develops this individuality of its vocation. (Beaudoin 1989, 236)

Mounier's personalism formed the basis of the *Novelle Théologie* which was emerging in France. It appeared in the work of numerous Roman Catholic scholars: M. D. Chenu, Yves Congar, Henri de Lubac, and Teilhard de Chardin (Hellman 1981). This philosophical trend appealed to Christians and non-Christians alike. Mounier's influence can also be found in the radical pedagogy of Paulo Freire (Elias 1976).

Mounier's personalism, however, is not to be confused with individualism, a lifestyle and attitude that neither Michel nor Mounier would endorse. Rather, individuals within the personalist viewpoint live lives that affirm initiative and responsibility as well as maintain an active spiritual life. Moreover, this way of living is to be accomplished through community with others. To Mournier, living your life meant active participation with others, to be in relationship with others.

Accordingly, the paramount value of the person was sacrosanct in the context of criticizing institutions and competing spiritual and political ideologies that

sought to construct a coherent system which they try to impose upon human history by the sheer force of the ideas themselves. Whenever living history or the realities of human life resist their attempts, they consider themselves the more faithful to truth if they shrink back completely into their system, and the more pure and unadulterated if they insist blindly upon the geometric fixity of their utopias. (Mounier 1938, 4)

In the concrete, Mounier's personalism criticized both Communism and liberal capitalism for their potential to depersonalize individuals.

Michel reflected Mounier's ideas in his thinking on "the imposed system of doctrinal formulas [as] expressed in his numerous articles concerning the theory and practice of religious education" (Beaudoin 1988, 238).

In personalist thought, persons are called to be critically reflective of their actions. They are to embark on a course of validation and renewal of themselves. Thus, life is to be looked upon as a journey towards betterment, enlightenment, and openness to new possibilities and learning. For Catholics this journey through life is to begin in childhood with proper upbringing and Catholic instruction. Moreover, this formation is to be built upon for the rest of one's life through continual learning from the liturgy. Michel advocated this viewpoint as early as 1925 in an essay, "A Religious Need for the Day," in which he linked his trinity of correct teaching, liturgy, and the living manifestation of living one's faith. He contended that the truths of the faith "must be taught . . . in . . . their living appeal to the whole man" (454).

Mounier's personalism considered the education of the child of primary importance. To this end, Mournier proposed three fundamental "living ideas": the purpose of education is not to fashion the child into rigid conformity with any social environment or with any doctrine of state; education ought to be concerned with the life of the whole person in a value-oriented context; education should influence one's conception of life and one's attitude toward life. The child must be educated as a person through the path of personal experience and the apprenticeship of free actions. The entire education of the child, like every influence in the life of the adult, should receive the guiding inspiration of some authority whose teaching is progressively interiorized by the subject who receives it (Beaudoin 1989, 236-37). These maxims had a deep impact on the educational philosophy of Dom Virgil Michel. Marx noted that Michel's article

> "Are We Educating Moral Parasites?" written in 1927 was the application of the philosophy of personalism to the training and education of humans being in an enticing, secularized culture, from the necessary dependency of childhood, through the inevitable unsteadiness of adolescence, to the rich and responsible personality of adulthood. Sound education, he

wrote, is not indoctrination nor is it "a struggle for overlordship." To educate is more than merely to instruct. (363)

The Chippewa Missions

Another significant influence upon Michel was his experiences living with the Chippewa, Native Americans of the Cass Lake area of northern Minnesota. Given to overwork, Michel's superiors had often warned him to slow down. Marx summarizes the five years following Michel's return from Europe in 1925:

> He taught philosophy at the seminary, wrote on a variety of subjects, organized the liturgical movement, in collaboration with his community and others founded and edited *Orate Fratres*, established and directed the Liturgical Press, edited some twenty publications, translated Grabmann's *Thomas von Aquin*, lectured and conducted about a dozen retreats, acted as Prefect of Clerics (1927-1929), carried on a large correspondence, organized the liturgical summer school and the first National Liturgical Day, directed and edited *With Mother Church*, and began an entirely new series of religion textbooks for the grades. (161)

In 1930, after years of arduous and productive work, Michel's eyes gave out and he suffered a breakdown. He was admitted to the hospital where insomnia and severe headaches plagued him continuously (Marx 1957, 161). He was unable to say Mass or his divine office and so for two years his daily obligation was simply three rosaries (Marx 1957, 162). Upon his discharge from the hospital, Michel was sent to the Native American Indian missions near Cass Lake in the northern part of Minnesota. Marx writes that Michel was supposed to engage in light work among the Chippewa, but in typical fashion "he embraced with zeal the apostolate to the Indian" (162).

Though still suffering from headaches and depression, he never ceased working. After one year, Michel was recalled to Collegeville but he soon returned to the missions at White Earth after realizing he was still ill (Marx 1957, 163). During his three years among the Native Americans of northern Minnesota, he learned their language, hunted

with them and ate their foods. He lived simply and admonished the
Chippewa to live Christian lives. He learned about poverty by
experiencing it (Marx 1957, 163). In 1933 he was once again called to
return to St. John's in the capacity of dean. He was most reluctant to
leave the peaceful home he had found. Evidence of how well loved he
was by the Chippewa was the large delegation that later attended his
funeral (Marx 1957, 164).

In the missions, Michel began to make connections between
liturgy and culture (Whelan 1996, 70). This experience among the
Native American people engendered in him an even deeper
commitment to social justice. Although interested in social justice
issues prior to 1930, after he left the reservation and returned to
Collegeville Dom Virgil became even more convinced of the strong
link between liturgy and society.

Liturgy and Religious Education

For some religious educators, the words "religious education" and
"catechesis" are interchangeable. To others, they are distinct concepts,
each with its own purpose. Although Michel began by using the term
"Christian education," he later utilized the terms, "religious education,"
"religious instruction," and catechesis almost interchangeably. Michel's
thought regarding religious education/catechesis "is one which evolved
organically, that is, while Michel continued to refine and elaborate his
initial insights, he at no point regulated them or recharted his course of
thought" (Whalen 1996, 110).

Michel was familiar with the work of Thomas Shields of Catholic
University, especially his innovative summer school. In 1929 Michel
started his own liturgical summer school at St. John's. He scheduled
classes in liturgy, pedagogy in religious education, church music, and
Christian art and symbolism. The school had an enrollment of
seventy-five in its first summer. It was through this experience that
Michel realized that there was a need for improved textbooks for
schools based on the liturgy as the heart of the curriculum (Bryce
1978, S-49).

Michel was involved with the American catechetical movement,
which began in the late 1920s. Prior to this time there was no organized
and unified method of religious instruction throughout America:

"During the years of Michel's' life the theory and practice of religious education in Europe and in the United States was reflective of a popular theology which separated body and soul, intellect and emotion, sacred and secular" (Beaudoin 1989, 239).

At this time, the *Baltimore Catechism*, first published in 1895, was widely in use. This method of teaching religion depended on the memorization of answers to questions regarding the doctrines of the Catholic faith. These memorized doctrines were to be applied to one's daily life by acts of the will with the grace of the Holy Spirit. For years some religious educators, including Frs. Edward Pace and Thomas Shields, viewed this method as rigid and narrow.

Virgil Michel suggested a different approach to religious instruction. Instead of memorization, he offered a liturgical approach to religious education. In his comments one can easily see the influence of personalism:

> The liturgy makes its appeal to the whole man, to understanding and to the senses, to the emotional and the esthetic life and to the will, and furnishes both the basis and the inspiration for constant spiritual growth of the integral man in all the elements of his nature. (Michel 1940, 532)

In this case, the continual growth of the individual, basic to personalist philosophy, was made manifest in Michel's view of religious education.

Central to Michel's thinking was the idea of community. He said: "To this must be added the collective nature of the liturgy, which makes legitimate use of the best possibility of what is today often known as mob or crowd psychology (1940, 531). Moreover, Michel believed that a person also learns by doing, thus he advocated a religious education grounded in the traditional pedagogical device of active participation. Michel was not against the acquisition of abstract knowledge. However, he believed the method of the *Baltimore Catechism*, with its emphasis on memorization of doctrinal issues, begged for better educational methods to be employed. Michel wrote:

> This . . . is not to disparage the acquisition of abstract knowledge; but it does stress the evident fact that abstract knowledge, especially about natural and supernatural living, cannot be

inculcated unto good fruits of life by mere abstract
instruction. (Michel 1940, 530-31)

Before examining what Virgil Michel thought religious education
ought to be, it might be helpful to understand what he thought it
should not be. In his articles "Religious Education" (1937a),
"Rediscovering the Obvious: Liturgy and the Psychology of Education"
(1940) and "Liturgical Religious Education" (1937b), Michel outlined
what he saw as some of the failures in religious education. He lamented
the "almost universally accepted atmosphere of individualism,
naturalism and materialism that pervades the culture of today" (1937a,
218). To counter these, Michel advocated the absolute value of the
human person as delineated in personalism, with spiritual values at the
very heart and center of human reality. As a result, the human person
exhibits a capacity for freedom, responsibility, knowledge,
consciousness, and love. While the individual is held in high esteem,
individualism is not to be prized. For Michel, personalism is
diametrically opposed to any system of doctrine, formula, and control.
Therefore Michel was adamant that catechetics, first and foremost,
respect the person. To this point, Michel wrote about "Our one-sided
stressing of intellectual grasp of doctrine, which has only too frequently
turned into mere memorizing without too much understanding (1936,
218). Michel believed in the practical application of religious truths,
pointing out that too often class activity was separated from the
celebration of the liturgy. Furthermore, Michel insisted that the moral
teaching of the Church should be presented not as a mere intellectual
exercise but rather as lived experience.

Another criticism Michel offered was that Catholic religious
education in his day had become too Protestant: "Much of our
teaching of Catholic religious education has confined itself to the
Protestant conception and delimitation of Christianity. This is true
even of many sermons preached from Catholic pulpits" (1937a, 219).
Dom Virgil saw in the adoption of the *Baltimore Catechism* the specter
of Protestant influence:

We have followed the method popularized by Luther in his
catechism of short questions and answers. We have aped
Lutheranism! Not so much that we copied his short question

and answer method–which might be unimportant, though some say it is not; but we have followed Protestantism in separating dogma from the living liturgy of the Church. For the Protestant reformer, who repudiated all visible priesthood and liturgical mystery, this is intelligible, for the Catholic, it is not! (1937b, 268)

The antidote to this, according to Virgil Michel was to teach the faith while "doing" faith. He decried, "We thereby separated both our teaching efforts and the learning efforts of the children as far as possible from the sources of divine grace in the liturgy" (1937b, 269). Unfortunately, in this article as in others, Michel does not provide a practical application of how one is to go about doing this. However, as a theorist, he could be quite vocal. It is only in his catechetical books that he gives expression as to how these ideas were to be implemented.

Michel argued that the liturgy was not only the vehicle for receiving God's grace but also provided sound pedagogical principles for religious education. It was through the liturgy that catechesis was made real and concrete with the ultimate goal of appropriate action in the world by members of the church:

> Now what does it mean to say that the liturgy must be made basic in our religious education? It means just this (and perhaps much more): that we must teach the truths of our religion in their practical relation to that living religion, to the actual living out of these truths in the church both by the church as a whole and by each member as an active participant. It means that the truths in their interrelation of dogma and worship must also be taught in their mutual relation to the everyday life of the Christian, which must ever be but an extension of the sacrificial dedication of himself to God at the altar. It means that the truths must be taught with all the interrelations they have in the living itself, psychological, emotional, intellectual, volitional, natural and supernatural. (1937b, 267)

Moreover, Michel asserted that unless and until we teach from this fundamental worldview we would teach an abstract form of

Christianity. In short, religious educators would not be teaching the truths that Jesus taught. Jesus as the way, the truth, and the life was fundamental to understanding the worldview of Virgil Michel. He, in turn, maintained that this was the path that all Catholics should follow. The guiding principle of his religious educational views was this:

> Just as Christ is the Way, the Truth and the Life, or King, Teacher and Priest so all religious education consists of morals, truths and worship; to teach Catholic truths without relating these truths, both theoretically and practically, to actual worship, which is a living of these truths in real union with Christ, is a terrible neglect of the duty of religious education. (1935, 495-96)

In his article, "Rediscovering the Obvious," Michel explained his views on religious education:

> Similarly, the science of education about which there has been such a to do in the past decade, has in many respects been no more than "discovering" and formulating in technical terminology principles which were taken for granted by our forefathers. This is especially true of psychology of education. Applying these principles to religious instruction, we find that they have been part and parcel of the Church's traditional method of teaching through the liturgy—but we have lost sight of the fact with our loss of liturgical spirit. (1940, 529)

Michel described the "rediscovered" pedagogical principles that ought to be applied to religious education. Although he predates the "experiential learning" generation, he did however comment on what the probable results could (and have, to a degree) become:

> The consequence has been that while we taught something of the Mass, for instance, we did not teach it in relation to proper attendance at Mass. And when we taught and drilled attendance at Mass (by means of the rosary, of litanies, of popular hymns or else silence), this "praying" of the Mass had at least the possible principle of "learning by doing," but in

regard to the focal center of all Catholic life we had the
children learn without doing on the one hand, and on the
other do without learning. Is there any wonder that the truths
learned had no vital meaning for them and did not stick, and
that the mechanical doing only too often ceased when there
was no longer any pressure of external circumstance to bear on
the grown-up children? (1937b, 268)

It is clear that Michel was working to formulate some type of middle
ground between theory and experience in his approach to
catechetics. What is striking is that the statement was written in
1937. Religious education professionals are still tying to find that
middle ground. To this end, Michel delineates the following
"rediscovered" pedagogical principles that ought to be applied to
religious education (1940, 529-32):

1. *Method and materials should be adapted to the learner.* Michel
maintained that the connection between education and liturgy is integral
to the Christian tradition. He asserted that this principle has been
applied at all times within the liturgy of the Church. More important,
this has been made manifest in the Incarnation. Further, Jesus instituted
the Church and provided it with the sacraments and the liturgy. By this,
Jesus gave the liturgy as a means of worship that is innately pedagogical
and serves needs of human nature to praise its Creator.

2. *Religious education should proceed from the concrete to the abstract.*
This principle is true because learning is best achieved by moving from
the concrete to the abstract. In Virgil's view, people understand more
clearly the "what" they were doing if they understood the "why" as well.
Toward this goal, Michel thought the materials used at Mass and other
sacramental celebrations were the concrete outward signs of inner grace:

The materials used in sacraments and sacramentals, water,
wine, oil, bread, ashes, salt, palms, various colors, the audible
words, the visible gestures, all of these are so many concrete
signs that convey their message to the soul in accordance with
the natural aptitudes of man. (1940, 530)

3. *One learns by doing.* Since he viewed learning as an interactive
process, Michel urged active and intelligent participation by

individuals in order to realize the full value of educational processes. Michel lamented the "state of apathy and indifference" (1940b, 530) that was prevalent during his time and urged the faithful to take an active role in the liturgy. As an example, Michel urged that during the celebration of the Mass the faithful recite prayers, genuflect, and sing: "The simple sign of the cross, in word and action, is a striking example that is not only intelligible but also appealing to the lowly and the great alike" (1940, 531).

4. *Learning is best done through group processes and dialogue.* Liturgy, for Virgil, should be a collective action on the part of the faithful, who should not be present merely as passive observers: "Once rightly instructed, the faithful member of Christ cannot but enter into its action with mind and heart and thus absorb its lessons ever more intimately" (1940, 531). To Dom Virgil, the Mass is the primary symbol of individuals being in community. Liturgy, conducted according to sound liturgical rubrics, should also foster the development of each person within a communal context. Thus Michel brings to bear the basic principle of personalism to an understanding of members of the Christian community and their participation in the liturgical actions of the Church.

5. *Repetition enhances learning.* Although Virgil argued against the over reliance on memorization of the *Baltimore Catechism*, he did favor repetition when it came to liturgical participation. He saw value in the weekly or even daily repetition of the prayers and the rituals of the Church. In Michel's view, the memorization of doctrinal statements, often poorly understood or even misunderstood, is not to be compared to the repetition of prayer and actions in which one has proper understanding and plays an active part.

6. *Learning involves progressive development and growth.* From Baptism and continuing throughout one's life, Michel maintained that the individual under the influence of the love of God advanced further along on the path to perfection day by day. He made clear the importance of the liturgical year:

> Such progressive advance on the path of Christ is seen in the development of the Advent liturgy to Christmas, and again in the development of Lent through Passiontide to Easter. It is also evident in recurrent daily and yearly cycles of prayer,

whose repetition calls, not for mechanical sameness, but a constant spiritual advance towards the greater realization of the Christ-life. (1940, 532)

This idea later became foundational to the catechetical books developed by Michel and his colleagues.

Catechetical Textbooks

In addition to publishing articles for the adult laity, Michel developed a series of catechetical manuals for schools of all levels, elementary through college. He was involved with the creation of five liturgical and catechetical publications, four of which will be reviewed here: *A High School Course in Religion* (for secondary schools); *With Mother Church Series* (for primary and secondary schools); *The Christ-Life Series* (for elementary school) and *The Christian Religion Series* (for high school and college). In each endeavor, Michel was the creator, author, or collaborator of a particular series of texts. Whether his involvement was direct or indirect, Michel's thought was the guiding light of each project (Whalen 1996, 166-214). In these works his idea of liturgical catechesis receives concrete application.

High School Course in Religion (1924)

This course was introduced in the College Preparatory School of St. John's University in Collegeville, Minnesota, during the school term year of 1923-24. This curriculum was designed for two class periods of religion per week. In his introduction, Dom Virgil described the basic outline for this course as the concentration on religion as a reality for the whole person, both interior and exterior. Michel saw religion as interior but he did not see it as a privatized form of practicing one's faith. Nor did he want the faithful to confuse external forms of faith expression as representative of what true religion was all about. Michel explained:

Religion with many persons takes on some external forms of action and remains at them. Such religion is but a faint shadow of true religious virtue. It is but a cloak that hides the true poverty existing in heart and mind—a blind that covers up before the eyes of others the true nakedness of the soul. If this fact is lost sight of, religious education and religious training easily assumes the form of an inculcation of external forms to the neglect of the vital core. (1924, 408)

When Michel speaks of "religion as interior," he is referring to the truth that religion must permeate every fiber of a person. Virtue must become a part of thinking, acting, and a way of life to the extent that the person is no longer thinking about what he or she is "doing." Instead, virtuous living ought to become instinctive. Michel wrote:

Only where positive religious virtue has previously been acquired and cultivated until it has become second nature, until it has entered the very life of individuals, will such external exhortations reap much fruit, and then they will become unnecessary. (1924, 409)

By claiming that "religion is of the whole man," Michel is suggesting that religion is not a solitary aspect of a person's life but is to permeate every aspect life. It must be possessed by the whole person and "therefore be rooted in and find a response in everything that makes up human nature" (411). For him, faith is more than "a mere affair of momentary sentiment" (410).

Each year of the high school curriculum concentrated on four distinct areas: 1) memorization of prayers with the addition of mental prayer in later years; 2) doctrine—commandments, government of the church, religious books, gospels, sacraments, the Creed, the Epistles; 3) history—the life of Christ, history of the Church, history of the Church in the United States; and 4) practice/reading—mental prayer, the lives of the saints, and selected pamphlets on religious topics.

In his article, "A High School Course in Religion" (1924), Dom Virgil explained his methodology and choice of subject matter. He stated that one of the prime purposes of the coursework arrangement was to teach the students not to rely on textbooks as the source of all knowledge. Above all, he wanted students to understand religion as "a spontaneous and personal possession" (484). It was with this goal in mind that Michel devised the curriculum for each study area:

memorization of prayers and texts from the Bible must be accompanied by understanding and doctrinal study should include the usual teachings of the Church as well as a study of the gospels and epistles. In an interesting development he placed other New Testament texts in the area of memorization. He mapped out his rationale:

> The multitude does not long merely for academic dissertations or verbal dissections of divine truths in all their telling simplicity. No better form of such doctrinal exposition can be had than that coming from the lips of Christ himself. (476)

The coursework involving history did not stress the memorization of dates, places and names. In fact, Michel advocated that teachers dispense with a textbook for this area of coursework. He felt the course material ought to be presented to the students orally and the students were to take notes as they saw fit (478). What Michel hoped to achieve in teaching was this:

> It is essentially an unfolding of the divine plan in the life of human society. It is not secular study; it presents Christ in the Church not figuratively but literally, as he is the life of that body, personally dwelling therein. The development of history should be the varied manifestations of Christ, His work of the redemption; it contains the same struggle with evil that Christ exemplified during His visible sojourn on earth. (478)

For the area of readings/practice, Michel exhorted teachers to make students aware of a variety of Catholic periodicals. Since he believed that Catholic families had little knowledge of Catholic literature, he felt it was the duty of an "educated Catholic to foster Catholic literature and by word and example to help spread its influence" (484).

The *With Mother Church* Series (1929)

The *With Mother Church* series had unique origins. This series was originally conceived by Sisters of Saint Dominic, Estelle Hackett and Jane Marie Murray of Grand Rapids. According to Whalen, Michel worked as a collaborator on this project. He provided the lessons on the liturgy and the church calendar year (1996, 171-72). However, it was the sisters who actually wrote the texts. From the beginning the series was not designed to be a formal textbook or textbook series. Nor was it designed to be an all-inclusive form of religious education. Instead, it was written to address a specific issue: to initiate children to the liturgical feasts within a catechetical environment. This series explained the feasts within the liturgical year and how their celebration helps to illustrate God's plans within the life of the church.

There were several reasons why the authors felt this type of series was needed (Whalen, 171-72). The liturgical movement, which was beginning to grow in popularity, emphasized the "Mystical Body" and its view of grace as life in Christ. Second, the collaborators sensed that the *Baltimore Catechism* did not sufficiently address the areas of feasts and seasons in their texts. To make up for this neglect, the authors began to design this series of five manuals. These texts were not meant to supplant an existing curriculum, but they were designed to be a set of experiential laboratory manuals and not a complete religion curriculum. The authors recommended that the series be used in conjunction with other materials.

Whalen (1996) assessed both the positive features and drawbacks of this series. He noted that

> On the one hand, these manuals constituted an integrated catechetical process in that they are designed ideally to be used sequentially and in whole. On the other hand, they could readily be used in isolation from one another. (175)

The series' inability to be integrated with the existing catechetical series used in schools was its Achilles heel. Ultimately, the clash of objectives and approaches was to be, at once, the manuals' success story and their major drawback. Although the series revealed deficiencies in liturgical foundation in the catechetical manuals then in use, the manuals were not enough to overcome the fundamental lack of liturgical catechetical instruction in the classroom.

The Christ–Life Series (1934)

Michel collaborated with Basil Stegmann, OSB, and the Dominican Sisters of Grand Rapids, Michigan, most especially with Sister Jane Marie Murray, to produce *The Christ-Life Series in Religion*. By 1934 all eight volumes for primary school were completed. In an article in *Origins*, Monsignor Roach remarks on what was paramount to Michel:

> Liturgy equals life. That equation of Fr. Virgil's is apparent from the titles alone of his major works: *The Christ Life Series*; *Our Life in Christ*; *The Christian in the World*; *Liturgy and Catholic Life*. He understood we are embodied spirits, and we don't just attend worship, but we are a part of worship. (Roach, 20)

Michel set the tone of the series in the opening paragraph of the *Teacher's Manual: The Christ-Life Religion Series*: "Michel speaks of the Church as the Mystical Body and refers to the vine and branches imagery found in John 15 when speaking of the abundant fruit that every Christian is called to bear" (Beaudoin 1989, 237). Thus, the focus of this series is upon understanding the Church as the Mystical Body of Christ where each person as a result of his or her baptism into the faith is graced to carry out God's will. Marx noted:

> This was Michel's profound conviction: if every student could be taught the liturgical life of the Mystical Body of Christ and his active share in it with all its implications for daily living, then he would have in the liturgy a lifelong teacher accompanying him as a kind of adult educator; in various life situations-truth, inspiration, and grace would be imparted as needed. (1957, 22)

Moreover, as Michel imagined it, the true instructor was the Holy Spirit, Christ's spirit, instructing through the liturgy.

This series incorporated doctrine, Scripture, art, liturgy, and music into a text that was meant to present the faith not as formulas to be memorized, but rather as a lived reality. According to Marx (1957), "If other texts had embodied parts of the liturgy as auxiliary aids, the *Christ–Life Series* was an avowed attempt to build a primary school religion curriculum based on, and inspired by, the liturgy, but without neglecting doctrine" (234-35). The series had eight volumes, one for each of the grade levels in primary school.

This catechesis is grounded in the study of the Mass, sacraments, and the liturgical year. Each topic area progressively leads one deeper and deeper into the liturgy. Furthermore, according to Whalen (219) the same themes, albeit in an expanded format, can be found in the texts Michel helped develop for the high school and college levels.

The Christian Religion Series (1938-52)

In this series Dom Virgil collaborated with Sister Jane Marie Murray. From the outset, this series was to be a continuation of *The Christ–Life Series*. The authors initially intended this series to consist of six volumes: four high school texts and two college-level volumes. Because of the death of Virgil Michel in 1938, only four volumes were actually published: two for high school and two for college.

In the preface to the first high school text, Sister Jane provided details on the shape the series was to take: Grade 9 *The Life of Our Lord;* Grade 10 *Living in Christ;* Grade 11 *Christ in His Church;* Grade 12 *Restoration in Christ.* The two college-level texts written by Michel were *Our Life in Christ* and *The Christian in the World* (Whalen 202).

As to the direction of the series, Murray wrote, "The series is written in the spirit of the Catholic revival of the day and specifically of the liturgical movement" (Whalen 202-03). Additionally, she pointed out that

> the books of the series consequently stress the vital truths of the Christian tradition in their relation both to the worship of the church and to the daily life of the Christian-and always in reference to the special characteristics of our present civilization. (Whalen, 202-03)

The Christian Religion Series was a companion set to *The Christ-Life Series.* In theory these two separate series could be used independently of each other. *The Christian Religion Series* coupled the liturgical and sacramental foundations in *The Christ-Life Series.* This dual basis is important for understanding the content or purpose of *The Christian Religion Series* and the philosophical approach to catechetics by Virgil Michel and his collaborators.

In this regard, Whalen makes an interesting observation: the locus of *The Christ-Life Series* and *The Christian Religion Series* is founded on the idea of "experience," since both series took for granted that students were engaged in a conscious and full participation in the liturgical experience (206-07). The co-authors' pedagogy was simple: they were training young minds to grow to adulthood and to be prepared to take their place in society. Consequently, the high school texts were geared toward the social teachings of the Church, while giving the liturgy and sacraments a prominent place in teaching. In his summary, Whalen synthesizes Michel's methodology in five foundational points: 1) The Foundation of the series, its philosophy and psychology of education, is Dom Virgil's philosophy of personalism, which places great importance on the absolute value of the human; 2) the Content of the catechesis in the series is the entire liturgical life of the Church as lived in its sacraments, the Mass and the liturgical year; 3) the Context in which catechesis took place is the liturgy as celebrated within the family and the church, which were viewed by Michel as the primary foci for the celebrations of feasts, sacraments the liturgy; 4) the Experience of liturgical catechesis is participation in the Mass. Also important for Michel was conveying an understanding of the colors, rubrics, music, and vestments; and 5) the Integrating Principle of the catechesis is the community (209-12). Whalen notes, "As such his approach to liturgical catechesis correlated liturgy and life, sacrament and society, worship and world, Eucharist and community" (213). It was Michel's hope that catechetical study would lead to a commitment to social justice, since the liturgically instructed would be enabled to maintain horizontal and vertical relationships with God and with community.

Expectations for Religious Educators

In such an ambitious course of instruction, Michel obviously had great expectations for religious educators about how they were to go about their duties.

According to Marx,

> not only must the teacher know his subject matter thoroughly, use the best pedagogical methods and skill, be acquainted with human psychology and needs at the various ages, and understand the prevalent environment and culture, but above all, he must *live* (emphasis in the original) what he teaches. (1957, 238)

Furthermore,

> Death to self, a profound and joyous living of the Christ-life-
> that is the essential lesson that must be caught from, if not
> taught by, one who must be seen by the student as a co-victim
> with Christ as a happy messenger of good Tidings from God.
> The teacher of religion, unless he lives thoroughly what he
> professes to teach, implicitly denies what he would have his
> students carry over into their lives. (Marx 1957, 238)

In two essays published in the *Journal of Religious Instruction*,
Michel explored what he considered to be minimal knowledge necessary
for a religious educator to teach religion, especially the Mass. This editor
of textbooks decried that teachers lacked the basic knowledge that is
foundational to teaching religion. In his response Michel concentrated
on upper grades and high-school level teachers. He held that a teacher
ought to have a well-rounded, liberal arts college education. In this
regard, he was critical of the offerings of Catholic higher education and
expressed his hopes for better college courses, saying

> I do not mean the motley secularized mosaic of a course that
> even some Catholic colleges offer, but really a Catholic college
> education, one that has mastered knowledge and views of life
> in terms of a living Catholic philosophy. (1938b, 765)

Michel believed the Mass was not a separate activity in a person's
life but "should be intimately related to everything a Catholic says and
does and thinks." He continued:

> Furthermore, any teacher who ignores, or is ignorant of this
> essential truth, while it is possible they would be imparting
> correct knowledge about the Mass the possibility exists they
> could miss the whole purpose of the Mass. (Michel 1938b, 765)

For Michel this would produce students well-versed in the rubrics of
the Mass, yet ignorant of its meaning. In Michel's judgment, not to
understand the Mass would be to fail to understand Christianity and
what it means to be a Catholic. He explained that

What happens in concentrated form in the Mass when it is intelligently and wholeheartedly participated in must unfold itself in detail through all the moments of our life between Mass and Mass, regardless of whether we can attend the Sacrifice daily or only on Sundays. The Mass is at once cult, creed, and code-worship, dogma, and life-and no teaching of it that does not embrace it in its totality is in any sense adequate. (Michel 1938a, 596)

What else would Michel ask from a religious instructor? He desired that the Mass be taught as embodying all the mysteries of Christ, as praying the doctrinal truths of revelation. He wanted every participant in the Mass to be joined with Christ (the vertical relationship] as well as with other Mass attendees (horizontal relationship) in knowingly giving themselves to God in the offering and receiving of Christ in the Eucharist.

Michel believed the Mass enacted all the mysteries of Christ, and was "the central-prayer action" of the Mystical body of Christ. Further, the Mass should be taught as the praying of the doctrinal truths of revelation. Ideally this means that at Mass each person joined in the collective offering of the entire community to Christ and, in return, received Christ in Holy Communion. Ultimately the Eucharist was taught and therefore understood in true Catholic fashion. That is, the emphasis was placed on the Real Presence, sacrifice, and sacrament of Communion.

For Michel, therefore, the Catholic instructor must be well versed in the Old and the New Testament. This knowledge is fundamental if the teacher is to teach the real meaning of grace. Grace is not to be understood, or taught, as a free pass to heaven. Rather, it is to be seen as truly living with Christ. If this were understood properly and lived out in the person's life, then heaven could be thought of as being present in the here and now.

Logically, the teacher must effectively connect the Mass with the doctrinal teachings of the Church. Michel continued:

To assure the application of this doctrine by students to present and future life, the instructor must teach always in terms of immediate participation in the Mass; otherwise the students will be learning without doing and doing without learning-and in the end, perhaps, neither learning nor doing. In other words, if the truths and the spirit of the Mass are to suffuse daily living, the Mass must first be meaningfully lived and experienced at the altar in church. If, then, the learner intelligently shares in the Sacrifice according to this capacity, carry over will be assured, especially if the teacher has related the "inspiration projection" of the Sacrifice of Christ to daily student living, while obviously living the Mass himself. (Marx 1957, 233)

In "Knowledge Requirement for Teaching the Mass," Dom Virgil wrote:

[These] requirements are not even what the teacher of the Mass should know by reason of his specialization in the Mass. They are what every intelligent layman should know as a matter of course; and they are also, I hope, what every graduate of a Catholic high school and college will know *ipso facto* in the next generation. (Michel 1938b, 767)

Writings on Religious Education

The best way to understand Michel is through his articles on education. Because of his enormous output, this section will concentrate on his views regarding the education of youth.

In an article with the interesting title "Are We Educating Moral Parasites?" Michel treated moral education of youth at home and in school. In a theme that resounds even today as many young people seem to abandon their faith after receiving the sacrament of Confirmation, Michel voiced similar concerns:

Much has been said in our day of the leakage in Catholic ranks in our country, of the way in which our youth succumb to the allurements of a life of pleasure, or the inspirations of non-Catholic thought, of how the training once received withers at almost the first instant of contact with the heat of the excited life today. (1927a, 147-55)

Michel opined that once youth are away from school or home their Catholic moral values are in danger of being abandoned or at least compromised as they enter society: "They live or die morally with the surrounding conditions. In other words, they are in the moral life what most parasites are biologically–they give all indications of being moral parasites" (1927a, 149). Michel posits two reasons for this. First, young people's hearts and minds are overly protected by their parents from the realities of the world. Young children are shielded from the temptations of their surrounding environment: "In the home the child lives in a moral environment that is not to be found later in the world at large. The young mind and heart are carefully shielded against the words and actions of an older world" (150).

The second reason is that children are often threatened into behaving well. Michel had little patience with the "big stick and the stern command" (Michel 1927a) method of instilling moral virtue and good behavior. He thought that

> In both cases the growing child learns to be good by reason, chiefly, if not solely of its environment. In so far as neither of these conditions can last throughout life and in so far as the world and the flesh will under all circumstances be with us at all times, this type of education is a grave injustice to the youth. (150)

Then how was one supposed to teach children moral values? Michel responds: "Education is to assist young people in their period of transition from a state of helplessness and direction by others to one where they are in control and are able to make their own decisions" (150). This necessary transition becomes clear especially when Michel asserts that "The two points ever to be kept in mind under pain of dire failure are simply what a youth is, and what he or she is to be. He is to be a full-fledged man, but at present is only trying to become one" (151; emphasis in the original).

Thus, Michel suggests that parents are to rear children within an atmosphere of acceptance and care that respects them as individuals. There was no room for a prescribed set of rules and formulas for every child growing into adulthood. He recognized and respected the uniqueness of young people and had an appreciation for their tender, impressionable, and confusing stage of life. Michel recommends that youth be treated

> with the kind, sympathetic understanding that was Christ's, an unselfish sympathy that is willing to make sacrifices of personal comfort and time, miseducation is the natural result and the fault of it lies rather with the adult than with the youth. (152)

Throughout his work and writings, Michel's personalist philosophy is evident. While he insists that "definitive objective, universal standards of conduct must be insisted on at all times" (152), Michel wants parents and educators to respect the value and dignity of the person. In such an atmosphere, education for self–direction, self control, and freedom are no longer seen as valueless concepts. Instead, they are valued resources nourishing the individuality of the person. Michel argued that children have the right to an education that assists them to gradually develop into adulthood as morally self-controlled and self-dependent individuals. Moreover, since children are individual persons, the education process should endeavor to respect their uniqueness. Thus, the aim of religious education is not to form "a creature that has become set it its ways of acting and its habits of thoughts and ideals, but a creature that is guided by reason and free will in its best actions" (152). Seemingly, Michel anticipated later educational reformers in his concern for education for freedom, self-direction, and self-control. He differs from them in asserting that this education for freedom should not be value neutral or subjective, but committed to objective moral values. Beaudoin analyzes Michel's thought noting that

> His concern as a personalist is the most appropriate way to educate persons for a free assimilation of the universal and objective values while respecting the absolute value of the person. He proposes a dialectical process which is truly a developmental enterprise. (1988, 245)

Michel proposed education as "an interpersonal dialogue involving both teachers and parents" (Beaudoin 1988, 240). Hence a primary goal of education was to raise children to a position of social partnership, in which there is something of the relation of give and take, since there are always on both sides, or in both parties, duties or obligations as well as rights. There are no relations between men on this earth, in which all the rights are on one side and all the duties on the other. Any education that neglects this fundamental truth is a menace to human society. It results in a product we wrongly called individualism. (Michel 1927a, 155)

Michel's rejection of indoctrination in teaching is a concrete example of the influence of personalism on his educational philosophy. While other religious educators of his generation did not hesitate to advocate indoctrinating students in the truths of faith, Michel warned teachers not to impose the truth on students nor force them to engage in mindless religious rituals. He counseled that

If this fact is lost sight of, religious education and religious training easily assumes the form of an inculcation of external forms to the neglect of the vital core. Young souls may be marched regularly to the reception of the sacraments, to frequent devotion, and still not get beyond the acquisition of external habits which is upheld by the dint of the pressure of eternal circumstances. (1924, 419)

Michel's Legacy

No doubt the liturgical movement left a significant impact on the Church in this country. Pecklers notes the movement was not without ecumenical and ethnic influences (1998, 283). Virgil Michel's stress on the Church as the Mystical Body of Christ gives meaning today to the multicultural elements and changing global demographics in the Catholic Church. Pecklers concludes his study by commenting,

The multicultural liturgical communities of the 1990s are quite different from anything the American liturgical pioneers might have imagined, but the principles and goals advocated by those pioneers remain as valid and relevant today as they did in 1926: to find in our liturgical prayer the impetus for social action in the face of rising inflation, unemployment, and a growing problem of homelessness; to see the Eucharist as modeling a pattern of more just, more dignified human relationships. (1998, 286)

Bringing people closer to the liturgy brings them closer to the universality of the Church. Michel knew that a deeper understanding of liturgy led believers to its practice in daily life. Still today the goals of liturgical catechesis, a vibrant faith and a hunger for worship, are fostered by a sound understanding of the proclamations, rites, symbols, and rhythms of the Mass. Michel knew well that the interplay of liturgy, catechesis, scripture, and witness through actions for justice are essential to handing on the faith. This interplay becomes of even more importance in today's growing secular culture. Catholic religious education would greatly benefit from a return to Michel's deeply spiritual and psychological understanding of this kind of liturgical catechesis.

Yet as a result of the reforms of Vatican II and subsequent changes in methods of catechesis, much of what Virgil Michel advocated has lost its visionary glow. However, the age in which he wrote must be kept in mind. To say he was a man ahead of his time seems trite. However, Dom Virgil gave voice to ideas that are still very much with us today. He advanced a philosophy that places great emphasis on the dignity of the person. Michel challenged a doctrinaire method of education in favor of one where the laity also learned the reasons why they held certain beliefs and performed certain rituals. To this end, he endeavored to synthesize different areas of study (liturgy and social justice) into an educational model that would teach the laity–young and adult–what it means to be a Catholic in the world and what they are called to do.

Virgil Michel stressed that teachers should endeavor to convey the message that revelation is God speaking in the present and that from this insight discernment of an earthly vocation is possible. This doctrine of a present revelation began to be more commonly held following the Second Vatican Council.

Dom Virgil sincerely wanted Catholics to understand and practice their faith. He was also convinced that they needed some type of education to grow into the fullness of adult faith. It is impressive that sixty years before Vatican II, a Benedictine monk would make it his life's work to teach the faithful what the Church had not previously taught clearly about the role of the laity. He was a pioneer who wanted the laity "to possess" their own church. While Michel did not provide an entire syllabus to flesh out his theories, he did leave behind a wealth of ideas and ideals.

As a result, the Church is blessed today with Michel's vision of the absolute value of the human person, the right of the laity to be full participants in the Church and its liturgical life, their right to understandable religious texts, and their responsibility to live their faith in the practice of social justice.

Sister M. Rosalia Walsh and the Parish Catechetical Apostolate

LUCINDA A. NOLAN

If Bishop John Lancaster Spalding of Peoria had lived long enough to see the vast numbers of lay and religious women receiving degrees in theology and religious education beginning in the 1950s and continuing today, he would have realized one of his most deeply held visions for the future of Catholic education in the United States. In 1964, a small, frail Sister of the Mission Helpers of the Sacred Heart received a Master of Arts degree in Theology from Fordham University at the age of sixty-eight. This moment was the culmination of a life lived in service of the catechetical mission to the Catholic children in this country who for one reason or another were unable to attend Catholic schools. Sister Mary Rosalia Walsh (1896-1982), along with her community that had been founded by James Cardinal Gibbons in 1890, ministered to poor immigrant and African-American non-Catholic school children in this country and later in Puerto Rico and Venezuela. As a result of their widely recognized and successful methods, thousands of children came to be catechized in their faith.

Scott Appleby, in an edited volume on the American Catholic intellectual tradition, defines intellectual traditions as "multi-generational arguments . . . about the nature of 'the good'–that is about what constitutes 'excellence' in the practice of education, art, the sciences, theology, literature, cinema, philosophy, history, ecclesial life and so on" (2004, xx). The written records of the theory and development of catechetical methods in the U.S. and the manner in which catechists were trained to carry them out may be considered an essential part of the American Catholic intellectual tradition. It might have surprised Sister Rosalia to find herself the subject of a chapter in this volume along with such notables as Bishop John Spalding, Edward Pace, Virgil Michel, and Jacques Maritain. However her long service and scholarship in the Catholic Church testify that she belongs. Her story is about living out the many facets of her vocation–writing, teaching children, training catechists, and studying the educational theories and methodologies of her time. Paradoxically, Sister Rosalia taught alongside learned professors in institutions of higher education while finding time to pursue her own studies only episodically.

Sister Walsh and the Mission Helpers of the Sacred Heart developed and shared their successful method under the title the Adaptive Way. Their story unfolds in the years of the transition of catechetical instruction from the age-old method of text-analysis and memorization to one of text explanation and presentation in light of the newly emerging field of educational psychology. The catechetical method of the Mission Helpers was based on principles developed in Europe, but was more deeply rooted in the Sisters' practical catechetical experiences.

Three main streams of catechetical history converge in the study of the work and writings of Sister M. Rosalia Walsh. First, she was instrumental in the adaptation of new methods of catechetical instruction to the situation in the United States. Her long tenure of teaching children and her studies in psychology enabled her to usher into the field of catechetics the progressive ideas of secular education and educational psychology. Second, she was intensively involved in the development of catechetical materials for the Confraternity of Christian Doctrine (CCD) in the U.S. Sister Rosalia was the first Director of the Mission Helpers' Department of Catechetics and was involved with development of teaching materials through the National Center of the CCD in Washington, D.C. for over twenty years (Spellacy 1984, 121). Third, she was responsible for increased awareness of the need for improving catechetical training in this country for religious and lay teachers alike. Her great concern for the careful preparation of members of her own community, other religious sisters, and lay catechists is evident in the detailed manuals she prepared, her efforts in conducting national workshops and training sessions, and in her addresses at national catechetical congresses. In each of these three streams of catechetical history, Sister Rosalia emerged as a pioneer and leader, a woman in a field heavily populated by male clergy, and a humble servant of the non-school catechetical apostolate. She would take no personal credit for these achievements, seeking always to name the Mission Helpers as the community to which all these triumphs should be attributed.

Following a brief biographical overview of the life of Mary Rosalia (Josephine) Walsh, this chapter examines the key ideas that emerge from her work and writings. In both theory and practice, much of the thought of Sister Rosalia remain salient in Catholic religious education. The chapter concludes with a survey of the contributions of Sister Rosalia's and the Mission Helpers' of the Sacred Heart Catholic religious education in this country from 1924 to 1966. Over the course of these forty years, Sister Rosalia came to be so closely identified with the catechesis of non-Catholic school children that one was overheard to say at one of the congresses, "Sister Rosalia *is* the Confraternity" (Bryce 1985, 321).

Becoming a Teacher of Those Who Teach Religion

The Walshes of Cumberland, Maryland, were a large Catholic family, loyal participants in the life of the Church and dedicated to helping the immigrants of like faith who came to settle in their area of the country. Josephine, born April 26, 1896, was the fifth of nine children born to William E. and Mary Concannon Walsh, and one of four who would later dedicate their lives to the Church. William Walsh was a devoted Catholic who led his family in morning and night prayer at home in front of the images of the crucifix, the Sacred Heart of Jesus, and the Holy Family. Josephine Walsh attended St. Patrick's grade school and high school. She was very bright and like her father, to whom she was devoted, loved to read (Spellacy 1984, 69-70).

William Walsh was president of the Saint Vincent de Paul Society at St. Patrick's Church in Cumberland, Maryland. He was active in the work of addressing the needs of the poor. A lawyer by profession, he voluntarily traveled on weekends to minister to the needs of Italian, Polish, and German immigrants and their families. Josephine was happy to accompany her father on such visits. No doubt those visits were instrumental in shaping her vocational dreams. William later expressed to the Mother Superior of his daughter's religious congregation that he would be most happy to see all nine of children enter religious life. Josephine would not need much in the way of persuasion. She loved the opportunities to teach the catechism to the children of the families they visited. Later recalling the influence of her family on her decision to enter religious life, Sister Rosalia wrote:

> My vocation was certainly fostered by the example of my parents who were exemplary Catholics and noted especially for their charity toward the poor. . . . My Father sometimes associated me with him in visiting the poor and the sick, and in catechetical work. From this, probably came my desire to enter a religious community devoted to work similar to that which my Father did as a Vincentian. I believe firmly that God called me to a congregation with these four characteristics:
> 1. The Sisters would visit people in their homes;
> 2. Teach religion to those not in Catholic schools;
> 3. There would be no lay Sisters, and
> 4. The Sisters would not visit their homes every year. . . .
> The regularity . . . did not appeal to me. (AMHSH, Personal Recollections, 3)

Josephine Walsh entered the Congregation of the Mission Helpers of the Sacred Heart on January 5, 1916, at the age of nineteen. Her pedagogical gifts were soon recognized and she was soon given the opportunity to give lessons on the catechism. These lessons were written as they should be spoken to children and were then read to novices while Josephine, now Sister Mary Rosalia, was still a novice herself. Shortly after making her first vows (October 2, 1918), Rosalia was given her first mission to Staten Island, New York. Residing in New York City, she traveled on Sundays with other Mission Helpers to teach religion in kindergarten and to older children all week. Sister Rosalia recalled in writing the difficulty of starting a new mission and the lack of resources for their work. She remained involved with the Staten Island mission until 1923 (Sister Rosalia's personal notes, AMHSH).

The Mission Helpers of the Sacred Heart were concerned about furthering the education of their Sisters and in 1923 sent Sister Rosalia to the Fordham University School of Social Service. After completing one year of the two-year program, Rosalia developed a severe eye condition that threatened her ability to see. She was hospitalized and eventually lost all sight in one of her eyes. She was unable to complete the course of study, and returned to the motherhouse in Towson, Maryland, where she turned her efforts toward teaching in the Novitiate. Shortly thereafter Rosalia was chosen to organize and direct the congregation's first Catechetical Department (Spellacy 1984, 113). While the Mission Helpers of the Sacred Heart had long been involved in the catechesis of children (their efforts were recognized as early as 1895), Sister Mary Rosalia Walsh would lead them into the catechetical renewal movement and in the preparation of teachers to carry it forth in the early decades of the twentieth century (Spellacy 1984, 71).

During the post-World War I period in the United States, Catholics were still struggling to assimilate into the culture. Having contributed heavily to the war effort, Catholics now focused their attention on national organizations to provide services for the growing numbers. The organization of catechetical ministry became the task of the National Catholic Welfare Conference (NCWC), which had been formed out of the National Catholic Warfare Conference when the war ended. The 1920s saw the rise of national efforts to educate the vast numbers of Catholic children who were not attending Catholic schools. Archbishop Edwin O'Hara was instrumental in the formation of the Catholic Rural Life Bureau, a branch of Catholic Social Action of the NCWC, which introduced correspondence courses in catechesis and religious vacation schools. By the 1930s, branches of the Confraternity of Christian Doctrine (CCD) began springing up all over the country and in 1935 the National Center of the CCD was formed as a bureau of the NCWC. Both the CCD and its National Center would impact the life and work of Sister Rosalia and the Mission Helpers of the Sacred Heart in the coming decades (Spellacy 1984, 77, 100 ff.).

In 1930, Rosalia studied the latest teaching methods in religion at Loyola College in Baltimore and enrolled in a correspondence course with Father Leo McVey through the Catholic University of America. While short of earning a degree, Sister Rosalia became immersed in both the study of methods in religious education and in how best to train catechists to use them. While studying and teaching in the motherhouse, Rosalia began to put into writing the method the Mission Helpers had been developing since their beginnings in the late years of the nineteenth century.

Child Psychology and Religion (Walsh 1937) became the community's first published catechetical text and the first specifically designed for those involved in the Confraternity of Christian Doctrine (CCD). It was a compilation of talks given by Sister Rosalia on catechetical methodology for the purpose of educating lay and religious catechists who would be working with non-Catholic school students. The text was also later translated into Spanish (1941). Because few women were writing catechetical texts at the time, the publishers advised Sister Rosalia not to list her name as author. Instead, she humbly chose to call herself "A Teacher of Those Who Teach Religion." The language of the text is easily understandable and the tone friendly and conversational. It is directed toward those who want to teach religion to the young but have no formal pedagogical training. It combined method and practice with some basic principles of educational and psychological theory. The topics include: prayer, apperception, catechesis in the home, the use of pictures and stories, class preparation and student motivation. The small volume of sixteen short lectures was well received and the name of the gifted author was soon commonly known in catechetical circles (Spellacy 1984, 119).

In 1937 Sister Rosalia also audited courses at the Catholic University of America with William Russell and Felix Kirsch in order to study the most current methods being used in religious education. It was also at this time that she first became associated with the National Center of the CCD (founded in 1935) and was named chairperson of the Teacher's Division of the National Shrine of the Immaculate Conception. The appointment was providential. Spellacy said of it, "Rosalia's association with the Center would last over twenty years and impact the entire catechetical movement in the United States" (1984,

121). Her work on revising the Center's *The School Year Religious Instruction Manual* was among the most notable of her many efforts on behalf of the Center.

In 1938, Rosalia wrote *The Correspondence Course for Lay Catechists*, a text drawn from her talks in the summer Catholic lecture series at Cliff Haven, New York. These were her first public lectures outside her congregation. The correspondence course was commonly used as a means of disseminating catechetical materials across the country, including the most rural of areas. Toward the end of that year and into the next, Sister Rosalia worked on rewriting the methods text of the Mission Helpers. The sisters also envisioned a graded text and Sister Rosalia prepared two volumes, one for grades one through four and one for grades five through eight, for trial use. These were published as *The Adaptive Way Course of Religious Instruction for Catholic Children Attending Public Schools* in 1941. Six years later this work was in use in forty-four U.S. states, Puerto Rico, Hawaii, and fourteen foreign countries (Spellacy 1984, 123). In the spring of 1944, a rewrite of the method text appeared as *Teaching Confraternity Classes: The Adaptive Way.* Shortly thereafter Rosalia was invited to assist in the work on a three-volume religion course being prepared by the Maryknoll priests (1943-47). These were eventually published in 1947 under the title, *The Religion Teacher and the World.*

Sister Rosalia continued her untiring efforts in the field of catechetics throughout the decade of the 1950s. From 1939 to 1959, Rosalia's writings were published by such distinguished journals as *The Journal of Religious Instruction, The Catholic Educator* and *Lumen Vitae* (Clement 2000, 61). Continually updating and revising teaching manuals for the Adaptive Way and her work at the National Center of the CCD occupied much of her time.

Rosalia taught summer methods courses at the Catholic University of American from 1947 to 1957 with such "well-known experts as Godfrey Diekmann, Gerald Ellard, S.J., Aloysius Heeg, S.J., Rudolph Bandas, and Joseph Collins" (Spellacy 1984, 180). From 1953 to 1961, she trained catechists through a mission at St. Paschal's Convent in New York. She continued to write and publish catechetical manuals including one for vacation religious school and a new version of *The Adaptive Way* in 1955. From 1957 to 1958 Rosalia conducted an advanced course in methods for training lay catechists at the request of Most Rev. Walter Curtis, Director of the CCD of the Archdiocese of Newark, New Jersey. Reorganization in 1948 and again in 1952 of the Catechetical Department of the Mission Helpers of the Sacred Heart shifted Sister Rosalia's role from Director to Promoter to overseer of correspondence on a few manuals. These changes gradually reduced Rosalia's "direct influence on the sisters and her contact with national leaders" (Spellacy 1984, 149).

The 1950s brought increased pressure for teacher certification and most colleges and universities required their instructors to have master's degrees. In 1963, Rosalia completed work on a Master of Arts degree in theology at Fordham University. She was awarded the degree on February 1, 1964. Later that year, Sister Rosalia was reassigned to the motherhouse in Towson, Maryland. In 1966 she completed a post-Vatican II revision of *The Adaptive Way* and celebrated her golden jubilee. Sister Mary Rosalia Walsh served as the librarian of the motherhouse and became involved in social justice groups, including the League of Women Voters. She spent her last years in the infirmary and died on January 21, 1982.

Sister Rosalia and the Mission Helpers had "their greatest influence on the catechetical field from 1948 to 1960" (Spellacy 1984, 240). Today the Sisters are involved in other endeavors to help the poor, but no longer are involved in addressing or publishing catechetical materials. Sister Rosalia accomplished much in the field in spite of the many challenges she faced: "She influenced teachers, religious, clergy, parents and children for decades" (Spellacy 1984, 247). Sister Rosalia worked with a humble heart for the glory of God and in unity with her community to develop and hand on better catechetical methods. This chapter now turns to the theoretical and methodological foundations underlying the catechetical ministry of Rosalia Walsh and the Mission Helpers of the Sacred Heart.

Theory and Method in the Adaptive Way

In 1905, Pius X's *Acerbo Nimis* (*On Teaching Christian Doctrine*) called on the Catholic hierarchy to make alleviating widespread ignorance of the faith their common concern. Without religious instruction, the Pope wrote, it is impossible to "expect a fulfillment of

the duties of a Christian" (n. 5). Pius urged bishops and priests to see
to the weekly instruction of boys and girls from the text of the
catechism for an hour (n. 19) in addition to separate sessions for
sacramental preparation (n. 20). Every parish was to establish a society
of the Confraternity of Christian Doctrine (n. 22). Emphatically, Pius
X added that no one, regardless of intelligence or oratory skills, would
ever be able to teach Catholic doctrine to children who had not
availed him or herself of extensive and careful study and preparation
(n. 26). *On Teaching Christian Doctrine* is often referred to as the
catalyst for the catechetical revival movements of the twentieth
century. The Catholic Church in the United States responded with
serious attention to the document, though it would be a gradual
process before the undercurrents, stirring first in Europe, would reach
this continent.

The Mission Helpers of the Sacred Heart had been involved in
catechetical ministry for twenty-five years by the time Josephine Mary
Walsh became a novice in 1916. Their past work had been in the areas
of ministry to the "publickers" (Catholic children attending public
schools), African-American mothers and their children, and the deaf.
Besides their Sunday school efforts, the Sisters sewed and collected
clothing for the poor, set up shelters for women, and established
industrial schools. By the mid- to late-1890s, the Mission Helpers were
recognized for their catechetical successes. They learned their teaching
methods from their own experiences in dealing with the needs of those
they encountered. As early as 1895, the Sisters were using Bible stories
to enhance the catechism lesson and recognized the need to involve
parents as much as possible in the religious instruction of children
(Spellacy 1984, 48).

These were years of a growing impetus toward certification for
Catholic school teachers and the preparation of catechists, both lay and
religious. It was of no less a concern to the Mission Helpers. The way
one learned to teach was to apprentice under a master teacher. Those
outside of religious teaching communities needed to be trained by
those who had experience, especially in the case of preparing catechists
to teach in the special situation of the "publickers," as the public school
Catholic children were called. Catholic school historian Timothy
Walch described the difficulty teachers had in finding schools for this
kind of training: "To be sure, [Thomas] Shields had established his

model college and several Catholic universities had opened
departments of education, but these programs could provide training
for only a few hundred teachers each year" (Walch 1996, 145).

Sister Mary Rosalia's natural affinity for working with children was
already well honed and the Sisters quickly recognized in her an
advocate and potential leader in their efforts to bring the faith to
Catholic children attending public schools. Through her efforts, the
Adaptive Way was organized so that it might be systematically shared
and taught among the Mission Helpers and later across the nation
(Spellacy 1984, 104). Sister Rosalia wrote:

> Teaching the catechism . . . means more than teaching the
> definitions contained in the catechism. It means teaching
> religion in all the ways in which the child learns, and in which
> the divine truths of revelation will become vital forces in his
> life. We sum it up in one brief principle, called the principle
> of adaptation: *All teaching must be adapted to the nature and the
> needs of the child.* (Walsh 1944, ix)

The theory and the method of the Adaptive Way were adapted *from* the
experience of the Mission Helpers and other catechetical sources as well
as adapted *to* the nature of the child.

Sister Rosalia's work with Catholic children attending public
schools and those who would be their catechists occurred during a time
of widespread dissatisfaction with catechetical practices both in Europe
and in the United States. Methods of teaching the faith remained
largely unchanged for four centuries, focused as they were on rote
memorization of catechetical formulae written in the dry, abstract
language of Scholastic philosophy. Catechetical journals and reviews in
the early decades of the twentieth century reflected a growing
discontent among scholars with the teaching methods being employed
and the inadequacy of the catechism as a textbook.

The most commonly used catechetical method at the end of the
nineteenth century was one of text explanation followed by
memorization. The explanation of the text was analytical and exegetical
and sought to help students understand the words and concepts of the
questions and answers they were to commit to memory. The following
instruction for catechists is descriptive of the aridity of this method:

In the explanation the catechist should keep exactly the wording of the catechism without adding other matter, for example, from other catechisms. The content of the prescribed catechism is in itself so rich that the catechist need not waste time searching for subject matter outside it. . . . [The catechist] should divide the answer into its component parts, first by singling out the subject and the predicate of the sentence and their modifiers and then by stressing the relative clauses pertaining both to the subject and the predicate. (W. Pichler 1907, quoted in Jungmann 1959, 177)

While the aim of the lessons was still the memorization of the catechism, this method added a deductive explanation of the abstract doctrinal formulae of the catechism. Although it expressed the admirable concern of helping the children understand what they were memorizing, this method was clearly not in tune with what Sister Rosalia and the Mission Helpers were discovering about how children best learn.

At the turn of the century in Europe, The Society of Catechists in Munich and Vienna looked to secular education and educational psychology for ways to revitalize catechetical method and provide students with deeper and more meaningful applications of faith to life. Catholic historian of religious education, Raymond A. Lucker, views this shift in catechetical aim as one moving from catechesis as information to catechesis as formation (1966). The method developed by these European catechetical societies, known as the Munich (or Psychological or Stieglitz) method "was popularized in the United States by students who studied under the successors of the originators of the plan" (Collins 1966, 20).

As early as 1908, Mother Demetrias of the Mission Helpers was in conversation with Thomas Shields of Catholic University about his methods of teaching religion (Spellacy 1984, 101). Later the Sisters were introduced to the work of the German Jesuits, Michael Gatterer, and Felix Krus, who together in 1914 wrote *Theory and Practice of the Catechism.* The text addressed the key question: "Shall we keep the catechism as it is, or shall we teach it by means of Bible History?" (Gatterer and Krus 1914, 103). Within their text, Gatterer and Krus identified twenty-seven principles of catechetical instruction. These twenty-seven principles form the heart of the Adaptive Way. The authors sought to harmonize the use of the catechism for instruction with modern pedagogical methods and the teaching methods of Jesus and the early Church:

> Under the guise of returning the method of Christ, to teach religion chiefly in parables and according to psychological methods (the two are held to be one and the same thing), there is a tendency, the authors notice to do away with the catechism as no longer up to the requirements of present-day pedagogy. . . . While strong advocates of all sane modern theories in pedagogy by which catechetical teaching may benefit, the authors of the present work, however, with insight and discrimination, hold the balance evenly, and show from history, reason, and experience that the *teaching methods* of the Church, sanctioned by twenty centuries of practical results, are not to be lightly discarded; that the teachers however, need to be frequently aroused to a full and clear realization of their duty to be self-sacrificing "Apostles of Jesus Christ." (Gatterer and Krus 1914, 6)

Sister Rosalia's writing reflected the principles of Gatterer and Krus as well. These Jesuit priests accepted the processes that came to known as the Munich method. Their principles analyze and logically address the new method point by point and offer the authors' reasoning and proof for the acceptance of each principle into the catechetical practices of the Church. Following and incorporating these ideas, Sister Rosalia's writings proposed in theory that catechesis is primarily for the building of a living faith that becomes evident in the actions of the learner. While the catechism remained the central core of the content, Bible history as well as liturgy, Church history, hymns, and the lives of the saints should augment the doctrinal lessons. The enhanced catechetical endeavor made its way through the whole catechism at least every two years, with a review every year. The teachings of the catechism should be clear and easily understood by the listener. While memorization was important, application and practice of the doctrines was essential. The training of the heart was more important than the instruction. The virtues were to be taught to the children and their practice encouraged.

Children should be trained in the virtues of work, prayer, obedience, truthfulness, and chastity. It was of extreme importance that the catechist maintained discipline, order, respect, and reverence in the classroom of religion in order to gain the hearts of the children. Finally, each lesson was to be a "methodological unit and made to appeal to the children from the outset" (Gatterer and Krus 1924, 395-404).

The Mission Helpers' Adaptive Way, in theory and in practice, was in actuality an adaptation of several methods. The "adaptation" in the Adaptive Way referred to the Mission Helpers' understanding that "all teaching must be adapted to the nature and needs of the child, to the subject matter, and to the circumstances under which it is taught" (Walsh 1955, 57). As noted earlier, Sister Rosalia and the Mission Helpers also "adapted" the principles of the twenty-seven catechetical principles of Gatterer and Krus addressed above and combined them with other catechetical methods of the time (the Sulpician Method and the more progressive Shields Method) to formulate the aptly named Adaptive Way method (Spellacy 1984, 130-31).

Factors in Successful Planning and Teaching

The factors of successful teaching in a religion class were "first and most important" order and discipline (Walsh 1944, 1). Second, what Sister Rosalia called "vivid teaching" would serve to "happily engage" children in their learning and curtail any disruptive behaviors that may result from boredom. Reverence and courtesy is considered basic to all good teaching. Finally, the use of rewards should be to "stimulate further effort" and should be used only "sparingly and with caution" (1).

Sister Rosalia wrote extensively on the process of lesson design in the Adaptive Way. Every teaching manual included a section on developing the lesson plan for the public school children in Confraternity classes. While the catechism supplied the content, and was gradually memorized over the years, the method of the Adaptive Way stressed that children first be helped to understand the material,since "learning presupposed far more than memory work" (Walsh 1944, 40).

The process should begin with the identification of both teacher and student aims. For Sister Rosalia, these aims must be clear in the catechist's mind to insure the focus and clarity of all the elements of the lesson. Doctrinal content for each lesson is provided in the graded course text that every catechist using the method would have. Also in the early stages of planning, the catechist should locate visual aids and materials for the class and prepare a list of the words the children will need to know in order to understand the doctrine being taught. These vocabulary words might be put on flashcards or written on a blackboard. The catechist might use charts, pictures, story, or discussion to familiarize the children with the vocabulary for the lesson.

The five steps of the lesson plan as explained by Sister Rosalia in *Teaching Religion the Adaptive Way* (1966) are: 1) Orientation, 2) Presentation, 3) Assimilation, 4) Organization, and 5) Recitation (Walsh 1943, 677ff). A description of what is entailed in each step follows, with special attention to the use of story in the Presentation phase, which was an important hallmark of the Adaptive Way.

Orientation

The first step of the lesson did not involve teaching. The orientation was devised in order to help the child recall knowledge that he or she already had on the topic for the day. The educational principle involved in this stage is apperception, "the act or process of adding a new idea or series of ideas to an old one" (Walsh 1937, 22). The linking of the new idea to one already known by the child helped the new information to be retained and assimilated. In this stage the teacher established the necessary connection between the religious concept to be learned and the child's experience. This could be done by tapping into the knowledge a child might already possess on the doctrine to be taught. A closely-related doctrine could be called to the mind of the child or an ordinary experience that the child might have had could be brought out to help the child understand what is to come later in the lesson (Walsh 1957, xvi).

Techniques that enhanced the orientation process included pre-testing, discussion, and use of images, words, or symbols that may stimulate recall and recognition for association of past experiences or previously learned related doctrines with the new idea. Walsh believed this stage to be of critical importance in motivating the student for learning and for the teacher to be able to grasp the full attention of the child. This part of the lesson ended with an evocative question that would stimulate the student's interest in the lesson for the day (Walsh 1966, 321-22).

Presentation

The presentation constituted the most important part of the lesson. All elements of good pedagogy applied to the teaching of the main idea, doctrine, scripture passage, and so on. The presentation may also occur within the context of liturgy or Christian witness. The purpose of the presentation was "to teach some aspect of the Mystery of Christ in ways that will engage the whole child in the desired response" (Walsh 1966, 323). Moreover, the presentation should teach the children how to live in light of the lesson learned and "motivate them to live that way; that is, to give them supernatural reasons or motives for living in that manner" (Walsh 1957, xviii).

The four sources of catechesis–Scripture, Liturgy, Doctrine, and Witness–provided the content for the topical focus of the presentation. The catechist considered what was essential and appropriate for student learning in the doctrinal subject matter. The "means" of transmitting the content might vary from catechist to catechist. Many teaching manuals supplied the appropriate subject, methods, and teaching aids for each lesson. Sister Walsh promoted the use of a variety of techniques to stimulate student interest in the presentation including the use of "story, filmstrip, discussion, song, drama, pictures and others" (Walsh 1966, 323). The doctrine and practice at hand should be woven into the story or presentation and there should be time allowed for questions and discussion, especially with older children (Walsh 1957, xix).

In this part of the lesson, Walsh stressed participation especially to stimulate students who are likely to be tired in religion class after a full day in public school. She also maintained the importance of the use of story and visual image in capturing the children's religious imaginations. Several key themes may be culled from Rosalia's writing on the use of story. She devoted entire chapters in texts and manuals to encourage catechists to the use of story and story telling. Grounded in Jesus' use of story for teaching, the principles of apperception from educational psychology, and many years of personal experience in teaching children, Walsh was convinced that stories were the key to opening up the religious sensibilities of the child and led to a deeper understanding of doctrine that in turn facilitated transformation of the will and actions. She wrote, "The story arouses interest and holds attention. It fires the imagination, stirs the emotions, aids the understanding, and influences the will" (Walsh 1959, 69).

The story was one of the most important aspects of the presentation part of the Adaptive Way lesson plan: "The story should arouse wonder, awe, it should deepen faith and love" (Walsh 1966, 240). Scripture stories hold the place of prominence for Walsh because salvation history is the story of God acting in love for the salvation of humankind and thus is the basis of all doctrine. The purpose of telling a story is, for Walsh, the teaching of doctrine and the motivating of the child to live it (Walsh 1959, 81): "Through a well-told story the abstract definitions of the catechism become concrete, living realities to the child and he learns with ease and joy" (Walsh 1959, 81). However, it must be noted that the story was always a means to an end. At the conclusion of the lesson it was the catechism question that should be remembered, understood and recited by the children: "The abstract definitions of the catechism must become living realities in the mind of the child, and in his life. Stories help to effect this; that is why we tell them" (Walsh 1944, 150).

The catechist should exercise care in choice and preparation of the story. The choice of story should highlight the doctrine to be taught and never overshadow it. Nor should it be so dramatic that the child recalls only the story and not the teaching. One story should suffice and should not be overcrowded with unnecessary detail or diversions. Stories should be selected from the Bible, from Church history, from

> the lives of saints, and from practical, everyday Catholic life. The chief source of stories for all ages . . . is the life of Christ. Selection is made on the basis of the doctrine to be taught and the grade to which it is to be taught. . . . Doctrine, presented in action in the life of a child saint, is easily understood by the children and appeals strongly to them. Stories of saints should be told so that they are Christ-centered. (Walsh 1944, 150)

Some stories in the Old Testament were deemed unsuitable material for young children. The story should be age-appropriate and its language and content adapted to the age of the child. The language used in a story shapes the picture it creates in the child's imagination. The characters should stand out and the message should not be obscure. Sister Rosalia believed that pictures used to illustrate a "revealed truth should be 1) theologically correct; 2) historically correct; 3) beautiful; 4) reverent; and 5) adapted to the student" (Walsh 1966, 250).

Other sources of stories suitable for use in the presentation were nature and human experience "in which case the story should embody only such events as have or may actually happen" (Bandas 1935, 27). However, fairy tales and imaginative narratives were to be avoided, as they were not seen as enlightened by the grace of God. Even stories of the lives of the saints, whose catechetical value was addressed by the early Church, must be used with great caution so not as to hold up lives of exaggerated virtue and superhuman feats that the children might not themselves achieve or take to so emotionally that stories of everyday life may come to be seen as drab. The catechist was called to use great care in the selection of Scripture passages.

In the method of the Adaptive Way, only the well-planned and rehearsed story would be successful. Attention should be paid to its structure, organization, and suitability for the age group. Sister Rosalia perceived the overall purpose of teaching religion as bringing children into relationship with the Divine through a gradual process of introducing the doctrines of God in a way that helps them to lead their lives in a new way. No amount of creative lesson planning can surpass the power of a well-told story.

As well as encouraging use of story in the presentation of the religion class, sound proof or apologetic defense of doctrinal materials may be included with older children. Walsh had the sensitivity and experience to acknowledge that many questions about a particular doctrinal teaching are attempts to understand the teaching more fully, not necessarily to challenge it. A confident catechist will not be ruffled by the children's questions.

One of the most important parts of the presentation was its application. The teacher assisted the child in drawing out implications of the presentation for life when this did not occur naturally. The application of the lesson may come spontaneously from the children without any prompting; it may be drawn out by the catechist with questions or it may be simply and directly taught. Whatever method employed, the catechist was to strive to help the students see the value of the teaching for Christian living. Walsh wrote:

> The effectiveness of our presentation of Religion to the child depends on the degree to which, with the grace of God, we succeed in making Religion the paramount value in his (her) life, that which he (she) appreciates and loves beyond all other desirable things, and therefore lives. (1943, 779)

The value of the presentation for the pupil was its ability to stimulate growth in knowledge, to aid in appreciating revealed doctrine, and to motivate for Christian witness (Walsh 1966, 323).

Assimilation Exercises

The third step involved activities that helped the pupil to more deeply comprehend the meanings of the presentation. This stage also provided some information for the catechist concerning how effective his or her teaching was in effecting student learning and comprehension. Further questioning, working with the text, or having students fill out worksheets aided the assimilation process. Such activities were oral or written and provided opportunities for exercises "in which the child judges, chooses, arranges, answers questions, gives reasons and motives, matches, identifies, associates, completes—in other words, thinks about and works over the content of the presentation" (Walsh 1943, 780). This step of the lesson also helped the catechist to see where he or she might need to do some re-teaching or further explanation of the doctrine

Many catechisms of the day, including the *Baltimore Catechism* (revised edition) contained exercises for student assimilation at the end of each lesson. This stage assisted students in becoming familiar with the structure and vocabulary of the text they had committed to memory. Assimilation exercises were done in class or were extended into some form of home study assignment.

Organization

The fourth step in the lesson may be understood best as re-organization of the material after it had been broken down, back into the original whole of the presentation: "The purpose of the Organization is to train the children in developing well-connected thought and speech concerning their religion" (Walsh 1957, xxi). Ideas from the presentation were placed in order by the class as a whole or by individual students on their own. When time was limited, as it often was for public school children in a parish religion class, this step may have been omitted. It was not generally recommended for younger elementary school children.

The value of organization is that it allowed for student expression of independent thought and fostered logical, ordered thinking. The means of achieving this included written or oral summaries by the students, arrangement of flashcards or key sentences, and analysis of the scripture or liturgical ritual (Walsh 1966, 324-25).

Recitation

The fifth and final step of the lesson actually occurred at the start of the next religion class. It was the time when "the class gives back to the catechist the material she (he) presented, and answers the catechism questions in which the doctrine is summarized" (Walsh 1943, 784): "The purpose of the Recitation is to find out whether the children understand and remember what they have been taught, and whether they have studied at home the material that was assigned" (Walsh 1957, xxi). The catechist could check the accuracy of the children's learning and evaluate the home study process. When the recitation was faulty, the catechist would provide remedial help. Where recitation was satisfactory, the catechist gave approval and recognized the achievements of the pupils. Sister Rosalia taught catechists that

> In Religion class it is extremely important that the pupil should want to answer well. When a spirit of achievement and success is built up in class, it helps to solve the problems of interest and attention, and the greater problem of study at home. One way to build it is to encourage. (Walsh 1943, 785)

Sister Rosalia ends her text, *Child Psychology and Religion,* by noting that when the children could tell in their own words what they should do as a consequence of the lesson learned, the teaching had most likely been clear. "Sometimes, though," she admitted, "they need a little help" (Walsh 1937, 133).

From her earliest experiences of catechizing immigrant children alongside her father to the time of her illness and death, Sister Rosalia was tireless in her efforts to promote catechetical advancement. Several major contributions made by Sister Rosalia Walsh to Christian education follow. She entered the field at the time the catechetical renewal movement was occurring in the U.S., and therefore is a rich study for students of American Catholic catechetical history. Because she incorporated principles of progressive education and insights from educational and developmental psychology, many of her methods of teaching and planning still have currency.

The Family as the Primary Center of Religious Education

Her own family upbringing deeply instilled the notion of religious education by the family into the core of Sister Rosalia's pedagogy. The ideal Catholic home exuded a catechetical atmosphere, where a "practical Catholic mother and father" had "received the Sacrament of Matrimony with all the graces this gives for living together in peace and union" (Walsh 1937, 29). This sacrament instills the duty of instructing the children in the faith and morals, which should begin very early on in the life of the child. Conversation, prayer, and patient addressing of the child's questions help the parent form the child's faith. For Walsh, religion must be correlated with Christian living and therefore the child's primary environment for socialization is the home. When this ideal home life is coupled with the attendance of the child at a parochial school, "the child has a splendid beginning for a life of practical Catholicity" (Walsh 1937, 35).

Not all families offered this ideal catechizing environment. Sister Rosalia believed in home visitations to assist catechists in understanding the situation of the children whom they taught and allowed for the education of parents in matters such as their responsibility to bring their children to Mass and to catechetical classes regularly. The teaching of the catechist, according to Sister Walsh, was secondary to that of the parents and the parish priest. She noted:

> Our teaching is classified differently. We are to supplement what the parents give in the home. It is we who should co-operate with the home, even while we seek actively to win the home to co-operate with us, and where right order reigns, where parents are fulfilling their God-given duty of teaching their children to know, love and serve God, this is done. (1952, 174)

The goal of such "fishing" (home visitors were called "Fishers") was to create mutuality between the parents and the religion teacher so that the children would register yearly and attend regularly. Appreciating the work of each other went a long way to foster the spirit of cooperation between parent and catechist. Sister Rosalia proposed the formation of Confraternity Parent-Teacher Associations, similar to the PTAs of public schools. These associations not only benefited the religion center by supplying parent support for classes, field trips, and libraries, but also afforded the parents opportunities to learn how to better teach their children religion and assist with their lessons in the home. In some cases, as Sister Rosalia well understood, the "work of giving effective instruction to the children includes what we may call the spiritual rehabilitation of the home" (Walsh 1946b, 508).

Catholic Pupils of Public Schools

Sister Rosalia clearly understood the missionary quality of religious education with those Catholic children who, for a myriad of reasons, were outside the parish and/or the parish school community. She was sensitive to the causes, among which were: 1) there was no parish school at all or it was overcrowded; 2) the parents' marriage was mixed, and the Catholic parent conceded the idea of Catholic school for the children; 3) indifference to religion; 4) lack of transportation to the parochial school; and 5) poverty.

Sympathetic to their needs and experiences from her childhood visitations with her father to the children of immigrants, Sister Rosalia decided early on that her vocation was to teach these children who, in the eyes of many, were so deprived. She described them as children who are

> children of the Church, members of the parish, called to be saints even as their more favored brothers and sisters of the parochial school, but faced with more obstacles in striving for that blessed consummation. . . . Each has a right to know the truths of religion that form a complete whole and make it possible to live as a child of God and member of the Church. (Walsh 1951a, 475)

If the catechists are to adapt the lessons to the situation of the learners, they must be familiar with the home environment, but not only that. Catechists must also have a great sensitivity to the unique needs of the public school student and great love for what they are doing. The students should be placed in a graded class, the same as the grade in public school, regardless of the amount of previous instruction or number of sacraments received.

Additionally, religion classes for the public school student should not be a synthesis of the parish school classes. Careful consideration of the environment, the length of days and class time, late comers, and sporadic attendance are all special considerations for students who are coming to religious education after long hours in the public school classroom. Often, the CCD classes were not given the quality and quantity of supplies that the parish school classes received. Sister Walsh, while never failing to uphold the unique value of the Catholic school, took exception to such practices:

> Effective religious education of the Catholic child of public school is a missionary work that helps to preserve, to build, or to revivify Catholic family life and parish life; it is a task that challenges the best that is in us, and should be given only the best. (Walsh 1946b, 153)

Sister Rosalia and the Munich Method in the U.S.

Sister Rosalia was only one of several proponents of the Munich Method in the United States: "Such writers as J. J. Baierl, Rudolph G. Bandas, Joseph B. Collins, S.S., Aloysius J. Heeg, S.J., Anthony N.

Fuerst, and Sister M. Rosalia, M.H.S.H. were among the leaders to make the Munich Method intelligible to American readers" (Lucker and Stone, in Hofinger and Stone 1964, 243). The radical shift in catechetical method in the United States during the early years of the twentieth century from memorization and text analysis of the catechism to the Munich Method was grounded in the principles of the educational psychology of Johann Herbart (1778-1841).

The Adaptive Way was based largely, but not solely, on the Munich Method. Sister Rosalia systematized her method for the catechetical instruction of Catholic children not attending parochial schools and wrote manuals so that catechists might be trained to use it (Nolan 2006, 1-2). The lesson plans and teachers' manuals prepared by Sister Rosalia and the Mission Helpers largely reflected the strong influence of the Munich Method. Based on the educational psychology of Johann Herbart, the steps for lesson preparation (presentation, explanation, and application) parallel the steps of learning (perception, understanding, and assimilation). The Munich Method did not intend to radically alter the content of the catechetical lesson. Yet the new psychological method opened the door for a more suitable way of addressing Church doctrine with children and by giving the Bible a place of primacy, actually began to reshape the landscape of catechetical content.

The hallmark of Sister Rosalia's catechetical manuals and lesson plans was their organization around a central theme. The graded courses were concentric in content, meaning that all major doctrines were addressed each year with increasing development according to the level of understanding of the learners (Walsh 1956b, 92). As the students progressed, the doctrine was treated in more detail and Scripture and history were added for the older students. The lessons were based on the principle of apperception (proceeding from the known to the unknown) and on the concept that all knowledge comes to the learner through the senses.

In later years the Munich Method would be criticized for its lack of student participation and its teacher centeredness. It began with a Bible story rather than the actual experience of the child. It failed to note the limitations of the catechism in passing on the entirety and fullness of the *kerygma*, the Good News proclaimed. However, over the years the revision of Sister Rosalia's texts on the Adaptive Way showed a developmental increase in her reliance on Scripture. Ultimately, the method consistently relied most heavily on the teaching experiences of the Mission Helpers.

The Importance of Proper Teacher Preparation

For Sister Rosalia, the first step in preparing children for what she called "complete Catholicity" was to prepare oneself to teach religion. To this end she dedicated her life's work. Her professional life was lived out in the era of the development of standardization and certification requirements for teachers of religion. Early in her career, Sister Rosalia saw the wisdom and necessity of training lay catechists. She began the work of training catechists in the novitiate and never abandoned it. Her personal sense of vocation and love of God seemed to energize her work. Hers was a natural gift, a special calling that preceded any special training which she always responsibly sought for herself. She wondered if the Church could afford to neglect any opportunities to train the catechist who is

> a brave person indeed–or should we say presumptuous?–who is willing to engage in a work in which right orientation of life in this world and the issue of eternity are always influenced and often decided. (Walsh 1951a, 476)

Regular class attendance, a high level of student learning, and drawing out appropriate responses from the children all depended on a well-trained catechist. For Sister Rosalia, there was no more important work. In an inspiring talk she said:

> It is excellent to be a catechist; one may hope in the course of the years to teach religion to hundreds of children. What of training as a leader who will in turn train catechists? One such leader may train fifty or a hundred catechists within a year. These will teach thousands of children. Hundreds of thousands wait. (1951a, 476)

Each manual written by Sister Rosalia expressed the care she would have her catechists put into preparing to teach. Though the manuals contained complete lesson plans, they also expressed the need for catechists to do background reading and to write out their own plans each week. As she insisted, "Careful preparation enables them to teach with strength, simplicity and clear cut accuracy" (Walsh 1951b, 119).

In 1956, Sister Rosalia recommended to the National Catechetical Congress that two thirty-hour courses, one in content (*The Revised Baltimore Catechism* No. 3) and the other in method, be offered as a standard course of study for advanced preparation of lay catechists: "'You ask a great deal of the catechists,' a priest said to me, and the answer was, 'We would rather have a few well trained, than a larger number inadequately prepared'" (Walsh 1956a, 114).

Conclusion

Sister M. Rosalia Walsh was a pioneer and a leader in the field of catechetics in her day. Yet she was also a humble soul, dedicated to her calling and to her community. She exercised humility and obedience to her community and vows throughout her long life. She asked nothing of others that she would not ask of herself. There was no group too small for her to go to in order to share her experiences of teaching and learning. She sought no personal credit for the initiatives she embarked on in behalf of her community. She lost no opportunity to make explicit the role of her community in the development of the Adaptive Way. Her image as model catechist was always kept within the context of the communal work of the Mission Helpers of the Sacred Heart.

In addition to her practical contributions, this chapter has traced the importance of Sister Rosalia's educational theory and, in particular, its relevance for catechesis with children educated outside the Catholic school system. Her strong convictions about the practices of catechesis were based in sound educational theory and child psychology. Early on, she recognized that a difference in context meant a difference in materials, methods, and overall approach. Moreover, in working with children, she emphasized the social and religious role of the parents and family in the shaping of the children's religious sensibilities and their understanding of faith as a way of life. She realized also the importance of a mature educator who recognizes the need for ongoing growth in faith for all members of the church.

Sister Rosalia wrote an article for the journal *Lumen Vitae* (1947) in which she highlighted the power of religious education to bring about the transformation of society and the world. She recognized in the years just after World War II that the future really lay in the hands of the children that were being taught in the churches. This is a rare article, not addressing practical concerns, but theological truths that must emerge through the study of all the disciplines and subject areas of Catholic education if a bond of world unity is to be achieved. She wrote: "True knowledge is a living growth . . . and this growth must be fostered and guided" (268). This is accomplished by teachers who

> stress the great germinal truths, those truths of which knowledge and love and love and practice should grow and expand in the child with each year of life. God as our loving Father is the first and all men as our brothers is the second. (269)

Militating against this growth are totalitarianism and racial discrimination. The first envisions humans "in terms of a servant or slave" and the second "evaluates on the basis of the color of skin" (270). Both demean the dignity of the human person. To overcome these biases, Rosalia thought that adding more content to the religion course would be a mistake. Rather, "effective teaching of religion requires even more than thought and assimilation: it requires presentation of religious truth in ways that will give clear understanding, deepen convictions, develop appreciation, teach right values" (274). It falls to religious education to produce apostles—those "who radiate the peace of Christ and the strength that goes with it. World unity cannot come otherwise" (277).

Sister Mary Rosalia Walsh of the Mission Helpers of the Sacred Heart is remembered for her many contributions to the Confraternity of Christian Doctrine in both the training of catechists and the writing of catechetical materials that ultimately fostered the missionary spirit and compassionate dedication for so many Catholic children who did not attend Catholic schools. The challenges she faced remain the challenges of the Church today.

In our time, the numbers of Catholic children who do not have the opportunity to learn about their faith in Catholic schools or Catholic religious education programs is staggering. The Church continues to deal with a shortage of well-prepared catechists. In the words of Sister Rosalia:

Teaching the small earthly sons and daughters of our
Heavenly Father is a very beautiful work, but like everything
worth while, has its own difficulties. . . . We do not work
alone. For all teachers there is the true source of confidence: "I
am come to cast fire on the earth: and what will I but that it
be kindled" (Luke 7, 49). (Walsh 1937, 135)

Jacques Maritain and His Contribution to the Philosophy of Catholic Education in America

LUZ M. IBARRA

Among modern Christian educators, Jacques Maritain occupies a preeminent place because of his reflections on the philosophy of education, elaborated through the use of Thomistic philosophy. Maritain proposed a general theory of education in which the concept of person stands at the center. Indeed, education according to Maritain depends on one's view of human persons—their values, destiny, relations to God and society, as well as the way they come to know themselves.

Given that Thomistic philosophy is usually Christian philosophy, Maritain's philosophy of education constitutes a suitable tool for reflecting on the ends specific to religious education. It is my contention that the contribution made in the twentieth century by Jacques Maritain in philosophy of education is still valuable for developing a Catholic philosophy of education. Not all scholars are in agreement that Maritain's Thomism is suitable for this task. This essay, however, will argue that it is up to the task of providing a sound basis for the philosophy of Catholic education.

Maritain was convinced that to ignore the task of reflecting philosophically on education—in particular Christian education—amounts to weakening education's foundation and core. In his view, the very act of reflecting on the nature and aims of Christian education constitutes an important step in providing a correct and meaningful education in a quickly evolving world.

Though he was French it is appropriate to include Maritain in a book about American Catholic educators. First, it is important to recall that Maritain spent many years in the United States holding a faculty position at Princeton University. He also lectured at many prestigious universities in this country, as will be indicated later in this chapter. Perhaps most important, his principal writings in philosophy of education were written in this country and in the context of United States education. His *Education at the Crossroads* (1943), the Terry Lectures given at Yale University, remains a classic statement of Thomistic philosophy. This work represents a defense of liberal education and is a strong critique of the utilitarian education proposed by educational progressives in this country. In it Maritain also made a strong case for the teaching of religion in the public school curriculum. Furthermore, Maritain was invited to contribute a substantial essay on the Thomistic view on education in the 1955 Yearbook of the National Society for the Study of Education (NSSE).

His Life

Jacques Maritain was born on November 18th, 1882, in Paris, France. His mother, Geneviève Favre, was the daughter of Jules Favre, a famous republican who was opposed to the policies of Louis Napoleon. Geneviève raised her son in a liberal Protestant environment. After she divorced Paul Maritain in 1884, before Jacques's sister was about to be born, she gained the right to raise Jacques and Jeanne, on whom she had an enormous influence (Mougniotte 1977, 11).

Young Jacques's family situation was so difficult that he was later reluctant to remember the days visiting his father at Château de Bussière. As a young man, he had already developed religious, pedagogical, and political ideas. He entered the Lycée Henri IV and then the Sorbonne in Paris. There he met Raïssa Oumançoff, a fellow student at the Sorbonne and the daughter of Russian Jewish immigrants. They wed in a civil ceremony in 1904. She was his spiritual and intellectual collaborator all of her life (Viotto 2000, 4).

Not long before Maritain's birth, the ideas of Marx, Comte, Huxley, Spencer, Darwin, Nietzsche, Balzac, and Zola had become an important part of the intellectual milieu in which European intellectuals lived in the late nineteenth century. However, philosophical positivism did not answer the larger existential issues of life for Jacques and Raïssa, both of whom had once contemplated suicide. They attended lectures of the French idealist philosopher Henri Bergson at the invitation of Charles Péguy, a socialist writer opposed to traditional philosophy. Peguy later had considerable influence on Maritain's thinking. Finding Bergson's lectures in aesthetics, philosophy of religion, and ethics to be a series of revelations exposing the many mistakes of the new scientism, the Maritains stopped thinking about suicide (Viotto 2000, 127).

Jacques and Raïssa started a real conversation about Catholicism with Léon Bloy, a writer who represented a version of French anti-bourgeois Catholicism and was known for his anti-Semitic polemic. They were impressed by the sincerity of one of his books, a novel entitled *La Femme Pauvre* (*The Poor Woman*), which was reviewed by Maurice Maeterlinck. Through Bloy's influence, both Maritains sought baptism in the Roman Catholic Church in 1906. With baptism both assumed the natural stance of "philosophical intelligences." They believed that only God could heal the spiritual aridity of their intellectual lives and fill their lives with a larger meaning (Viotto 2000, 127).

Maritain obtained a scholarship to study biology at Heidelberg, which offered him an opportunity to abandon philosophy. But Humbert Clérissac, a Dominican, introduced Maritain to the *Summa Theologica* of Thomas Aquinas. In the philosophy of St. Thomas, Jacques and Raïssa found clarity and order, depth and moderation, and above all a sense of mystery. They also found in Aquinas an uncanny predisposition to get to the essence of matters. Their in-depth reading of the *Summa* freed their spirits.

This intellectual encounter was decisive. It was as if Maritain had forged a deep and lasting alliance with St. Thomas Aquinas, the Angelic Doctor, born six centuries before his own. The encounter impelled Maritain to become a Christian philosopher for his church. Following his encounter with Thomas of Aquinas, Maritain's preferred Thomistic axiom was "distinguish in order to unite." With this idea in mind, he started a dialogue that engaged and embraced different modern ways of thinking and initiated a revival of interest in the Angelic Doctor. To be sure, Maritain was also influenced by the writings of the mystic Carmelite, St. John of the Cross, to whom he dedicated his beautiful essay *Todo y Nada* (*Everything and Nothing*) (Lacombe 1991, 37).

In 1912 Maritain became a professor at the Collège Stanislas in Paris, causing much controversy because of his use of Thomistic methodology. In 1919, he obtained the chair of History of Modern Philosophy at the Institut Catholique de Paris. In 1921 he became a full Professor of History of Modern Philosophy, Logic and Cosmology at the same institute (Viotto 2000, 128).

By the late 1920s, Maritain's attention began to turn to social issues leading him to develop principles of a liberal Christian humanism and a philosophical defense of human rights. Jacques and Raïssa founded the Cercles Thomistes (Thomistic Circles), a group dedicated to the study of Thomism. Leading lights from the intellectual and artistic circles of Paris attended the group, including Jean Cocteau, Francois Mauriac, George Rouault, Manuel de Falla, Paul Claudel, and Étienne Gilson (Viotto 2000, 128).

Maritain did impressive philosophical work between 1922 and 1931, writing on a great variety of topics found in the writings of Thomas Aquinas, such as religion and culture, political and social thought, and Christian philosophy. In 1932 he published his most important work entitled *Distinguish to Unite: The Degrees of Knowledge*, which focused on epistemology.

Étienne Gilson, a renowned Thomistic philosopher, invited Maritain to give courses and lectures at the Institute of Medieval Studies in Toronto. On his way to Canada, he visited the United States and met Mortimer Adler and Robert Hutchins, prominent philosophers at the University of Chicago. There Maritain first established his reputation as a philosopher in the United States with his lecture on "Some Reflections on Culture and Liberty." This was further confirmed with lectures on various philosophical themes at Notre Dame, the University of Chicago, New York University, and the Catholic University of America (Viotto 2000, 132). In these lectures Maritain defended a metaphysical approach to philosophy to counter the reigning pragmatic philosophy in this country.

In 1936 Maritain wrote *Humanisme Intégral* (*True Humanism*) based on lectures given in Santander, Spain. This book, which focused on a new lay and pluralist Christendom, was criticized in some circles, by socialists for not sufficiently embracing socialism and by others for adopting too many socialist ideas. The same year he gave an important lecture in Chicago entitled "Socialist Humanism and Integral Humanism," which demonstrated that a Catholic philosopher could be a major contributor to the serious dialogue about the growing acceptance of socialist ideas in the academy.

Maritain returned to the United States in 1938 where he gave lectures in New York, which furthered his reputation in this country. While visiting Fordham University he met a group of young Catholic professors, including Harry McNeil, Emmanuel Chapman, and Dan Walsh (Florian 2000, 43). In January of 1940, he gave a series of conferences in New York, Chicago, Buffalo, Princeton, Washington, Annapolis, Charlottesville, and Philadelphia. At this time he decided not to return to Paris because of the Nazi occupation of France, settling in New York (Mougel 1988, 9) and becoming an established figure in Catholic thought in the United States (Mougel 1988, 7-28).

Maritain's ideas were also very influential in Latin America, as well as in Europe and the United States. He was noted for his conferences on anti-Semitism. As a result of the "liberal" character of his political philosophy, which included certain socialists concepts and a defense of liberal democracy, Maritain came increasingly under fire from both the left and the right both in France and abroad (Mougel 1988, 8).

Maritain wrote two anthologies in English: *Scholasticism and Politics* (1940) and *Ransoming the Time* (1945). The former made the case that there was no incompatibility between Christianity and liberal democracy because of the Christian ideal of universal love. The latter presented a strong case against anti-Semitism. Maritain also founded the "École Libre des Hautes Études" in New York and published *Human Rights* and *Natural Law* (1942), in which he defended natural law ethics and an ethics of human rights. In 1943, in lectures at Yale University on education, he confronted American pragmatism and published his Yale lectures under the title *Education at the Crossroads*. This major educational work will receive extensive treatment later in this chapter.

Following the liberation of France in the summer of 1944, Maritain was named French ambassador to the Vatican, where he served from 1946 to 1948 under Pope Pius XII. While there he befriended Giovanni Battista Montini, the pope's secretary of state, who later became Pope Paul VI (Viotto 2000, 131).

In 1948, Maritain resigned from his diplomatic position because of an invitation by president Harold Dodds of Princeton to teach moral philosophy at the university (Maritain 1955b, 150). The following year he gave six lectures at the R. Walgreen Foundation of Chicago, later published as *Man and State* (1951). Maritain frequently returned to France to give short courses on philosophy. At the same time he continued to write on politics and social matters, and was actively involved in drafting the United Nations' *Universal Declaration of Human Rights* (1948) (Viotto 2000, 136).

In 1954 Maritain suffered a heart attack and had to limit his teaching (Viotto 2000, 132). His writing continued apace, however. In 1958 he wrote *Reflections on America*, a paean expressing his gratitude to the United States for what the country had done for him and his wife. In 1960 Maritain and his wife returned to France, where he received the Grand Prix de Littérature awarded by the French Academy. Following Raïssa's death later that year, Maritain moved to Toulouse where he decided to live with the Little Brothers of Jesus, a religious order founded by Charles de Foucault. There he wrote his famous polemic and cry of a broken and bitter heart, *The Peasant of Garonne*, a critical reply to the Second Vatican Council. He died in Toulouse, France in April 28, 1973.

Since his death several institutes have preserved the intellectual legacy of his works: The Jacques Maritain Center founded in 1958 at Notre Dame University; Institut International Jacques Maritain founded in 1964 in Rome, with a second branch called Centre International d'études et de recherches in Treviso, Italy; and the Cercle d' Études Jacques et RaVssa Maritain founded at Kolbsheim, France in 1962, to which the philosopher gave all rights to his works, which were published as *The Complete Works of Jacques Maritain (Oèuvres Complètes)*.

His Philosophical Sources

Maritain's philosophy was influenced by Henri Bergson, Aristotle, St. Augustine, and most of all St. Thomas of Aquinas. Maritain described his philosophical sources during a conference in New York on January 9, 1943, saying:

> An old lady who I venerate, spoke about me to one of my friends, some time ago, saying: he is Catholic, you know, but from a particular sect; he is Thomistic as well. My God, Thomism is not a sect such as Christian Science; it is simply the philosophy of Aristotle baptized by Saint Thomas of Aquinas. It relies on a synthesis of the principles of reason and faith to face the sharpest problems of our time. It has been

twenty-five years since I have let Thomism go out from the historic chests or from manuals of the seminars in order to construct a vivid philosophy, and this was an absurd enterprise, an enterprise for people in despair. I want to believe that our adventure turned out well, because from its very beginning it was led by the freedom of the spirit." (Maritain 1947, xi-xii)

Maritain considered Thomism a philosophy that was anchored in a strong foundation of common sense and intellectual insight. He saw Thomism as a true, evolving philosophy with vitality and openness to all questions, not a closed doctrinal system. Fernand Brunner said of Maritain, "His work represents an important tendency in Neo-Thomism and showed an ambition to extract the thought of Thomas Aquinas from its theological context in order to consider it as philosophy" (1975, 5).

Maritain knew how to combine medieval thought with contemporary ways of thinking, especially about education. For Maritain, Thomism was not a dead philosophy of the past but a key to the present and the future. Consequently, one cannot classify Thomism as "anti-modern" simply because it opposes some ideas and philosophies of the twentieth century, such as voluntarism, pragmatism, or intellectualism. Maritain addressed this matter himself:

What I call anti-modern here could just as well be called ultramodern . . . anti-modern against the mistakes of the present time and ultramodern because of the multiple truths to be developed in the future time. . . . Thomas' thought is not a thought of a century or a sect. It is a universal and timeless thought elaborated by the natural reason of humankind. (1922, 14-16)

What separated Maritain from the philosophers of his time were his strong affirmation of the "primacy of the spiritual" and the belief that reason is not against faith but a legitimate way to seek God. In this manner, Thomism was decisive for Maritain's work; his philosophical effort was to reestablish the real hierarchy of being, both human and divine, and give rightful priority to spiritual and metaphysical values (Hovre, in Gallagher 1963, 41). Maritain's philosophy built a bridge between reason and Christian mysticism, according to Philippe Filliot (2007). In other words, Maritain's thought possesses a double frame, one theological and the other philosophical. For Maritain, philosophy is no longer the "hand maiden" of theology, as it was regarded in medieval times; rather, theology is a useful tool for philosophy.

Maritain's work in the United States was appreciated and well recognized by such philosophers as Donald and Idella Gallagher, who wrote:

> Maritain has much in common with the sages of the ancient and medieval periods–with Platonic and Aristotelian views of rational human nature and the dignity of contemplation, with Augustine and Aquinas on the final end for humans and the primacy of love-in-contemplation. Still, his is a twentieth-century philosophy of education and not a mere recapitulation of classic ideas and ideals. (1963, 29)

Maritain and the Thomistic Revival

Jacques Maritain is rightly considered a key figure in the Thomistic revival which flourished in the United States before and after World War II. This revival featured translations, articles, and textbooks. Between 1911 and 1935, the Dominican Fathers from the English Province issued a translation of the *Summa Theologica,* which helped raise interest in Thomism in the United States. At the beginning of this revival only Catholics were interested; later other philosophers took serious note of Thomism. From the 1930s to the early 1950s Thomism was the locus of philosophical action for Catholic philosophers and a number of prominent scholars in secular universities. New journals provided a forum for those exploring Thomism in depth or attempting to relate it to modern philosophies. In 1927 the American Catholic Philosophical Association started to publish the journal, *New Scholasticism,* while the American Dominicans started *The Thomist* in 1929.

This renewed interest in Aquinas's thought before Vatican II was called "neo-Thomism," with two schools of interpretation. One was Aristotelian Thomism, whose distinguished adherents included James Weisheipe, William Wallace, Vincent Smith, and Benedict Ashley. The other school was Existential Thomism, which claimed Étienne Gilson (born in 1884) and Maritain, both French philosophers living in the United States.

In the estimation of John Knasas, there was also a third school called Transcendental Thomism, which was represented by Jesuit theologians Karl Rahner, Henri de Lubac, and Bernard J.F. Lonergan. Knasas (2003, 30-31) argues that although the Thomistic revival continues in the work of major Catholic systematic theologians from the school of Transcendental Thomism, the metamorphosis of the Thomistic revival from Neo-Thomism into Transcendental Thomism had been disaster for Thomism itself, since it takes into account Immanuel Kant's idealism, and thus is not "pure" Thomism. Not all scholars take this negative view of Transcendental Thomism (Kerr 2007, 111-12).

Maritain and Gilson were the most important figures representing the revival of Thomistic philosophy in the 1940s and 1950s (Elias, 1999, 93). Though some have called Robert Hutchins and Mortimer Adler Thomists, Donohoe states that, "They would themselves have very likely disclaimed this attribution" (1968, 16). As laymen, both Maritain and Gilson made Thomism appear less the forbidding clerical preserve. Gilson was the peerless historian of medieval thought while Maritain the preeminent Thomistic commentator on contemporary epistemology, political philosophy, metaphysics, culture, and education.

The combined impact of Gilson and Maritain has been greater in the United States than in France. French and Belgian interest in Thomism goes back to the time of Pope Leo XIII. He urged the restoration of the wisdom of St. Thomas and helped Belgian bishops create a chair of Thomistic philosophy at the Catholic University of Louvain. In 1888, Abbe Desire Mercier founded the Institute Superieur de Philosophie, which became an important center of Thomistic research. Leo XIII was also instrumental in establishing the pontifically recognized Catholic University of America, whose philosophy department was committed to Thomism for many years.

Maritain galvanized the movement of Neo-Thomism. This was especially true with the educational issues he raised in his Terry Lectures at Yale in 1943. In these talks "the most vital phase of his work . . . was . . . carrying scholasticism beyond seminary walls and into the world. . . . Maritain came . . . like a breath of air into a room long sealed" (Fecher 1953, 340).

Maritain's neo-Thomistic Catholic philosophy of education was a reaction to progressive or pragmatic philosophies of education. It aimed at helping persons to achieve a supernatural destiny as its primary goal, and at placing "emphasis on the inner resources of the student and the vital spontaneity of the child" (Elias 1999, 84). Neo-Thomism offered "a rigorous and a coherent synthesis of human nature, society and God" (Bryk, Lee, Holland 1993, 36). It also sought to recover truths and to bring these perennially valid principles to bear on the moral dilemmas of the present day.

Equally important, neo-Thomism reconnected with Aristotle and St. Thomas. After all, it was the Angelic Doctor who supported and then advanced the Aristotelian ideal of science in which many of the mysteries of human life could be revealed through the application of human reason to faith. Neo-Thomist philosophy therefore draws its principles from religious and philosophic sources. It sought to recover truths, valid principles, and moral values and incorporate them into current philosophical discussions.

The revival continued under the aegis of Pius XI. Inspired by ideas similar to those of Maritain, he claimed:

> Christian education is to co-operate with divine grace in forming the true and perfect Christian; that is, to form Christ Himself in those regenerated by baptism. . . . Christian education takes in the whole aggregate of human life, physical and spiritual, intellectual and moral, individual, domestic and social, not with a view of reducing it in any way, but in order to elevate, regulate and perfect it, in accordance with the example and teaching of Christ. (Pius XI, in Treacy 1945, 64-65)

In Maritain's thinking, Christian humanism and personalism came into play. Both philosophies bore significant influence for the encyclicals of Pope Paul VI and Pope John Paul II. The latter wrote the *Angelicum* in commemoration of the hundredth anniversary of Leo XIII's *Aeterni Patris*:

> The philosophy of St. Thomas deserves to be attentively studied and accepted with conviction by the youth of our day by reason of its spirit of openness and of universalism,

characteristics which are hard to find in many trends of contemporary thought. . . . Such openness is also a significant and distinctive mark of the Christian faith, whose specific countermark is its catholicity. (John Paul II 1980, 130-40)

For Knasas, Aquinas's philosophy does not claim to embrace the totality of truth but to be "open" to all truth: "Christian philosophy, of which Thomism is a model example, follows a methodology in which faith prompts one's thinking to the limits and so helps to avoid the limitedness of viewpoint that plagues historical, that is, secular, forms of philosophy" (2003, xiii).

A Philosopher of Education

For Maritain, philosophy is a witness to the supreme dignity of thought, pointing to what is eternal in a person, and a stimulant to the thirst for pure knowledge. By vocation the philosopher seeks knowledge of those fundamentals "about the nature of things and the nature of the mind, and man himself, and God" (Maritain 1961, 7). Indeed, for Maritain, people do not live on bread or technological discoveries alone, but on the

values and realities which are above time, and worth being known for their own sake; they feed on that invisible food which sustains the life of the spirit, and which makes them aware, not of such or such means at the service of their life, but of their very reasons for living. (Maritain 1961, 7)

Maritain constructed a philosophy of education that focused on reflection about the nature of education itself–its motifs, *raison d'être*, objectives, meaning, and methods. The basis of Maritain's philosophy of education can be found in the answers to four questions he raises regarding education. These are: What is education? What is the person? What are the fundamental dispositions of the student? and What is the role of the teacher?

It should be noted that Maritain's responses to these questions take him into the realm of metaphysics; he presents largely but not exclusively a metaphysics of education. John Dewey criticized

Maritain's view by attacking metaphysics, which Dewey thought was the basis of Maritain's philosophy of education. Dewey rejected what Maritain proposed as the perennially valid truths about reality and education. He also pointed out "the elitist social condition that gave rise to it" (Elias 1995, 14), the Greek world in which the philosophies of Plato and Aristotle were formulated.

The major questions concerning the philosophy of education focus on the aims of education, the role of the educator, the dynamics of education (i.e., the relationship between teacher and student), the specific role of the school, as well as the spirit, curriculum, and values of education. If the aim of education is steering persons toward their own human achievement and happiness, then education cannot escape the problems and entanglements of philosophy, for it presupposes them by its very nature.

After writing in branches of philosophy ranging from metaphysics and epistemology to philosophy of nature and philosophy of history, it seemed only natural that Maritain sought a practical field for applying his theories. This field was education. An early letter he wrote to Françoise Baton in 1898 reveals Maritain's keen interest in education: "And of course all that I shall think and know, I shall devote to the cause of the proletariat and to mankind; I shall use it completely for the preparation of the revolution and the education of mankind" (Allard 1982, 8).

Maritain's own childhood provided him with a wealth of material that formed his approach to education. Early in his life he raised many questions, such as: What does education mean? What are the aims of education? What are the principles that inspire education? What is the role of the student in relation to the teacher? Is there an *élan vital*, a vital impetus, inspired by the grace of God? Is there such a thing as liberal education? Do we really know what freedom is? Is it possible to be wise? Because of this holistic and measured approach to education, it is indisputable that Maritain enjoys an important role in the history of pedagogy. Maritain answered these questions in *Education at the Crossroads* and other educational essays.

His fresh approach to the subject can be seen in a series of pithy remarks, such as "Education is an art" (1943, 2), "Education of man is a human awakening" (1943, 9), and "Education is the conquest of internal and spiritual" (1943, 11). Maritain's purpose in entering debates about education was to provide a philosophy of education based on Christian thought and suited to the needs of contemporary persons. Guy Avanzini would later write of him, "I know that not everyone shares his faith, but we have to recognize that a faith is indispensable to initiate a dynamic education. We are losing sight of the true purposes of education and thus we have the contemporary crisis in our schools" (1978, 365).

Maritain's writings on philosophy of education are regarded as possessing enduring value (Elias 1999, 93), a value especially evidenced in *Pour une Philosophie de l'Éducation* (Maritain 1959b, 10). The work collects three essays, written first in English and later translated into French in this book.

The first essay was developed from a series of conferences given at Yale University in 1943. "The Thomist Views on Education," the second essay, was a study written at the request of the National Society for the Study of Education in 1955. Maritain was familiar with the American educators known as the "Chicago group," which included Robert Hutchins (president of the University of Chicago), Mortimer Adler, Stringfellow Barr, Scott Buchanan, and John Neff, then director of the Committee of Social Thought at the University of Chicago. This esteemed group advocated that an integral liberal education replace the elective system established at Harvard. Maritain agreed with its ideas, values, and desire to integrate liberal arts and humanities with scientific and technological based studies while broadening the so-called "specialization" approach, which according to Maritain, kills a more global approach to thinking (Maritain 1959b, 10).

The third essay, "On Some Specific Aspects of Christian Education," was derived from a paper given at a seminar on the Christian Idea of Education at the Episcopalian Kent School, in Connecticut, in 1955. The original English language version is found in Fuller (1957). A revised edition of this work appeared in 1969. In sum, the book constitutes an organized statement of Maritain's cogent philosophy of education.

Another of Maritain's compelling works is *The Education of Man* (published by Donald and Idella Gallagher in 1963). This volume contained two of the earlier essays "The Thomist Views on Education" and "Specific Aspects of Christian Education," as well as "Moral Education," "Education and Humanities," "Moral and Spiritual Values in Education," "The Education of Women," "Conquest of Freedom," and two appendixes entitled "Education for the Good Life" and "The Crucial Problem of the Education of the Human Being." Evans and Ward considered this collection "a token of the courtesy and generosity extended to a French philosopher by this great country, a country in which he has lived for a long time and in the cultural life of which he is proud to participate" (1995, xii). Of Maritain, Donald and Idella Gallagher said:

> The philosophy of education issuing from this half century of teaching, and from meditating upon the principles of education and the practical problems involved in schooling the young, is undoubtedly one of the lasting contributions of this eminent Thomist to twentieth-century thought. (1963, 9)

Although Maritain's writings on education are not a large part of his work, they are significant and enduring in classical value. His writings on education reflect deep personal insights and clear solutions to frequent questions. There is also a unity in his thought that is remarkably contemporary. Furthermore, Maritain's originality was to establish an approach to pedagogy centered on the learner as a person, to reexamine the aims of education, to emphasize the importance of culture for balanced human development according to moral virtues, to assume democratic responsibilities in society, and to search for truth.

An integral humanism and a liberal education for all are components of Maritain's democratic dream. The welcoming of theology in the classrooms, emphasizing the dignity of manual work, and the seeking of wisdom are all part of a pedagogical ideal that is centered on the "formation of a true moral conscience and the formation of man as an image of God" (Cassata 1953, 98).

Christian Pedagogy

In Maritain, as in Thomas Aquinas, there is an impressive marriage of rationality and spirituality. His philosophical reflections on education proceeded along the two paths of theology and philosophy. But his Christian reflection on education transcended the limits of the Christian society. It encompassed the whole world and proposed an answer to the crisis of modern society.

In this context Maritain's work is outstanding. His Christian convictions are always at hand, never hidden. In writing his work *Pour une philosophie de l' éducation*, he dedicated an entire chapter to the Christian idea of the human person, providing a foundation for a Christian pedagogy.

It should be noted that in a pluralistic world, Christian pedagogy has been often been characterized as being discreet or silent. Guy Avanzini (1996, 555) analyzed this phenomenon by describing two types of Christian educators. Some practice what they teach by embodying virtues like commitment, competence, readiness, respect for others and equity, which resonate with gospel teaching. The other group claims that Catholic doctrine is the unifying principle of their teaching. Of these two groups, it is the first that has taken a dominant role in our society. The reasons are many: the prohibition of religious proselytism in society, the pervasive spirit of secularism, the respect for other faiths, and so forth. Consequently the second group has been excluded and Christian pedagogy has been a silent presence. Maritain falls into the second group in his public arguments for the inclusion of the religious in all forms of education.

Education is twofold–philosophical and spiritual–throughout Maritain's writings. Even in addressing secular civilization, his philosophical and religious ideas are always present. In particular, the Christian idea of the person is presented in these two senses: "I say philosophical because this idea pertains to the nature or essence of man; I say religious, because of the existential status of this human nature in relation to God and the special gifts and trials and vocation involved" (1959b, 151).

According to Filliot, it is possible to say that Maritain has a "spiritualist pedagogy," because of the questions he raises about education (2007, 2). The first question is "What is education?" (1943, 2-28) and the second is "What is man?" The two essential questions define the fundamental principles of education considered as a dynamic process where the student is primary and teachers play an integral but facilitative role. The second question, which also concerns the aims of education, asks if it is possible to be wise and if an education for wisdom is possible. According to Maritain, "Education and teaching can only achieve their internal unity if the manifold parts of their whole work are organized and quickened by a vision of wisdom as the supreme goal" (1943, 48).

According to Allan Mougniotte, Maritain–due to his Thomistic philosophy melded with modern theories of education–holds a balanced and open position. In addition, even if he acknowledges the Christian belief of sin in human nature, he does not lean at all toward a repressive pedagogy (1997, 115).

Also noteworthy in Maritain's philosophy is the integration of culture in education according to a healthy hierarchy of values and knowledge. Christian pedagogy is based on *intellectus quaerens veritatem* (intelligence seeking the truth) and finding through the light of faith the real sense of human knowledge. "Art, science, and wisdom are the intellectual virtues" (Maritain 1959b, 152), which, when coupled with a liberal education, can equip, cultivate, liberate, and give the intelligence needed for their development.

For Maritain, education is an ongoing process which also has a social dimension. Indeed, education, in the broad sense of the word, will "continue through all our life in every one of us" (Maritain 1959b, 155). By the action of God's grace, education helps us find the "supreme perfection which consists in love" (156). And it is only because of love that we give ourselves to others who have the same image of God as we do and share a common good. In Maritain's penetrating words, "Education ought to teach us how to be in love always and what to be in love with" (1943, 23).

Maritain asserted that "The educational adventure is an incessant call to the intelligence and free will of the youth" (1959b, 166). However, Christian pedagogy is not to be limited to the learner. Ideally, a teacher possessing deep personal convictions, not to mention intellectual openness and generosity, accompanies the learner as a companion. This implies a context where school, common life, and fraternal charity are involved and integrated.

Maritain's educational philosophy is a Christian pedagogy that constantly reiterates a conception of liberal education. Liberal education for Maritain includes the traditional liberal arts as well as philosophy and theology. The aims of this education are intellectual understanding, moral development, aesthetic cultivation, and religious formation through the inculcation of perennial truths and values. This education takes place in three stages of life: rudimentary or elementary education attends to the development of the imagination and intellectual skills; secondary education in secondary schools and colleges focuses on the liberal arts; advanced graduate education entails specialization to prepare a person for professions and careers.

For Maritain it was important to foster spiritual flexibility needed in the search for the truth, in accordance with the Church's mission to teach, as interpreted by St. Thomas (Mougniotte 1997, 117). Mougniotte concluded that Maritain built a very modern educational practice on a traditional anthropology: "The paradox of his thought consists in presenting a Christian pedagogy, faithful to its Christian sources, but at the same time, a pedagogy that offers the best warranties of respecting their faith" (1997, 118). To J.L. Allard, Maritain's pedagogy reflects his conception of philosophy, and "It could surely contribute to an enrichment of contemporary pedagogical thought and education" (1982, 115). His ideas also contribute to Christian education–or religious education as some would call it today.

The Concept of Education

According to Maritain, "The task of education is above all to shape man, or to guide the evolving dynamism through which man forms himself as a man" (Maritain 1943, 1). In other words, education helps us to become who we really are or "to become a man" (1943, 1). This goal is possible because human beings are educable. The idea of liberal education is founded on having an education available for every human being. In Maritain's words, "Every human being is entitled to receive such a properly human and humanistic education" (Gallagher and Gallagher 1963, 69).

Maritain emphasized that "Becoming who we are" stresses the broader purpose of education, which is "any process whatsoever by means of which man is shaped and led toward fulfillment" (1943, 2). If man becomes man, man enters into a dynamic process of creativity. This is why Maritain affirms that "Education is an art" (1943, 3) and everyone could become a work of art.

The primary goal in Maritain's philosophy of education is "the conquest of internal and spiritual freedom to be achieved by the individual person, or, in other words, his liberation through knowledge and wisdom, good will, and love" (1941, 11). But this liberation is not to be understood as merely unfolding potentialities without any object to be grasped or without a goal to reach. Rather, "No one is freer, or more independent, than the one who gives himself for a cause or a real being worthy of the gift" (Maritain 1943, 12).

The virtue of wisdom is also important in Maritain's philosophy and the pursuit of freedom is inseparable from the pursuit of wisdom. Wisdom appears as the supreme knowledge that embraces all realities of the person as well his or her aspirations, including freedom (1943, 48). Thus, Maritain writes that "Education and teaching can only achieve their internal unity if the manifold parts of their whole work are organized and quickened by a vision of wisdom as the supreme goal" (1943, 48).

Paradoxically, wisdom cannot be obtained directly by education, since education is only an indirect means to wisdom, providing the student with the basic necessity to obtain it. Maritain writes of education that "Its specific aim is to provide [humans] with the foundations of real wisdom" (1943, 48). He continues, "The purpose of elementary and higher education is not to make of the youth a truly wise man, but to equip his mind with an ordered knowledge which will enable him to advance toward wisdom in his manhood" (1943, 48).

The reason why wisdom cannot be obtained directly by education is that wisdom cannot be taught. Wisdom cannot be achieved by science alone (1943, 48), but also needs "human and spiritual experience," since "it is over and above every specialization" (1943, 48). Wisdom appears then as a practical experience, requiring not only the use of reason but also of intuition—or "intellectual insight" as Maritain calls it. This insight occupies an important place in his thought (1943, 43). The answer to the paradox of wisdom that cannot be taught lies in the appeal to intuition.

The formation of a person depends upon guidance. "Education, like medicine, is *ars cooperativa naturae*" (1959b, 165)," Maritain writes. Continuing, he says, "The principal agent in the educational process is not the teacher, but the student" (1959b, 65). (Thomas Aquinas developed this in *Summa Theologiae*, 1q.117, a. 1; *Summa Contra Gentiles* 75; *De Veritate*, q. II, a. 1.)

To be more precise, Maritain urges that "the primary dynamic factor or propelling force is the internal vital principle in the one to be educated" (1943, 31). There is an *élan vital*, in the famous Bergsonian formula, which can be defined as a "vital and active principle of knowledge" (1943, 31), that exists in each person. For Maritain, the teacher or educator–the secondary factor or agent–"has to offer to the mind either examples from experience or particular statements which the pupil is able to judge by virtue of what he already knows and from which he will go on to discover broader horizons" (1943, 31). Put another way, "His power of intuition will be awakened" (1943, 45). Therefore "education of man is a human awakening" (1943, 9), but the results of the human action of learning is attributed to God who created this vital principle, which in Christian terminology corresponds to "divine grace."

Education transforms the person, who moves from reality to a transcendent level. "Man does not merely exist as a physical being," Maritain wrote. "There is in him a richer and nobler existence; he has spiritual super existence through knowledge and love" (1943, 8). This spiritual conception of education in Maritain is contrary to the instrumental and technical views of education that came to prominence in the United States in the 1930s and 1940s and are still present in the postmodern world of today.

Through education one becomes truly human, according to Maritain. This humanity is not for the self alone but for the community and society. If education is the ability to think, it has to perform its task in a world which thirsts for the liberation of the human person (Gallagher and Gallagher 1963, 100).

It is significant that Maritain, a Frenchman, defined what a democratic education should be when he was living in the United States:

> A democratic education is an education which helps human persons to shape themselves, judge by themselves, discipline themselves, to love and to prize the high truths which are the very root and safeguard of their dignity, to respect in themselves and in others human nature and conscience, and to conquer themselves in order to win their liberty. (Gallagher and Gallagher 1963, 69)

The Concept of Person

Maritain's philosophy of education has a departure point: the human person. The goal of education consists in becoming who we are (1943, 1). The social and political implications of his personalism are expressed in his *True Humanism* (1946). Maritain has been considered a "personalist humanist" (Viotto 1991, 17), for his philosophy is person–centered.

The answer to the question "What is a man?" (Maritain 1943, 1) constitutes the basis for his philosophy of education. Maritain's idea of the person is the Greek, Jewish, and Christian concept of

> man as an animal endowed with reason, whose supreme dignity is in the intellect; and man as a free individual in personal relation with God, whose supreme righteousness consists in voluntarily obeying the law of God; and man as a sinful and wounded creature called to divine life and to the freedom of grace, whose supreme perfection consists of love. (1943, 7)

This unified view of the person needs to be considered in the work of education and teaching. That is why both education and teaching should unify in fostering the "internal unity in man" (1943, 45).

Maritain's consideration of the union of body and soul explains the person *ad intra*, or in relation to oneself. And for completion, Maritain introduces the concepts of "individuality" and "personality," which allow him to describe the person *ad extra*, in relation to the world. According to Maritain, a human being "is an *individual* in so far as he is part of the universe, the human being is a *person* in so far as he is a spiritual object" (Gallagher 1963, 214). Put another way, "Because we are individuals, we are subject to the stars. As we are persons, we rule them" (Maritain 1925, 28). Considered as a person, a human being possesses special dignity, or, as Maritain would say, "an absolute dignity because he is in direct relationship with the realm of being, truth, goodness, beauty, and with God" (1943, 8).

Therefore education can never be akin to mechanical training. On the contrary, it is a perpetual appeal to intelligence and free will (1943, 9-10). Guidance of a person requires a dynamism "which shapes him as a human person–armed with knowledge, strength of judgment, and moral virtues–while at the same time conveying to him the spiritual heritage of the nation and the civilization in which he is involved" (1943, 10). That is why education for Maritain cannot be merely utilitarian or pragmatic; it cannot be reduced to a social reality, a mere idea, or an act of the will. It must primarily be an effort to develop the intellect or intelligence of the person of the person, as is emphasized in the Thomistic tradition.

The Fundamental Dispositions of the Student

For Maritain, the power of learning is naturally present in the learner. He recalls the example of Pascal, who was kept away from books on mathematics when he was a boy but nevertheless became a great mathematician (1943, 49-50). Since Maritain believed that "What is learned should never be passively or mechanically received, as dead information which weighs down and dulls the mind" (1943, 50), he recommended that knowledge must be given to students in such a way that they can assimilate it in such a vital manner that it becomes their own. As Maritain puts it, "Teaching liberates intelligence instead of burdening it. . . . Teaching results in the freeing of the mind through the mastery of reason over the things learned" (1943, 49). Teaching is not forcing the students' minds to receive information; rather, the teacher touches their spirit of learning and motivates them to develop new dispositions and desires for learning.

Learners thus become human by virtue of their inner resources, enlightened by truth, animated by the love of the good, and by taking charge of their own destiny. The vitality and intuitiveness of the spirit, says Maritain, "should be relied upon as invaluable factors in the first stages of education" (1943, 61). Elias has commented that the imagination has to be guided by rules of reason, space, and time. He also argues that while Maritain's theory "does have a place for understanding the power of imagination," it does not emphasize the free play of imagination (Elias 1995, 85). Childhood is characterized by imagination (Maritain 1943, 62), but adolescence witnesses ascending natural reason. For Maritain, it is mainly in this second stage of adolescence that the "natural impulse [is] to be turned to account by education, both by stimulation and by disciplining reason" (1943, 63).

It is this abiding internal disposition that enables us to grasp the meaning of science or art in the specific truth or beauty it offers us: "I should say that the youth is to learn and know music in order to understand the meaning of music rather than to become a composer" (1943, 63). This is possible if young people grasp this truth or beauty by the natural power and gifts of their mind–including their intuitive capacity–says Maritain. He enumerates five natural dispositions to be fostered in the student.

The five dispositions are: the love of knowing the truth; the love of truth and justice, that is, the love of acting according to the truth; the love of simplicity and openness, or "the attitude of a being who exists gladly, is unashamed of existing, stands upright in existence, and for whom to be and to accept the natural limitations of existence are matters of equally simple assent" (37); the love of work, which does not mean hard work or laziness, but "a respect for the job to be done, a feeling of faithfulness and responsibility regarding it" (38); and the love of cooperation that is, a disposition against the tendency to rivalry and competition (see Filliot 2007, 7).

To foster these five dispositions in learners, educational norms are needed. In actuality these norms comprise the attitudes the teacher must take toward learners. The teacher must encourage individuals, be concerned above all with their inwardness, nourish internal unity of the person, and liberate learners' minds by leading them to mastery of the things learned (Maritain 1943, 35-39).

As such, education and teaching can only achieve their internal unity "if the manifold parts of their whole work are organized and quickened by a vision of wisdom as the supreme goal" (1943, 48). As stated above, there are no classes on wisdom (1943, 23), nor can wisdom, virtues, love, or intuition be taught; they are freely given gifts. Indeed, to acknowledge that not everything can be learned already counts as wisdom. Maritain criticizes the cultural milieu in which courses are served up for almost anything; he maintains this is not enough for acquiring the wisdom, love, and internal freedom that he wants education to accomplish.

Consequently, Maritain's philosophy–which unites a teacher who cooperates in eliciting the fundamental dispositions of the student, upon which education builds–acknowledges the practical level of a spiritual education, which may ultimately lead a person to wisdom.

The Role of the Teacher

Maritain proposed a list of four rules that ought to light the path of a teacher. First, the teacher must foster the good dispositions of students by liberating their best energies and repressing their worst ones, with repression being only a secondary means if other approaches do not work (1943, 39). His second rule is to focus on the interiority of students and their spiritual well being by stressing "inwardness and the internalization of the educational influence" (39). The third rule is to foster internal unity in humans by fighting against what brings dispersion and fragmentation in a person. In short, if persons do not overcome the inner multiplicity of drives and various currents of knowledge and belief and the diverse vital energies at play in their minds, they will always remain more slaves than free persons (47). Fourth, the cited dispositions have as their aim freeing the spirit of the person. For Maritain this formation happens not by the mental gymnastics of a person's faculties but by the truth that sets persons free, a truth that is vitally assimilated by the insatiable activity, which is rooted in the depths of the self (47).

Teachers cooperate with students in their learning because they act as instrumental causes, not as efficient causes of learning, in accordance with the view of Aquinas:

> Their duty is not to mold the child's mind arbitrarily as potters mold lifeless clay; rather, their task is to assist the mind and the living spiritual beings, which they are endeavoring to develop, and which in that process of development must be the principal agents. In like manner, the teacher's task is to cooperate with God. (1943, 43)

The art of education consists "in inspiring, schooling and pruning, teaching and enlightening, so that in the intimacy of human activity, the weight of the egoistic tendencies diminishes, and the weight of the aspirations proper to personality and its spiritual generosity increases" (35). Teaching is a subtle art in which teachers performs as artists in the role of awakening intelligence and will.

Maritain asserts that a special kind of child is best able to be educated; it is the one "whose intellect, before being fecundated by sense-perception and sense-experience, is but a *tabula rasa,* as Aristotle put it" (33). Therefore, knowledge does not pre-exist in the soul as Plato taught, for there are no innate ideas. The teacher possesses knowledge the student lacks; hence, teachers are required.

Maritain's conception of education is not mechanical, but spiritual. The old analogy of education depicts the teacher as a sculptor who imposes form on the previously formless marble of the student. But Maritain, like Aquinas, prefers instead the analogy of the doctor who exerts real causality in healing a sick person "by imitating the ways of nature herself in her operations, and by helping nature, by providing appropriate diet and remedies that nature herself uses, according to her own dynamism, toward a biological equilibrium" (30). According to Maritain's metaphor, a teacher is comparable to a doctor, and is not just an artist. Rather, the teacher practices science *and* art.

The teacher's role is to facilitate the process of education by trying to create the conditions so that students can find truth and wisdom. Teachers should awaken and heed the inner resources of the learner (35). The educator then has to stimulate the expression of the awakened mind by listening to and respecting the natural path of spiritual awakening and by doing this until the learner's "intuitive power is liberated and strengthened" (44).

The teacher's domain is the domain of truth, which is determined not by the masters but according to the value of evidence. Teachers are called to have a very special mission in which "What is most important . . . is a respect for the soul as well as for the body of the child, the sense of his innermost essence and his internal resources, and a sort of sacred and loving attention to his mysterious identity, which is a hidden thing that no techniques can reach" (9). This mission also consists in making learners think: "From the very start teachers must respect in the child the dignity of the mind, must appeal to the child's power of understanding, and conceive of their own effort as preparing a human mind to think for itself" (27). Therefore the teacher has to offer learners "either examples from experience or particular statements which the pupil is able to judge by virtue or what he already knows and from which he will go on to discover broader horizons" (31). The more the teacher frees the mind, the more students become eager to know and can aspire to wisdom.

According to Maritain, far more than pedagogical skill is required. It is very important to have a Christian inspiration when teaching. "I think, there are of course no Christian mathematics or Christian astronomy or engineering," Maritain allows. "But if the teacher has Christian wisdom, and if his teaching overflows from a soul dedicated to contemplation, the mode or manner in which his own soul and mind perform a living and illuminating action on the soul and mind of another human being." What will his impact be? He will "convey to the student and awaken in him something beyond mathematics, astronomy, or engineering" (Gallagher and Gallagher 1963, 136). Note how Maritain distinguishes between a teaching being Christian and teachers who are not. The difference is in how teachers approach issues and insights from students.

Teachers must guide pupils in becoming truly human and doing so with values such of love, generosity, service, and hope. Teachers must draw intelligence from the interior of their students. In doing so, wisdom can be attained as the supreme aim of education. The true educator has the important task of "centering attention on the inner depths of the human person and its preconscious spiritual dynamism, in other words, to lay stress on inwardness and the internalization of the influence" (1943, 39). An appeal should be made to the "sources of knowledge and poetry, of love and truly human desires, hidden in the spiritual darkness of the intimate vitality of the soul" (41).

It is by the truth that learners will be set free, and not by a mere gymnastic exercise of their powers. The human mind gains its freedom "when truth is really known, that is, vitally assimilated by the insatiable activity which is rooted in the depth of self" (1943, 52). Education is not about imposing truths on the learners, but about developing in them their own personal convictions.

Maritain's Legacy

Maritain's philosophical reflections on education have an important value for our modern world. Technology has achieved major advances, and globalization has torn down borders between people. But people have allotted precious little time to reflect on the world that is being created. As a consequence, issues arise that escape our control. One example of this lies in the field of Catholic education, specifically its philosophical underpinnings. What happened to this philosophy of education? This is a profound question that Elias raised (1999, 92). He noted the concept of transcendence and the effect of its disappearance from religious education. Earlier, Marie-Odile Metral (1969, 11) noted that education itself has lost its philosophical roots. It is important to reflect upon the meaning of education.

It is imperative that philosophers of education constantly assess and evaluate the aims and nature of education and adapt these to a changing world. For this reason, the contribution of Maritain is valuable. As Métral states, "It is for philosophical reasons, relying on a philosophically based humanism, that Jacques Maritain offers sometimes impertinent reflections because they are pertinent for a human and fully democratic education" (1969, 11-12).

The legacy of Maritain seems irrelevant in the contemporary scene. For evidence, we can cite how Thomistic philosophy of education–sponsored mainly by the Catholic Church–has essentially disappeared in educational theory. In an article he wrote in 1999, Elias offered some reasons for this. He cited changes within the Catholic Church and changes within the field of philosophy of education (101). Regarding the first, Elias noted that at Vatican II in *Gaudium et Spes* (13), the Church admitted to not having "the answers to all problems and expressed a willingness to work with others to discover solutions to the pressing problems of our times" (102). As a consequence, Catholic philosophers do philosophy "within a number of different perspectives: analytic philosophy, pragmatism, phenomenology, existentialism, and even Marxism" (102). This varied approach is motivated by the desire to leave behind the "dogmatic attitude" of Thomistic philosophy in order to pursue the apparent freedom and openness in other philosophies. Elias's second reason is linked to the first: philosophy of education has been taken up by other philosophical approaches besides Thomism. He avers that "By the 1960s, analytic philosophy of education had become the predominant mode of philosophizing in the English-speaking world" (104).

Interestingly, these reasons found support in the analysis on the future of Thomistic philosophy made by Maritain himself at the end of his life. Maritain expressed his disapproval in *The Peasant of the Garonne* (1966), which he wrote after joining the Little Brothers of Jesus, a Catholic congregation in Toulouse, France. In a bitter tone he pointed out that recent popes had not made an impression on the professors who have the responsibility for teaching in the name of the Catholic Church. He continued to think that if the Church insists on recommending a human doctrine, "She obviously could not possibly do so in the name of the divine Truth" (1968, 168). Such was the case when promulgating Canon 236, n. 3 after Vatican Council II, which states:

> There are to be classes in dogmatic theology, always grounded in the written word of God together with sacred tradition; through these, students are to learn to penetrate more intimately the mysteries of salvation, especially with St. Thomas as a teacher. There are also to be classes in moral and pastoral theology, canon law, liturgy, ecclesiastical history, and other auxiliary and special disciplines, according to the norm of the prescripts of the program of priestly formation.

According to Maritain, recommending St. Thomas's teachings was not a matter of preserving people's faith or a safe doctrine. Rather, he wanted St. Thomas taught because he viewed his insights as truth.

The Church was against positivism, rationalism, and pragmatism, which assert the existence of reason alone. The Church reacted to such philosophical movements by recommending the philosophical approach of Aquinas, an approach that acknowledged the existence of faith, which enlightens and informs the faculty of reason. The problem was that the Church's original recommendation of St. Thomas's system subsequently came to be seen as an imperative, with scholars and teachers not given alternatives. Maritain thought that Thomism (which he preferred to the term neo-Thomism) had to be adhered to because of its inner truth, not because it was imposed by some ecclesiastical authority. In fact, Maritain thought that this was the reason for the rejection of neo-Thomism in the twentieth century. Maritain suffered severe criticism for his *The Peasant of the Garonne* and his position against the alleged neo-modernist deviations of some of the theologies propounded after the Second Vatican Council, such as various forms of political and liberation theologies.

Maritain, however, held out hope for the future. He wrote, "I am dreaming of a day when the Church would turn, even in the most delicate matters, toward the road of freedom" (1968, 169). But he should not be misunderstood: he does not oppose freedom to obedience to the Church. Rather, he speaks of freedom because he intends to appeal less to obedience and more to the pursuit of truth. Socrates, who lived from 469 to 399 BCE, had defined philosophy as "the pursuit of truth," and many philosophers since have agreed. Similarly, for Maritain the truth of a Christian philosophy of education should be enough to ensure its preservation, progress, and expansion, which could become a reality if there were true freedom of expression and not the arbitrary imposition of authority.

Rethinking and reformulating a Christian philosophy of education has value in today's pluralistic and diverse world. It can be accomplished by employing rigorous reasoning. A Thomistic philosophy of education remains a valid option more than ever when the array of philosophies of education is considered. Even Elias, despite his critique of Maritain, believes that "The tradition of Thomism should be kept alive as one possible way of grounding this tradition" (1999, 105).

What can a Thomistic philosophy of education offer teachers and students in our time? Elias (1999, 106-09) suggests an interesting list of the enduring values of Thomism. He mentions Thomism's rich view of human persons, including its religious orientation; the depth of its social concern; its eloquent articulation of the aim of liberating the human spirit, its emphasis on having a liberal arts curriculum centered in philosophy and theology; its concern for methods of transmitting truths; and the stress it puts on the teacher in developing insight in learners.

Jacques Maritain's aim of liberating the human spirit is especially needed, given the present materialistic world that promotes an exaggerated individualism and exalts materialistic achievements or possessions as the ultimate end—what Aquinas called the *summum bonum*—of human existence. Maritain offers valuable insights on behalf of a Christian education, whose aim is to foster the Christian idea of what humanity is. He emphasizes the unity of the human being, body and soul, and sees the person as both a natural and a spiritual being.

Maritain does not maintain that Christian education makes humans perfect. Rather, it seeks to develop as far as possible natural energies and virtues, both intellectual and moral, depending more on grace than on nature, without separating divine and human love. According to Maritain "Christians must take risks . . . and, at the same time must be prepared to fight to the finish for their souls and lives in God, using the weapons of the Cross every day" (in Gallagher and Gallagher 1963, 132).

It should be noted that neo-Thomism, especially as a philosophy of education, took root more in America than in Europe. As Maritain noted:

> Neo-Thomism is one of the living currents in American Philosophy today. The National Society for the Study of Education asked a Thomist philosopher [Maritain] to write a chapter in its Yearbook for 1955, entitled *Modern Philosophies and Education.* So according to this Yearbook Thomism ranks among modern philosophies. Never did M. Emile Bréhier or his colleagues at the Sorbonne recognize the fact. (Maritain 1955, 150-51)

While the religious truth of the Church cannot be expressed through a single exclusive system, nevertheless, it is possible even today to establish a solid basis through Thomism; not to reduce truth, but to find it and love it. So, as Maritain did with his well-known work, *The Degrees of Knowledge*, where he demonstrated Thomistic epistemology and metaphysics had validity, I have tried to show in this essay that St. Thomas's theology has a "theological wisdom, structured by a perennially valid metaphysics" (McCool 1992, 213).

Such a revival is not without precedent. About Maritain and the Thomistic revival, Charles A. Fecher said, "No one man could have done the whole job; but Maritain certainly made the foundations firm, set the pace, pointed out the direction to follow" (Fecher 1953, 340). The Thomistic renaissance has gained much ground, as Fecher says, and has triumphed over many obstacles. Maritain has never been afraid of getting his shoes muddy or his knuckles bruised, and much less afraid of having his feelings hurt (1953, 346).

Conclusion

Maritain had been all but forgotten, not only in France but in the United States as well. But the publication in 1995 of a 16-volume edition of his complete works, *Oèuvres complètes de Jacques et Raïssa Maritain,* inspired scholars in France to appreciate anew his contribution to the fields of politics, culture, philosophy, art, education, human rights, and so forth. Maritain's writings are considered by many to contain the best philosophical work of Christian thought (Bressolette et Mougel 1995, 1). His writings on education show his personal insights and clear solutions to questions often asked about and reflected upon. Whether one agrees or not with his theology and philosophy, the lucidity of his way of approaching the problems, the topics of his analysis and the solutions he proposed must be acknowledged. His is a Christian philosophy, not in terms of excluding others but in terms of considering the full development of persons through Christianity and for his contention that a liberal education is valid for persons in every era.

From Maritain's perspective, it appears that education today lacks a clear understanding of its purpose and essence. Human persons are no longer considered subjects of education–persons who have to be educated. They are merely treated as objects or things to be studied and analyzed, Maritain noted. As he puts it, "By dint of insisting that in order to teach John mathematics it is more important to know John than it is to know mathematics–which is true enough in one sense–the teacher will so perfectly succeed in knowing John that John never succeeds in knowing mathematics" (Maritain 1943, 13-14).

Maritain makes explicit the objectivity of human knowledge–not to mention its aims and values–without offering a new educational theory. He renews Thomas Aquinas's thinking and applies it to the present educational situation. The originality of Maritain was to establish a pedagogy that centered on the learner as a person, reexamined the aims of education, stressed the importance of culture for a balanced human development through living according to moral virtues, fostering the ability to assume democratic responsibilities towards society, and encouraging the search for truth. Maritain motivates his followers to search for wisdom and to return to the sources of the Western European cultural tradition.

Thomistic philosophy can still show how to extend little by little the boundaries of philosophy itself, to go further into the problems of our time, and help us to express ourselves in a religious educational setting where Christian philosophy has always had so much to offer.

Neil G. McCluskey: A Public Voice for Catholic Education

HAROLD D. HORELL

In 1971, at the sixty-fifth anniversary banquet for the journal *Religious Education*, Neil G. McCluskey was recognized as a pioneering Catholic educator. At that point, McCluskey was well known for his outgoing and friendly manner and quick wit and for making significant contributions for over two decades to discussions about Catholic education and the nature and purpose of religious and moral education in the United States. His scholarly work in religious education would continue for another two decades.

How many people know Neil G. McCluskey's work today? Some religious educators are aware of McCluskey's classic work, *Catholic Viewpoint on Education*. The book is one of the best expressions of McCluskey's superb ability to shed light on educational trends and issues by examining their social context and guiding readers in envisioning how these trends and issues could continue to develop as we look toward the future. Yet, many people today are unaware of McCluskey's contributions to religious education.

This chapter explores McCluskey's life and contributions to religious education. Its overall purpose is to enable readers to become more familiar with a person whose teaching, administrative work, writing, and public speaking have helped to shape the ways religious faith, education, and public life intersect in U.S. culture.

A Brief Biography

Neil Gerard McCluskey was born December 15, 1920, in Seattle, Washington. He was the fourth of Patrick John and Mary Genevieve

(Casey) McCluskey's six children. McCluskey entered the Society of Jesus (the Jesuits) in 1938. In 1944 he received his A.B. degree from Gonzaga University in Spokane, Washington, with a double major in English and psychology. An M.A. in philosophy from Gonzaga followed in 1945. In 1952 McCluskey received an S.T.L. (Licentiate in Sacred Theology) from Alma College, now the Jesuit School of Theology at Berkeley. Once he completed his degree at Alma College, McCluskey went to live, travel, and study in Europe. In Europe McCluskey was mentored by Père François Charmot while he studied ascetical psychology at the Maison Colombière, Paray-le-Monial, France, in 1952-53. He then studied educational psychology under the tutelage of Jean Piaget in 1953-54 at the Université de Genève.

In September 1955, McCluskey moved to New York City to pursue new opportunities for personal and professional development. First, he became an associate editor of *America*, a position he held until August of 1960. *America* is a national Catholic weekly journal of opinion published by the Jesuits. McCluskey's articles and commentaries in *America* focused on educational concerns, but he also wrote about other timely religious and social issues. Second, McCluskey studied at Columbia Graduate School of Philosophy and Teachers College, earning a Ph.D. in social history in 1957. His dissertation was a comparative study of the educational philosophies of Horace Mann, William Torrey Harris, and John Dewey, with a focus on moral education in United States public schools. During his first of two extended periods in New York, McCluskey became a sought-after lecturer and presenter, addressing groups both within and beyond Catholic communities. He continued to be active on the lecture circuit for the next twenty-five years.

McCluskey began to address critical issues about Catholic education and religious education in U.S. culture as early as 1950 (McCluskey 1950a and 1950b). His reflections deepened and matured through his travels and studies here and abroad. The early fruits of these reflections were presented in two books published in the late 1950s. First, in *Public Schools and Moral Education* (1958), McCluskey addressed the lack of consensus in the United States about governmental support for religious and moral instruction (McCluskey 1958). The book was, in essence, a revised and somewhat expanded version of McCluskey's dissertation research. Second, McCluskey offered a broad analysis of education in the United States with a specific focus on Catholic education in *Catholic Viewpoint on Education* (1959).

In September 1960, McCluskey returned to Gonzaga University as an associate professor of education. In 1964 McCluskey was appointed Dean of the School of Education and then became Academic Vice President of Gonzaga. While serving in these positions, McCluskey played a central role in the administrative and programmatic reorganization of the university. During his time at Gonzaga McCluskey also helped to develop the Honors Program and originated the Gonzaga in Florence (GIF) study abroad program. At the present time, both the Gonzaga Honors Program and GIF continue to thrive and remain central to the educational mission of the university. While at Gonzaga, McCluskey also published *Catholic Education in America*, "a sampling of the important documents that explain Catholic education over the last 175 years," with a general introduction and introductions to each document by McCluskey (McCluskey 1964, 2).

In the fall of 1966, McCluskey became Visiting Professor of Education at Notre Dame University. The next year he was appointed Professor of Education and Dean-Director of the Notre Dame Institute for Studies in Education. The year after that, McCluskey founded the *Notre Dame Journal of Education*, a professional quarterly journal. Despite its positive reception, the journal ceased publication in 1976 because of lack of funding. While at Notre Dame McCluskey began to devote more time to addressing issues of Catholic higher education and adult religious education. He also became more actively involved in the Religious Education Association (REA) and the International Federation of Catholic Universities (IFCU).

McCluskey published *Catholic Education Faces its Future* in 1968. He began the book with the claim: "The explosive forces unloosed by the Second Vatican Council are forcing a complete reappraisal of Catholic education in the United States at all levels" (McCluskey 1968, 17). History has shown, of course, that this was indeed the case. Yet, Vatican II did not force McCluskey to reappraise completely his own approach to religious and educational issues. Rather, the stances McCluskey took in his early work (for example, his focus on ecumenical and inter-religious dialogue, his calls for freedom of religion and his emphasis on the social dimensions of Christian faith) foreshadowed many of the developments of Vatican II. Hence, even though he was writing in the light of the updated teachings of the Second Vatican Council, McCluskey's focus in much of *Catholic Education* was on further developing the approach to educational issues that he had first formulated in the late 1940s and early 1950s.

While at Notre Dame, McCluskey collected and edited scholarly essays to address questions about Catholic higher education. He contributed an essay on university governance to the collection and published it in 1970 as *The Catholic University: A Modern Appraisal.*

McCluskey returned to New York City in 1971 to become a professor and Dean of the Division of Professional Programs at Lehman College, part of the City University of New York (CUNY). While at Lehman College McCluskey oversaw an extensive administrative reorganization of the division he led and developed new programs in teacher education, most notably PACE (Program for Alternative Careers in Education). At this point in his career McCluskey focused his teaching, research, writing, and lecturing on addressing issues of adult education.

In 1975, McCluskey became the Professor of Gerontological Studies and Director of the Center for Gerontological Studies, CUNY. While McCluskey continued his research and lecturing in the fields of education and religious education into the 1980s, this new position provided opportunities for him to pursue developing interests in life-transition planning and life-quality for the aging (McCluskey 1979 and 1981, Borgatta and McCluskey 1980, and McCluskey and Borgatta 1981).

McCluskey resigned from the Society of Jesus in 1975 and in 1978 married Elaine Lituchy Jacobs.

In the fall of 1981, McCluskey was appointed Executive Director of BHRAGS, Inc. BHRAGS had been formed by combining Brooklyn's Haitian, Ralph, and Good Shepherd social service centers. BHRAGS focused on providing job training for people of all ages and social services for young people and older adults. Under McCluskey's leadership BHRAGS's total number of programs went from eight to twenty. Then, in 1986 McCluskey became the director of Mainstream, an Institute for Mature Adults at Westchester Community College, and he rebuilt the institute's programs. To ease his way into retirement in the late 1980s, McCluskey became a senior consultant with Retirement Advisors and offered seminars on mid-career/life assessment and retirement education. These seminars had a specific focus on issues of faith and spirituality and were often offered for Christian and Jewish groups. In 1990 he started the Westchester Literary Agency in Hartsdale, New York. The Westchester Literary Agency continued to assist writers and aspiring writers until 2004.

After Neil and Elaine McCluskey retired, they moved to Florida. They were active in their local community and maintained contact with a large network of extended family and friends. In late 2007, Neil McCluskey underwent intestinal surgery and died of complications on May 27, 2008.

Countering Anti-Catholicism in the United States

One of McCluskey's most significant contributions as a Catholic educator was to help many people in the United States to gain a better understanding of Catholic Christianity. When McCluskey was growing up there was a great deal of anti-Catholicism in the United States. Fear and distrust of Catholics was still quite common in the 1950s and into the 1960s. For example, Paul Blanshard's anti-Catholic tract *American Freedom and Catholic Power* (1958) was widely read and praised by many in the United States throughout this period of time. McCluskey was part of a loose coalition of Catholic intellectuals, many of whom were Jesuits, who sought actively to counteract the effects of anti-Catholicism and to make Catholic perspectives on social and religious issues understandable within the broad expanse of United States society. John Courtney Murray was one of the best known members of this coalition. McCluskey dedicated both *Catholic Viewpoint* and *Catholic Education* to Murray. While Murray focused mostly on political and social issues, McCluskey concentrated on addressing anti-Catholicism (what he tended to call "the shadow of bigotry") in the educational forums of the United States.

Reaching out Beyond the Catholic Community

McCluskey anchored his efforts to counter anti-Catholicism in outreach beyond the United States Catholic community. For example, in April of 1957 McCluskey was part of an inter-religious forum at the fiftieth anniversary celebration of the American Jewish Committee in New York. At a time when many Catholics would literally not set foot in a Protestant church let alone a Jewish synagogue, he called on Catholics and Jews to recognize parallels in their histories in the United States: both are minorities, both are often treated with suspicion in the broader culture, and both embrace firmly established faith traditions that they are trying to bring into dialogue with the democratic values and freedoms prominent in the United States. Generally, McCluskey demonstrated a profound respect for Judaism.

Similarly, in February of 1960 McCluskey delivered a paper at the annual convention of the American Association of School Administrators (AASA) in Atlantic City, New Jersey, on why public support should be given to parochial schools (McCluskey 1963). The beginning part of his paper focused on explaining why many Catholics preferred Catholic schools to public schools. In the last two-thirds of the presentation, McCluskey stressed what Catholics and non-Catholics have in common and he argued for public support for private schools primarily as a matter of respect for parents' freedom to choose the education that they think is best for their children.

Throughout his career McCluskey was a member of the REA, an organization whose membership is predominantly Protestant, though the number of Catholic members has grown in recent years. From 1967-89, McCluskey was a member of the REA Board of Directors, serving a number of years on the Editorial Committee for the REA journal *Religious Education* during this time. Additionally, through the REA McCluskey became involved with the National Council on Religion and Public Education (NCRPE), serving as president of the council from 1973-76. Throughout his work with the REA and NCRPE, McCluskey was sensitive to anti-Catholic sentiments among his religious education colleagues and worked to present an understandable and credible Catholic perspective on educational and social issues.

Presenting a Catholic Viewpoint on Education

As part of his efforts to counter anti-Catholicism, a great deal of McCluskey's scholarly writing was focused on presenting a Catholic viewpoint on educational issues using language that would be intelligible across the broad expanse of social and political contexts found in the United States. For instance, both of McCluskey's major books, *A Catholic Viewpoint on Education* and *Catholic Education Faces its Future*, were written to address the educational concerns voiced by professional educators and the general population from Protestant, Catholic, Jewish, and secular humanistic perspectives. Moreover, McCluskey's writings enjoyed a wide circulation because they were generally seen as clearly written, accessible, and scholarly. One commentator even describes McCluskey's introduction to *Catholic Education in America* as a "model essay" on U.S. Catholic education (Cross 1974, 127).

Religious Freedom and the Contribution of Catholicism to the Common Good

An analysis of McCluskey's work reveals that he used three primary arguments to help people understand and become more accepting of Catholicism. First, McCluskey argued that Catholics are linked to and could work cooperatively with other religious groups in the United States because of shared social histories. For instance, in his 1957 presentation to the American Jewish Committee McCluskey stressed, as noted above, the shared concerns of Jews and Catholics in the United States. Similarly, in *Catholic Viewpoint on Education*, McCluskey demonstrated how the evolution of U.S. Catholic education could be seen as part of the general development of education in the United States. He emphasized that Catholics share a concern for moral and religious education with many of their non-Catholic neighbors, even though they will always hold distinct religious convictions (McCluskey 1959, 15-34).

Second, McCluskey contended strongly throughout his career that popular stereotypes of Catholics as close-minded and authoritarian were unfounded, and he countered these characterizations by demonstrating that Catholics embraced, even championed, a commitment to religious freedom. More fully, while at Alma College, McCluskey enrolled in a seminar devoted to exploring recent U.S. Supreme Court decisions concerning state support for private schools. In the discussions of these cases, critics of state support for private, religiously-affiliated schools accused these schools, and Catholic schools in particular, of supporting a sectarian and separatist social outlook that was antithetical to the democratic values and freedoms of the United States. They argued that if the state supported these schools it would be undermining, rather than carrying out, its responsibility to ensure that civic education is provided for the nation's children. McCluskey was affected deeply by these discussions and made a commitment to respond to critics of private support for religious schools.

In addressing the charge that Catholicism and Catholic schools are antithetical to religious freedom, McCluskey began by going back to the First Amendment of the United States Constitution. It states: "Congress shall make no law respecting an establishment of religion, or prohibiting the free exercise thereof; or abridging the freedom of speech, or of the press; or the right of the people peaceably to assemble, and to petition the Government for a redress of grievances." The phrase "make no law respecting an establishment of religion" is generally known as "the no establishment of religion clause." Critics of public funding for religious schools charged that the authorization of such funding would violate the no establishment of religion clause. McCluskey countered this claim by focusing on the phrase "make no law . . . prohibiting the free exercise thereof [religion]." This phrase is commonly known as the "freedom of religion clause." In numerous public addresses and scholarly publications, McCluskey argued that to deny funding to religious schools would violate established laws and legal precedents, including the freedom of religion clause of the United States Constitution. For instance, in his 1960 address to the Association of School Administrators (ASA) McCluskey claimed that failure to support parochial schools should be seen as a hostile act against religious persons and families and as such is a violation of "freedom of choice in education" and ultimately of the freedom of religion clause of the First Amendment (McCluskey 1963, 3; 1959, 139-54).

In some of his work, McCluskey took his religious freedom argument one step further. He suggested (and we need to remember that he wrote at a time when Communism was the most feared enemy of the Unites States) that to eliminate all private schools and maintain only a public school system would be to foster a monolithic, state-controlled, narrowly ideological educational system similar to that found in what was then the Soviet Union. Thus, McCluskey suggested that Catholic schools championed religious freedom at a time when advocates of public education were calling for a Communist-like system of state dominance and control of all learning (McCluskey

1959, 41 and 1963, 1). Generally, in arguing for state support for religious schools as a matter of religious freedom, McCluskey helped to counter prejudices against U.S. Catholics by showing how Catholics could use the common language provided by the U.S. legal system to present their educational views, and in doing so, show Catholics as supportive of the democratic values and freedoms of our nation.

Third, in tandem with his argument for state support for religious schools as a matter of religious freedom, McCluskey also often claimed that Catholic schools should be supported because of the contribution they make to society. For example, in his 1960 address to the ASA, McCluskey cited Title I of the National Defense Education Act of 1958, which he summarized as holding "that the security of the nation requires the fullest development of the mental resources and the technical skills of its young men and women." He argued that Catholic schools had made and continued to make a significant contribution to the cultivation of the talents of the nation's youth and consequently deserved to be supported by the state (McCluskey 1963, 5).

Today, there is still a degree of anti-Catholicism in the United States (Massa 2003). However, because of the efforts of McCluskey and other Catholic leaders in the last half of the twentieth century, Catholics in the United States are usually accepted and treated as equals today by those from other faith and philosophical traditions. Moreover, McCluskey helped Catholics to be accepted and welcomed within a variety of forums in the United States, enabling them to contribute to discussions of significant educational and other social issues affecting the nation.

Educating for Catholic Identity in the United States

McCluskey contributed significantly to the education of United States Catholics in the last half of the twentieth century. In retrospect, the Catholic Church in the United States during McCluskey's childhood and early life was often deeply divided along ethnic lines. It was common at this time, for instance, to find an Irish Catholic parish and school, an Italian Catholic parish and school, a German Catholic parish and school and maybe as many as half a dozen other ethnic parishes and schools in a mid-sized or large U.S. city. The various Catholic ethnic groups often tended to avoid contact with one another just as they avoided their Protestant and Jewish neighbors. Some of those who lived within these ethnic communities had fairly narrow views of the world. In his lecturing, administrative work, and writing McCluskey sought to move U.S. Catholics beyond their divisions and to develop a broader, more expansive view of themselves and the world. McCluskey even suggested that in some cases Catholics who had never moved beyond the boundaries of particular Catholic communities should not receive all of their schooling under Catholic auspices so that they could have opportunities to gain a broader sense of U.S. culture (Lee 1969, 7-8).

McCluskey's interest in fostering a viable sense of Catholic identity in the United States was linked or related directly to his efforts to: draw attention to the distinctiveness of a Catholic viewpoint on education, explore the aims of education, educate Catholics to relate to non-Catholics and the broader culture, instill an understanding of the importance of critical reflection in education, and attend to immediate educational concerns while maintaining a comprehensive and holistic guiding vision of education.

A Catholic Viewpoint on Education

In articulating what he called a Catholic viewpoint or outlook on education, McCluskey noted that while public education in the United States tends to focus on the role of the state to provide educational opportunities, a Catholic viewpoint focuses on the interrelated functions of family, civil society (which includes but is not limited to the state), and the Church: "Each has distinct rights, yet all are properly ordered to ensure balance and harmony within the total educational process" (McCluskey 1959, 80). McCluskey suggested that a diminished sense of the role of the family in educating children has led at times to a failure to respect the rights of parents to send their children to private schools when the available public schools are offensive to the faith and moral standards of their family. He also called for Catholics to assert their right to educate their children in ways that are consistent with their faith and moral values.

To the United States Catholics who heard McCluskey's presentations or read his books or articles from the 1950s through the 1980s, McCluskey's articulation of a Catholic viewpoint on education offered both a reminder and a challenge. On the one hand, McCluskey's work reminded Catholics that even if they were separated into German, Italian, and other ethnic communities, they were united by their Catholicism, including common Catholic beliefs, values, and similar if not shared perspectives on family life and education. On the other hand, McCluskey challenged Catholics to work together to assert their rights in the broader society. As already noted, he even called Catholics to champion the core American value of religious freedom when this value was neglected by those calling for the creation of a monolithic public educational system.

Exploring the Aims of Education

In addition to discussing a Catholic viewpoint or outlook on education, McCluskey developed a philosophy of education in a number of addresses and written works. From a broad philosophical perspective, McCluskey held that a viable educational process needs to have a dual or twofold aim. It must attend to both the natural and supernatural dimensions of the human person. More fully, education, according to McCluskey, should be about our life here and now, and about our supernatural destiny as we come face to face with God after death. In *Catholic Education* McCluskey further developed his ideas about the dual purpose of education using the metaphor of time and eternity. He asserted that education needs to be focused on the now, the present time, and on preparing people to live in the present. Yet, he argued that any education that focused only on the now is incomplete. Education must also focus on eternity, on what we can contribute to what comes after us in this life and what awaits us after death (McCluskey 1959, 75-80 and 1968, 1-45).

McCluskey suggested that the various Catholic communities in the Unites States could retain and celebrate their ethnic roots as they focused on the now or present moment. He also contended that Catholics in the United States can and should affirm a sense of transcendent values and the eternal destiny of the human person as a foundation for working cooperatively amongst themselves and with others in the broader society. Additionally, the value of Catholic schools, McCluskey contended, is that they can provide an "atmosphere and values" that make it possible to attend to both the now and the eternal, each in "their proper place." Stated differently, Catholic schools can provide an environment in which educators can attend to the "total spectrum" of human "experience" and focus on the development of "the whole person" (McCluskey 1968, 35). Moreover, McCluskey suggested that as a united group, Catholics in the United States could help to correct an impoverishing neglect of the significance of the supernatural or eternal in United States public education.

Relating to Non-Catholics and the Broader Culture

In addressing the issue of how Catholics should relate to non-Catholics, McCluskey counseled Catholics to develop a reflective and discerning outlook, or what can be called prudential discernment. As envisioned by McCluskey, such an outlook on life should be based upon a holistic understanding of the human person and, as such, it should include respect for both the dignity of persons and legitimate social values. For instance, in one of the first articles he wrote for *America*, McCluskey explored the Jehovah's Witness faith. McCluskey noted that Catholics and Jehovah's Witnesses could relate to one another insofar as both groups have been persecuted minorities within the United States. Yet, McCluskey was critical of the unwillingness of Jehovah's Witnesses to enter into genuine dialogue with others because such unwillingness reveals a failure to respect the dignity of persons as reflective of the image and likeness of God. He encouraged Catholics to question secretive, and hence anti-social, Jehovah's Witness practices (McCluskey 1955). In contrast, when considering how Catholics should relate to Protestants and Jews, McCluskey suggested that whenever there is a genuine respect for persons as made in God's image, openness to dialogue, and a willingness to work together to address issues of common concern, Catholics should be willing to work with other groups to secure their own legitimate rights and to contribute to the common good of society (McCluskey 1959, 187-92).

McCluskey also called upon Catholics to exercise prudential discernment in the way they approached educational and other social issues. For instance, McCluskey encouraged U.S. Catholics to affirm individual rights as a way of respecting the unique God-given dignity of persons. Yet, he also asked Catholics to recognize limits to these rights. For instance, he noted that parents' rights to educational choice in providing for their children are not absolute, but subject to limits by a concern for the common welfare. He claimed that the state could legitimately interfere with parents' choices if parents opt for an educational curriculum that seeks to undermine the democratic freedoms and values of our nation (1959, 81).

The Importance of Critical Reflection

In his lecturing and writing McCluskey always affirmed the achievements of Catholics and Catholic education in the United States. At the same time, he always stressed the challenges faced by Catholics and Catholic educators and the need for critical reflection in addressing these challenges. A classic example of the mix of affirmation, challenge and call to critical reflection in McCluskey's approach to education is found in his April 1960 address in Chicago to the Conference of Diocesan School Superintendents of the National Catholic Educational Association. McCluskey began his presentation by comparing United States Catholic schools to dinosaurs. He stated:

> Since 1940, American Catholic school enrollment has increased 147 percent, so that today our elementary and secondary schools enroll slightly more than five million pupils. This is truly a remarkable achievement. There is little time, however, for the kind of preening and mutual admiration that induces euphoria. . . . There is always a temptation to look upon bigness as a guarantee of security and survival. It is not. Back in the good old days of the Mesozoic Era, nothing more grand and fearful strode the earth than the mighty brontosaurs and tyrannosaurs and stegosaurs. Yet, these fierce monsters with their tiny brains and huge bodies, along with the rest of the dinosaur family, suddenly disappeared. Paleontologists generally agreed that one reason these unwieldy giants became extinct is that they were unable to adapt to new conditions imposed by climatic upheavals. There may not be an ice age ahead for us, but if Catholic education is to continue to flourish in the decades ahead, those responsible for leadership must be keenly aware of present challenges and make required adaptations. (McCluskey 1965, 11-12)

Generally, the importance of critical reflection is an underlying theme in much of McCluskey's work. McCluskey argued that Catholic educators need to be critically reflective about the challenges they face in guiding Catholic schools and educational programs. He also encouraged Catholics educators to instill a sense of the value of critical reflection in those they taught.

A Comprehensive Educational Vision

From the 1950s to the end of his career McCluskey was an educator whose hand was on the pulse of Catholicism in the United States. This led McCluskey to address immediate educational needs as they developed in the U.S. Catholic Church and to consider educational issues at every stage of the life-cycle. In the 1950s when Catholics were moving into the United States mainstream, many Catholics were concerned about the education of their children. McCluskey responded by addressing issues about public and Catholic schooling. When Catholic concerns about issues of higher education became prominent in the 1960s, McCluskey again responded and addressed these issues. By the mid-1970s, many Catholics felt settled and "at home" in the United States; their concerns began to shift toward issues of mid-life transition and life in older adulthood. Once again McCluskey, perceiving this shift, began designing adult and older-adult educational programs to meet the needs being voiced within Catholic communities around the country. (McCluskey's educational outreach at this point in his life, however, was not limited to Catholic communities. In providing life-transition and life-quality seminars and educational programming that incorporated a focus on spirituality, McCluskey was also in contact with Jewish and Protestant communities and groups.)

As he attended to immediate educational needs, McCluskey always viewed educational issues within the light of a broad, comprehensive, and holistic vision of education. For example, the subtitle of *Catholic Education* is *The Background, Present Position, and Future Trends of Catholic Education*. The book discusses the educational issues faced by the Catholic Church in the United States in the post-Vatican II era. In examining these issues McCluskey explores their background,

that is, their social and historical context as seen from a distinctively
Catholic viewpoint. He also raises broad philosophical and
theological concerns about human nature, sin, and the
supernatural/eternal or transcendent dimension of human life.
Overall, McCluskey's analysis of Catholic education moves from a
consideration of the immediate post-Vatican II context to a reflection
upon the emerging challenges and opportunities facing Catholic
education as seen in the light of a comprehensive and holistic guiding
vision of education.

For United States Catholics in the last half of the twentieth
century, *how* McCluskey discussed educational issues was as
instructive as the analysis he offered. In essence, he suggested that
Catholics needed to be concerned about the immediate issues
affecting their lives and their relations with others. Yet, he
counseled Catholics not to be limited in their approach to issues by
narrow understandings of personal and group interests. Rather, he
conveyed that a broad sense of Catholic identity and an inclusive
concern for the eternal destiny of all people would provide a
guiding vision for a truly Catholic approach to educational issues.
Additionally, the corpus of McCluskey's work highlighted the need
to address educational concerns across the life-cycle from childhood
to older adulthood, and how to approach such concerns guided by
a sense of the central importance of religious education in any
educational process.

Generally, McCluskey is one of the Catholic leaders of the last half
of the twentieth century who helped to foster the sense of United States
Catholic identity that is often taken for granted today. Because of the
educational efforts of McCluskey and other Catholic leaders, many
Catholics continue to treasure their ethnic roots but no longer view
their ethnic heritage as separating them from Catholics with different
ethnic heritages. Many Catholics in the United States treasure the
distinctiveness of Catholicism, but are also committed to the
democratic values and freedom of the United States. Many Catholics
are able to reflect critically on civic issues and are willing to work with
people from other faith and philosophical traditions in addressing these
issues. Further, many Catholics in our country hold a strong sense of
the distinctiveness of U.S. Catholicism while retaining a commitment
to the universal Catholic Church.

Catholic Higher Education

Throughout his career McCluskey spent considerable time and energy addressing issues of Catholic higher education. This work was part of McCluskey's effort to contribute to the broadening of Catholic perspectives in the United States. Moreover, it is one of his most important contributions to the Catholic Church, both nationally and internationally.

McCluskey's contribution to U.S. Catholic higher education began when he wrote for *America*. For example, Edward J. Power cited McCluskey's *America* article on the lack of Rhodes Scholars at Catholic higher educational institutions as presenting a convincing argument for changes that helped to raise academic standards at U.S. Catholic colleges and universities (Power 1972, 458).

McCluskey's most systematic and influential discussion of Catholic higher education is found in *Catholic Education*. In this book, McCluskey challenged Catholic institutions of higher education to focus on serving the educational needs of the United States while retaining a distinct Catholic identity. He urged collaboration between clergy and laity in Catholic higher education administration. He spoke of the importance of financial assistance and cautioned Catholic institutions against becoming schools that only the wealthy could attend. Moving beyond a focus on Catholic schools, McCluskey discussed the value of establishing Catholic centers at public colleges and universities. Also noteworthy is McCluskey's advocacy for educational equality for men and women (McCluskey 1968, 215-55).

In *The Catholic University*, McCluskey presented a collection of essays by Catholic scholars and intellectuals addressing issues of higher educational administration. In the introduction to the book, McCluskey wrote,

> Of necessity the university leads a precarious life. If it responds too easily to social pressures, the university loses its leadership muscle. If it is impervious to the needs of the times, it becomes arteriosclerotic and is by-passed. It cannot be too far out in front; it dare not fall behind. (McCluskey 1970, 1)

Guided by McCluskey's comments, readers of *The Catholic University* are led to see the critical importance of issues such as academic freedom, institutional commitments, and a Catholic university's stance in an ecumenical, inter-religious and international world. The selection of themes and authors for the various essays of the book reveals McCluskey's realistic understanding of the challenges facing the Catholic university and his clear sense of the contribution Catholic universities can make when these challenges are well met.

In addition to his scholarly work, McCluskey made significant contributions to Catholicism as a Catholic higher education administrator and consultant. For instance, McCluskey went to Gonzaga University in 1960 with a well-developed educational philosophy and vision for the further development of Catholic education in the United States. Gonzaga provided him with a chance to test and refine his views in practice. Hence, in overseeing the revision of the university's academic programs and in contributing to the development of the Honors Program, McCluskey was able to implement and further develop his conception of a rigorously academic yet holistic education that included a focus on both the natural and supernatural development of a person. Similarly, McCluskey envisioned the Gonzaga in Florence study abroad program as offering Catholic young adults an opportunity to study and travel in Europe that would broaden their understanding of Catholicism and Western civilization. At the same time, McCluskey hoped that, as they conversed with people in Europe, young American Catholics would come to appreciate more fully the distinctiveness of both the American outlook on life and Catholicism in the United States.

While at Notre Dame, McCluskey was similarly drawn into conversations that contributed to the development of Catholic higher education in the United States. By the mid-twentieth century a number of frictions and rivalries had developed among U.S. Catholic institutions of higher learning as these institutions competed for students and resources. When Theodore Hesburgh became president of Notre Dame, he worked to ease these tensions. McCluskey quickly became Hesburgh's ally when he joined the Notre Dame faculty. Together, Hesburgh and McCluskey drew the leadership of Catholic higher educational institutions into conversation. Their efforts helped to foster a new climate in U.S. Catholic higher education that enabled many Catholic colleges and universities to overcome difficulties and thereby prosper in the latter half of the twentieth century.

During his time at Notre Dame, McCluskey also contributed significantly to the International Federation of Catholic Universities (IFCU). Shortly before McCluskey's arrival at Notre Dame, Hesburgh was elected president of the IFCU. Hesburgh invited McCluskey to help him prepare for IFCU executive committee and federation meetings. At Hesburgh's request, McCluskey planned a 1967 meeting at Notre Dame's ecological center in Land O'Lakes, Wisconsin, for representatives of major Catholic institutions of higher education in the United States and Canada, along with a few high-level administrators from ecclesial offices in Rome. The Land O'Lakes group prepared a statement on the nature and role of the contemporary Catholic university from a North American perspective that was then presented at the next IFCU meeting. This statement, entitled "The Nature of the Contemporary Catholic University," is more commonly known as "The Land O'Lakes Statement."

The Land O'Lakes Statement includes: a call for a strong commitment to academic excellence, especially in the branches of theology; encouragement for theologians exploring and critically reflecting upon the richness of Christian traditions; affirmations of the value of interdisciplinary study; and the articulation of a vision of the Catholic university as the critical reflective intelligence of the Church. Thousands of copies of the document were circulated, and it was discussed by faculties in dozens of colleges and universities.

In 1968, McCluskey participated in the eighth triennial conference of the IFCU at Lovanium University in Kinshasa in the Democratic Republic of the Congo. He and the other delegates discussed "The Land O'Lakes Statement" and other reports prepared by regional groups from around the world. Near the end of the conference McCluskey was elected chair of a committee that drafted the conference's final declaration. The brief declaration was entitled "The Catholic University in the Modern World" and became known as "The Kinshasa Statement."

As part of the follow up to the IFCU meeting in Kinshasa, McCluskey was one of six representatives elected by forty institutions of higher education in the United States to attend a 1969 consultation on Catholic higher education in Rome. The consultation, which has since become known as the "Rome Congress," concluded with the adoption of a position paper entitled "The Catholic University and the

Aggiornamento," more frequently referred to as "The Rome Statement." The Rome Statement was discussed at a plenary session of the Congregation for Catholic Education in October, 1969, and insights from the statement were incorporated in the Congregation's post-session report to Pope Paul VI. This report helped to shape a statement on Catholic higher education that Paul VI sent to the Catholic bishops of the world. ("The Land O'Lakes Statement," "The Kinshasha Statement," and "The Rome Statement" are included as appendices in McCluskey, 1970.) Finally, between January 1971 and November 1972 a series of follow-up discussions on Catholic higher education were held at Land O'Lakes, Caracas (Venezuela), and Grottaferrata (near Rome, Italy). McCluskey was present at each of these meetings. (McCluskey 1970, 1-28; and Galen 2000, 129-33.)

One well-respected authority of the development of U.S. Catholic higher education stated that Theodore Hesburgh, John Tracy Ellis, Neil McCluskey, and other nationally known Catholic intellectual leaders helped "to raise the quality of American Catholic higher education" (Geiger, "Faculty" in Hunt, et al. 2003, 203; Geiger, "Governance of Catholic Higher Education," in Hunt, et al. 2003, 120). Another scholar named McCluskey as one of Catholic leaders whose work led to the "inclusion of lay men and women on the boards of Catholic institutions" and who ultimately "urged the colleges and universities into the mainstream of American higher education." She also noted that, "now these institutions were perceived less and less as a subculture with its own symbols and language" (Gallin 2000, 43, 50).

Overall, McCluskey has had a significant influence on the development of both the theory and practice of Catholic higher education. His scholarly publications and work as a higher education administrator helped to foster greater creativity and ongoing discussion of critical issues in Catholic higher education. McCluskey's most noteworthy contributions to Catholic higher education were made through his involvement with the IFCU. First, McCluskey played significant roles in IFCU meetings that brought the leadership teams of United States higher educational institutions into greater conversation with one another, created a new level of international conversation about Catholic higher education, and influenced the way the institutional Church at the highest levels addressed Catholic higher education.

Second, the Land O'Lakes Statement became a foundational document for the further development of United States institutions of higher education. Because of its influence, the teaching of Christian theology remained a part of the core curricula offered at these institutions, and higher education administrators retained a focus on the distinctive Catholic identity of Catholic colleges and universities. At the same time, the guidelines offered in the statement have helped to ensure academic freedom for professors and contributed to the development of governance structures that gave Catholic colleges and universities the maneuvering room they needed to adapt to changing social and cultural conditions. (O'Brien 1995.) In helping to draft the Land O'Lakes Statement, McCluskey contributed to laying the foundation that Catholic institutions of higher education in the United States have built upon as they have become one of the great assets of our contemporary church and society.

State Support for Private Schools

In his efforts to educate non-Catholics about Catholicism in the United States and to foster a sense of Catholic identity, McCluskey was an advocate for state support for private, especially religious, schools. This aspect of McCluskey's educational ministry deserves special mention because of its influence upon and continuing relevance to contemporary debates of this issue. Today there has been a resurgence of interest in private primary and secondary schools as alternatives to public schools. There are also numerous debates about when and how public support can be provided for these private schools. The arguments advanced today in favor of private schools and public support for private schools build upon the arguments McCluskey presented in his work.

The National Catholic Education Association (NCEA) School Choice Initiative web page (http://www.ncea.org/public/ SchoolChoiceInitiatives.asp) is one of the best sources of information about contemporary arguments made in favor of private schools and public support for private schools. McCluskey's name does not appear on this web site. However, it is clear that the current position of the NCEA incorporates ideas that McCluskey was among the first to advance. Included among the arguments are freedom of religion as the foundation for educational choice, the rights of parents in choosing an education for their children, and the idea that private schools should be supported because of the contribution they make to the growth and development of the nation's youth.

Moral and Religious Education

Throughout his career McCluskey was a tireless advocate for moral and religious education in public and private education in the United States. Moreover, McCluskey's discussions of moral and religious education helped to shape public discussions of education in the United States from the 1960s through the 1990s, and continue to be relevant to current discussions of these issues.

McCluskey first became interested in moral and religious education during his studies at Alma College. At that time, he was introduced to an often fierce pubic debate about whether or not moral and religious instruction should be included in public and state-funded schools. On the one hand, from colonial times to the present many people have held that moral and religious education are essential to any educational process, and common (or public) schools have often assumed some responsibility for religious and moral education. On the other hand, as the United States has become more morally and religiously diverse and culturally pluralistic, more people have come to hold that moral and religious education should be excluded from all public and state-funded education so that the religious and moral views of any group or groups are not given preference over the views of others.

With the publication of his first book, *Public Schools and Moral Education*, McCluskey stepped into the middle of the debate and became a strong advocate for the positions that: 1) moral and religious education needs to be at the core of any educational process that seeks to encourage full human development; 2) ways can be found to introduce moral and religious education that show respect for the religious pluralism and diversity of the United States; and 3) moral and religious education can complement rather than detract from a focus on academic rigor.

Even though he advocated for the inclusion of moral and religious education in public education, McCluskey focused primarily in his early work on analyzing the flaws in existing proposals for religious and/or moral education in U.S. public education. For instance, he noted that trying to base moral and religious education on nonsectarian Christian truths (a proposal advanced by Horace Mann) or even nonsectarian religious and/or moral truths is not tenable. McCluskey saw that increasing socio-cultural and religious diversity in the United States made it impossible to create a consensus about what should be included in a listing of such nonsectarian truths. Additionally, McCluskey accepted the claim that all religious and moral perspectives were grounded in some specific social and cultural context, and granted the validity of the argument that to present any one religious/moral perspective as objective and universal would be to overstate that perspective and show a lack of sensitivity toward those who held other moral and religious perspectives (McCluskey 1958, 11-98; 1959, 21-26; and 1968, 49-50).

Similarly, McCluskey rejected the claim that public education could provide moral training by enforcing a disciplinary code. This claim was advanced by some influential U.S. educators, including William Torrey Harris. These educators objected to the existence of religious school systems and claimed that schools should be completely secular. Yet, they also often held that by applying disciplinary standards schools could provide moral training and encourage the development of moral habits, and that these habits could then become the foundation for more extensive moral education that is provided within families and faith communities. McCluskey pointed out that approaches advanced by Harris and his colleagues pushed moral and religious education to the margins of school life and failed to address adequately the central importance of morality and faith to human existence. He also contended that efforts to provide minimal moral training through school disciplinary procedures could only foster a negative, punitive, and impoverished understanding of morality (McCluskey 1958, 99-176 and 1968, 93-94).

McCluskey also rejected the approach to moral education advanced by the influential educator John Dewey. Dewey reenvisioned the nature of moral values. For Dewey, moral intelligence is social intelligence focused on achieving social interests and aims and alleviating social ills. Moral values are neither ultimately transcendent nor universal guides for living. Rather, they have a solely pragmatic value. They are tools whose value is determined by their usefulness when working on social issues. For Dewey, the only overarching value is democracy itself, primarily because it has proven to be the most useful political system for fostering fullness of human living. Schools, Dewey counseled, should provide moral education by teaching practical skills in democratic living. In critiquing Dewey's position on moral education, McCluskey remarked that Catholics and others who hold traditional Christian beliefs, including a belief in the transcendent or supernatural dimension of the human person, are not likely to find Dewey's approach to moral education to be satisfactory. In McCluskey's words, such people of faith are likely to "regret that Dewey's dedication to the immediate ills of human society caused him to underestimate the 'unpractical' world of saint and stargazer, wherein an immortal soul might seek union with a Spirit that transcends the . . . pettiness of earth" (McCluskey 1958, 258 and 1968, 196-98).

Building upon his critique of existing approaches, McCluskey spent nearly a decade exploring other ways of providing moral and religious formation in public and state-funded education. He then outlined a detailed proposal for addressing this issue in *Catholic Education*. In a chapter focusing on public education and values he states:

> If one accepts the secular character of the contemporary American public school, does it follow that this type of school should be altogether excluded from religious education? If the public school is considered an extension of the political state, the answer is yes; it would have to be, like the state, neutral. But functioning as an extension of the social community, the public school can and should work together with the community's legitimate undertakings in religious education. (McCluskey 1968, 211)

Essentially, McCluskey granted that the state needs to strive to be as neutral as possible. That is, those who represent the state need to be able to step back from the specific interests of any person or group so that they can evaluate issues with as great a degree of impartial fairness as possible. However, McCluskey argued that public schools should be seen not as part of the state, but as part of the social community, and in the social community another set of operational norms is needed.

In the social community people come together from diverse backgrounds. They are members of some religious community or tradition. They are from a variety of ethnic and national backgrounds. Therefore, McCluskey suggested, within the social community respect for difference and a willingness to work together on issues of common concern are both necessary. According to McCluskey, schools can foster respect for differences and provide foundational religious education by teaching about religious diversity. That is, if educators can identify the religious faiths and traditions that are present in a social community, they can lay a foundation for religious education by teaching about these traditions in schools. Then, if pressing socio-moral issues can be identified as issues of common concern (today, for example, drug abuse, driving under the influence of alcohol, the environmental crisis, and violence come to mind), schools can provide a foundation for moral education by offering an academically rigorous explorations of why these are socio-moral concerns. McCluskey also argued that schools can create an awareness of moral and religious issues that parents and churches can then build upon in providing more substantive moral and religious formation.

When he was actively involved in discussions of public and Catholic education, McCluskey was described as "one of the principal spokesmen" for the view that intellectual and moral/religious development could be effectively combined (Lee 1968, 32). As a result of the influence of McCluskey and other significant educators, it is fairly common in today's public and private elementary and secondary schools to have programs of character or citizenship education, to teach morality by focusing on broad social concerns such as preventing drug abuse, and in some cases even to have programs or courses in world religions or U.S. religions. Ironically, it is often taken for granted that contemporary programs in moral/religious education can be part of a rigorous academic curriculum. However, attention to McCluskey's analysis of the flaws of the moral and religious education programs of the past would greatly enhance many of the moral education programs found in both public and private schools in the United States today.

McCluskey's Educational Ministry

When Neil McCluskey was recognized as a pioneering religious educator in 1971, it was clear that his educational ministry had born fruit. As a journalist, scholar, administrator, and popular lecturer and presenter, McCluskey had crisscrossed the nation contributing to educational theory and practice, and helping Catholics and those from other faith and philosophical traditions to understand themselves, each other, and critical educational issues. Moreover, from our contemporary vantage point we can recognize that McCluskey's many achievements continue to shape educational attitudes, perspectives, and practices.

Yet, we should also realize that there are a number of notable weaknesses in McCluskey's perspective. First, McCluskey tended to synthesize ideas together to create comprehensive approaches to issues. In some cases this created unresolved tensions and confusions that have sometimes led McCluskey's work to be misinterpreted. For example, a discerning reader of *Catholic Viewpoint* will note that McCluskey used the term "supernatural" in two ways. On the one hand, McCluskey talked about "supernatural wisdom." For instance, he wrote, "The Church founds schools so that these persons as her communicants will better acquire the supreme integrating principle of supernatural wisdom in ordering the knowledge, skills, and attitudes they learn" (McCluskey 1959, 76). In McCluskey's discussions of supernatural wisdom as an integrating principle, there are echoes of the humanistic philosophy of secular, public schools. On the other hand, McCluskey discussed what he referred to as the "revealed supernatural order." For example, he asserted, "The starting point in the Catholic philosophy of education, then, is the reality of the supernatural as revealed through and in Jesus Christ" (McCluskey 1959, 79). McCluskey contended that there are fundamental supernatural truths that "form a perennial unchanging charter" that has from the beginning of the Christian era to the present "guided Catholic education" (McCluskey 1959, 78). In referring to supernatural truths as substantive principles to guide Catholic education, McCluskey's analysis resonated with established Catholic educational approaches of the mid-twentieth century (see, for example, John D. Redden and Francis A. Ryan, *A Catholic Philosophy of Education*). The tension between these two understandings of the supernatural is never fully resolved in McCluskey's many discussions of the aims of education, resulting in a certain amount of ambiguity in his thought.

McCluskey has also been criticized for being overly optimistic about the possibilities for mutual understanding and cooperative action among diverse groups. Critics of McCluskey have noted that he tended to downplay the difficulties that often need to be overcome to reach mutual understanding and he seldom if ever offered a method or practical suggestions for overcoming barriers to genuine dialogue. He also overlooked the fact that dialogue can sometimes deepen the divisions among diverse groups.

However, while we need to be aware of the limitations of McCluskey's thought, we can appreciate the continuing relevance of his educational ministry by focusing on his positive contributions. Currently, the institutions that once stood as symbols of stability and social and moral values are often questioned or even disregarded. Governmental agencies, political parties, schools, business corporations, and churches no longer command the respect they once did. We are more inclined today than in the recent past to "deconstruct" the religious and moral perspectives voiced by those in positions of authority or even by our neighbors and colleagues. McCluskey, who spoke of the value of critical reflection throughout his career, applauded the level of critical reflection people displayed at the dawn of the twenty-first century. Yet, he also noted that critical reflection can never be an end in itself, and that deconstruction must lead to reconstruction if it is to give rise to deeper understanding and action.

Undoubtedly, McCluskey's work can inspire us, as it inspired many people in the past, to reach beyond ethnic and religious divisions in search of deeper understanding. As a Catholic, McCluskey began reaching out to Jews in the 1950s, inviting Jews and Catholics to work together. Today McCluskey's work can inspire Catholics and other Christians to reach out to Jews, Muslims, and people of other faith traditions. McCluskey continually called people of diverse backgrounds to acknowledge their differences while working together to address issues of common concern. His work can inspire religious educators to acknowledge the increasing plurality and ambiguity of our times and, yet, to work with people from other faith and philosophical traditions in addressing pressing educational social issues.

Mary Perkins Ryan:
Visionary in Modern
Catholic Religious Education

ANN M. HEEKIN

Mary Perkins Ryan remains one of the least recognized of the twentieth century figures in the modern renewal of Catholic education in the United States. The reasons why are many but none satisfactory. Ryan was an intellectual without a scholarly credential beyond her bachelor's degree. She was an educator without an affiliation to an academic institution. A leading voice for professional standards in church religious education without ever serving in either a parish or diocesan role, Ryan worked alongside the giants of twentieth century Catholic educational history–Gerard Sloyan, Johannes Hofinger, Gabriel Moran, Berard Marthaler, Maria Harris, Gloria Durka, and Thomas Groome. Despite her leadership in the American liturgical movement and her visionary stance on adult religious education, Ryan still remains in the margins of Catholic educational history.

The purpose of this chapter is to illustrate how Ryan's intellectual corpus that includes twenty-four authored works and forty years of editorial direction at *The Living Light* and *Professional Approaches for Christian Educators* (PACE) justifies her place alongside the more established figures of her time. It is also intended to reclaim a leadership role for Ryan as a visionary in the modern renewal of Catholic education and in so doing to move her contributions from the margins to the main text of that history.

Nearly three decades before the Second Vatican Council (1962-65) convened, Ryan and other leaders of the American liturgical movement envisioned a pastoral orientation to the religious education of the laity. It was a renewal focused on the full and active participation of the laity in the liturgical life of the Church. Its aims were to correct the apparent sterility that had characterized Catholic parish life at the start of the twentieth century. As a catechesis for the liturgy, the early movement understood the liturgy in the broad sense of the public prayer life of the Church. It included all the liturgical practices of the Catholic tradition–the Mass, the sacraments, the praying of the Divine Office, and participation in the annual cycle of the liturgical year–as formative of the Christian life. Moreover, these early reformers advocated for popular liturgical education at the source of individual and social transformation in Christ.

Formative Influences on Ryan's Life and Work

Mary Perkins was born in Boston on April 10, 1912, to Charles Perkins and Elizabeth Ward Perkins. One of four children, Mary was a member of a highly educated Catholic family. Her father was an architect but it was the combined influence of Ryan's mother, Elizabeth Ward, and aunt, Justine Bayard Ward, that inspired Mary's early appreciation of the liturgy. In a pre-Vatican II Church, Elizabeth and Justine were progressive Catholic educators in the application of art and music to the liturgy. Mary's mother–an arts educator by training–collaborated with Dr. Thomas E. Shields of the Catholic University of America in his pioneering work of integrating religion and the general curriculum. Elizabeth's involvement with the National Liturgical Conference preceded her daughter's. In 1945 she addressed the conference with a presentation entitled, "The Perennial Art of the Liturgy." Also, Justine Ward, a renowned music educator, applied the directives of Pope Pius X's *Motu Proprio* (November 22, 1903) for sacred song in her publication of the *Ward Method of Gregorian Chant.* The Catholic Education Press began publication of Ward's method textbooks in 1910, establishing her as one of the early pioneers of the liturgical movement in America. In Elizabeth and Justine, Mary found strong role models for women's leadership in education for liturgical reform.

Mary was formally educated in Boston, Connecticut, and New York. Upon graduation from high school at age fourteen, she studied in Europe for two years before entering Manhattanville College of the Sacred Heart in New York City. She graduated with honors in 1933 with a Bachelor of Arts in English Literature. By this time Mary was fluent in both French and Latin. Her knowledge of Latin actually began in the Perkins' home around the practice of her mother, a Benedictine Oblate, reading the Breviary to her children. In the period prior to the Second Vatican Council when there was a need for accessibility to the Mass and other prayers of the Church in the vernacular, Ryan's command of the Latin language served her well as a writer and translator of popular liturgical books for Catholics.

With her sights set on a writing career, Mary found her first job as a secretary at the Catholic publisher Sheed & Ward in New York City. It was a brief tenure and Mary acknowledged that her meager secretarial skills made her perhaps Sheed & Ward's "worst employee." She returned to the publishing house two years later after a discussion with Father Leonard Feeney, S.J., who served on the editorial staff at Sheed & Ward. He convinced her to write a popular book on liturgical practices for Catholics. *At Your Ease in the Catholic Church* was published by Sheed & Ward in 1938 when Mary was also rehired by the publisher, this time as an editor. It was on an editorial assignment in 1940 that Mary met Father Michael Ducey, O.S.B, the chief architect of the Benedictine Liturgical Conference, which became the National Liturgical Conference in 1941. During the interview, Father Ducey described a presentation for an upcoming National Liturgical Week in Chicago on lay participation in the divine office. When he learned that Mary prayed the Breviary, he requested she lead the discussion following the session. For the next two decades, Mary was a leading figure in the National Liturgical Conference.

In 1942, Mary Perkins married John Julian Ryan, a Harvard graduate and professor at Holy Cross College in Worcester, Massachusetts. The couple shared an enthusiasm for liturgical reform, with John also participating in the National Liturgical Conference and joining Mary as a board member in 1953. Mary's publishing and active involvement in the National Conference continued as she and John raised a family of five boys. In 1963, the Ryans relocated to Granger, Indiana, when John accepted a faculty position at St. Mary's College, Notre Dame, Indiana. This move proved to be yet another fortuitous chapter in Mary's life and work. There she met Father Michael Mathis O.S.B., who founded the Liturgical Institute at Notre Dame in 1947, and was soon hired as a staff member. At the Liturgical Institute, Mary translated the works of European liturgical giants Louis Bouyer and Jean Danielou. Soon after Johannes Hofinger, S.J. arrived at the Institute as a visiting scholar, she edited his classic work, *The Art of Teaching Christian Doctrine* (1957). The experience at Notre Dame and her work with Father Hofinger helped to sharpen her vision for the close relationship between liturgy and catechesis and what she later described to friend and colleague, Sister Mary Charles Bryce, as the realization that "religious education was the missing factor in the whole picture of [liturgical] renewal."

By 1963, the Ryans relocated back east to Goffstown, New Hampshire, after John accepted a faculty position at St. Anselm College. The following year, during the closing sessions of the Second Vatican Council, Mary published her provocative work, *Are Parochial Schools the Answer?* (1964). Despite biting criticism of the book in certain Catholic circles, Mary was recruited by Father Russell Neighbor (then associate director of the National Center of the Conference of Christian Doctrine) to launch a new catechetical journal, *The Living Light.* Father Neighbor was a leading proponent of adult religious education and shared Ryan's vision for moving beyond the parochial school model of education in the Church. The two were founding members of The Catechetical Forum, a loosely structured think-tank of authors, publishers, academics, and practitioners in religious education who gathered annually in Grailville, Ohio, from 1964-72. Ryan spent nine years editing and writing for *The Living Light* (1964-73) before embarking on a new United States Catholic Conference (USCC) publishing venture, *Focus on Adults.* When the launch of the new journal failed to materialize, she joined the editorial staff at *Professional Approaches for Christian Educators* (PACE), a hands-on scholarly reference for religious educators published by St. Mary's Press. Mary became the principal editor for PACE in 1978. From 1988-93, she continued her contributions to PACE under the title of Editor Emeritus Senior Consultant until her death from Parkinson's disease in October, 1993.

The Early Liturgical Movement

Ryan's work in promoting the early liturgical movement in the United States can be described as educating to a new vision of Church. It is through the lens of Ryan's theology of church that her concept of education in the Catholic faith tradition comes into sharper focus. Her early writings, between 1930 and 1950, took place against the backdrop of the liturgical movement in America that had its origins in eighteenth-century Europe and the Benedictine spiritual revival focused on the liturgy. In its modern form, the origins of the European liturgical movement may be traced to the mid-nineteenth century (Reeder 1997, 806). By the turn of the century, the centers of European liturgical renewal had spread to monasteries in France, Germany, Austria, and Italy. With the publication of *Liturgy the Life of the Church* by the Belgium Benedictine, Dom Lambert Beauduin, the movement went beyond monastic enclaves with a distinct pastoral approach to the liturgical practices of the laity. Beauduin's work responded to the rise of popular devotions in Europe that had begun to overshadow participation in the liturgy. He emphasized the communal nature of the Mass and the role of the liturgy as the common prayer of the Church that unites the corporate body into the Mystical Body of Christ. In his work, the role of the liturgy in forming greater solidarity among the faithful as the Body of Christ was explicitly linked to Catholic social action and ecumenical unity. The metaphor of the Church as the Mystical Body of Christ resisted the growing tendency of passive participation in the liturgy with a pastoral approach to "a mystical body which overflowed with passion for justice [and] a mystical body united, where Anglican, Orthodox, and Roman Catholics might dwell together in mutual respect, open to dialogue" (Pecklers 2001, 11).

The European liturgical renewal sought a living engagement with the liturgy that had been diminished by centuries of a manual approach to theology as the dominant form of catechesis. Moreover, the concept of the Mystical Body of Christ pointed toward a new model of church. The expression of church as mystical communion was in sharp contrast with the institutional model of church that held sway since the Middle Ages. More precisely, it was not the Church as institution that Beauduin and other European reformers objected to. Rather, it was the institutionalism of the Church that had calcified the Catholic response to the Reformation. In its most extreme form, the institutional model of church manifested a culture of clericalism and juridicalism that the liturgical reformers saw as undermining the active role of the laity in the liturgical life of the Church and the connection between the liturgy and social transformation.

The reformers also attacked this lifeless and institutional model as lacking in biblical and early patristic traditions in its foundations. Following the European suit, Ryan was among those early formidable leaders in the United States–Virgil Michel, Gerald Ellard, Godfrey Diekmann, Reynold Hillenbrand, and Martin Hellriegel–who saw this model as promoting the laity as spectators rather than participants in the life of the Church. This static model was the culture of church that Ryan sought to reform with her early works in popular liturgical education. Her first published work, *At Your Ease in the Catholic Church* (1937), focused not only on adult education on the parts and meaning of the Mass but also the entire liturgical tradition of the Church. *At Your Ease* provided a history of these practices and an understanding of how conscious participation in the liturgy integrates the Christian "body and mind to the great mysteries of the Faith" (Ryan 1937, 4-5). Ryan argued that becoming knowledgeable in the language of the faith leads to the cultivation of a more intense spirituality that is necessary for any kind of social action. She wrote:

> Therefore, study and work towards the acquisition of Catholic poise and culture is part of our duty of Catholic Action. As we awake more and more fully to the terrible need for such action in the world today, we shall work more intelligently to discover and take our share in it. (Ryan 1937, 4)

Ryan's publishing in popular liturgical education continued with *Your Catholic Language* (1940) and *Speaking of How to Pray* (1944). In all three major liturgical works, Ryan wrote to the theme of a more intelligent participation in the liturgy among adult Catholics.

More than a decade before liturgical reform in the United States coalesced into a national religious movement with Ryan and others as its leading spokespersons, Dom Virgil Michel and his collaborators at St. John's Abbey in Collegeville, Minnesota, laid the groundwork. Michel encountered the liturgical movement while studying in Europe "and his contact with Lambert Beauduin who would exercise great influence on Michel's early liturgical thought and writing" (Whalen 1996, 6-7). Whalen observes, "Michel's real contributions did not revolve around an isolated liturgical theology" (1996, 64). Instead, Michel's distinct interpretation was an integrated vision of the relationships between liturgy and catechesis and liturgy and social justice. With the Mystical Body of Christ as the core theological concept, Michel taught how the communal aspects of the liturgy could be translated into full participation by the faithful in the action of the liturgy and shape the religious life of the Christian outside of the action of the liturgy as well.

In 1926, Michel and his colleagues provided the needed infrastructure for the birth of the liturgical movement in America with the founding of *The Liturgical Press* (originally called *The Popular Liturgical Library*) and the liturgical journal, *Orate Fratres* (later renamed *Worship*). Initially, Michel's work remained outside of institutional parish life. In the effort to reach a more popular audience for liturgical reform, he created the *Christ-Life Series*, a liturgically-based curriculum for Catholic schools and release-time programs. The series was developed along with Dominican Sisters Jane Marie Murray, Estelle Hacket, and Benedictine biblical scholar, Basil Stegmann. These educators were convinced that the traditional catechism approach was too abstract for communicating the essential sacramental message of Christianity. Their pedagogy was a progressive experiential one advocating that "the truths of the faith cannot simply be explained to children; children must experience these truths with the liturgy" (Whalen 1996, 76).

Whalen describes Michel's distinct contribution to the American renewal as the concept of the sacramental quality of all human existence that forges the relationship between the Christian life as celebrated in the liturgy and the Christian life as lived in the world. It was a theme that later expressed the mission of the national organization of liturgical reform—The National Liturgical Conference.

American Liturgical Renewal Comes of Age

The establishment of the National Liturgical Conference by the United States bishops in 1944 galvanized liturgical renewal into a national Catholic movement. Ryan was one of the dominant figures in the Conference from its inception and served on its board of directors beginning in 1950. The Conference reached a mass audience of adult Catholics through a program known as the National Liturgical Weeks that "gave liturgical study a popular, pastoral outlet" (Kinast 1997,

1242). The keynote address of the first Week given by Dietrich von Hildebrand ("Liturgy and the Cultural Problem") signaled the breadth of the renewal's mission.

The movement embraced a spiritual, historical, and social transformation in Christ. Ryan's comments, following Hildebrand's talk, were characteristic of her call for more intentional forms of popular liturgical education among a more educated and culturally assimilated generation of American Catholics. She explained:

> There are indeed, ways of bringing everyone, however old, however uneducated, into the life of the liturgy. Anyhow, there are now very few people in this country who are illiterate. We all have to go to school. We all have to learn how to read. Why then don't we take advantage of this, and show people how to use their education in God's service? If people can read the comic strips and the newspapers, they can be shown how to read the Missal. (Ryan 1948, 198)

Ryan's growing involvement in the National Liturgical Conference led to her editing *The Sacramental Way* (1948), a collection of the papers delivered by liturgical leaders over the first five years of the National Liturgical Weeks. Between 1940 and 1945, the Weeks grew in popularity, as did annual parish missions, a kind of traveling liturgical show-and-tell inviting leading liturgists and educators to gather at a local parish or diocese for a series of themed talks, small group discussions, and liturgical celebrations.

The National Liturgical Weeks were an undisputed success. The theme of the 1941 week, "The Living Parish," attracted "over 1200 bishops, priests, and lay people, gathered in a 'serious' manner but with 'enthusiasm and piety' to witness for themselves what the movement was recommending for parish worship" (Reeder 1998, 805). In her introduction to *The Sacramental Way*, Ryan cited the influence of Pope Pius XII's encyclical, *Mediator Dei* (1947), as the impetus for the growing audience of Catholics drawn to "the fruits of study, meditation and practical experience in the liturgy" (Ryan 1948, xi). *Mediator Dei* legitimized both the liturgical movement and the work of liturgical educators like Ryan in its call to promote the active participation of the faithful in the liturgy. Its publication signified that the liturgical movement had come of age. The modern liturgical movement, said Ryan, is not merely concerned with "the purely archeological or aesthetic preoccupations . . . of the outward aspects of Catholic worship," but more properly understood in the context of the full sacramental life of the Church (1948, x). Ryan wrote:

> We hope therefore that this book may do something to remove such misapprehensions and misunderstandings of the Liturgical Movement, as a whole. Perhaps the phrase, "the Sacramental Apostolate," now coming into use, better describes the same reality. For the many-sided work which both terms designate consists in the effort to make the full sacramental life of the Church once more appreciated and lived by our Catholic people, so that in closer, more vital contact with Christ Our Lord, they may begin more effectively to carry out their vocation of re-establishing all things in Christ. (Ryan 1948, x)

Ryan's thinking and influence on Catholic sacramental life reached another level in the 1950s, when the issue of the Catholic family in a pluralistic society emerged as a pressing concern of the Church. Both *Mind the Baby* (1949) and *Beginning at Home* (1955) reflected Ryan's life stage as a married mother of five boys and her growing pastoral interest in new forms of Catholic family catechesis. These factors reflected the social reality of American Catholics at mid-century. Catholics were now two generations removed from the immigrant church experience of the prior century and the assimilation of Catholics into mainstream society would pave the way for the first American Catholic president (John F. Kennedy) by the next decade.

Ryan's theological conviction held that the meaning of the Church in the metaphor of the Mystical Body of Christ directs the faithful towards increasing engagement with the wider culture. In a series of articles appearing in *Orate Fratres/Worship* on the theme of family catechesis, Ryan acknowledged religious pluralism as a reality of modern life. She urged parents to move beyond a sentimental longing for an idealized Christian past and to become engaged in the "sacramental way" in modern Christian family living:

To sum it all up, let us not be in any way afraid of the
manifestation of modern American culture, simply because
they are new, different from what we were accustomed to, etc.
But let us try, with the help of the Holy Spirit, to find
whatever is of value in them, and to show the children what
this is and how to use it, while rejecting what is wrong and
meretricious. Thus they will be on the way to becoming truly
sophisticated men and women of creative Christian taste,
ready, if God wills, to help in the formation of a true
American Christian culture. (Ryan 1952, 502)

The engagement by Catholics with the broader culture marked the
beginning of a characteristic stance on faith and culture that Ryan and
other reformers whole-heartedly embraced in the period leading up to
the Second Vatican Council. The shift represented a critical turn in
ecclesiology from the Church's "nineteenth-century defensive,
intransigent position relative to the world to a more affirming, open
stance" (Boys 1989, 177). While the social dimension of liturgical
renewal was central to European reformers and the early work of Virgil
Michel in America, this action-oriented theme gradually took on even
greater significance in the birth of American splinter movements under
the leadership of Dorothy Day of *Catholic Worker* and Catherine van
de Heuck of *Fellowship House*. By the 1950s, the social justice
dimension of liturgical renewal developed into "a crusade to establish a
Christian social order" (Hughes 1990, 15). Ryan likewise insisted that
the transcendent value of the liturgy culminated in concrete service and
Christian love of neighbor.

The Liturgical and Kerygmatic Movements

The modern reform of Catholic education in the United States
that began under the influence of the liturgical renewal took place at
the intersection of multiple but complementary movements. By the
mid-twentieth century, when Ryan had joined the staff of The Liturgy
Program at Notre Dame University, a second movement was underway.
The groundbreaking work of Austrian liturgist Josef Jungmann and his
principal spokesperson in the United States, Johannes Hofinger,
ushered in the kerygmatic orientation to catechesis, with its emphasis

on the proclamation of the gospel message. Hofinger offered a systematic approach to a pastoral education in the faith. He worked at restoring the proclamatory nature of the good news in the schema of salvation history, with its deep moorings in the ancient liturgy of the Church and the practices of the early catechumenate as a model of lifelong formation in the context of community. Hofinger frequently lectured at Notre Dame's liturgy program, where he helped to synchronize the liturgical and kerygmatic movements. At Notre Dame, Ryan collaborated closely with Hofinger in the editing of his classic, *The Art of Teaching Christian Doctrine* (1957). Ryan's own work, *Perspective for Renewal* (1960), also linked the liturgical and kerygmatic renewals in her thinking. Their collaboration was crucial and timely in the history of the liturgical movement. There was a growing opposition among traditionalists, who feared that the direction of liturgical reform had gone too far. In a later conversation with her friend and colleague, Mary Charles Bryce, Ryan recalled becoming acutely aware of the opposition to liturgical renewal and her growing realization that "poor catechesis was largely to blame" (Bryce 1975, 278).

For Ryan, Hofinger, and other leaders of the catechetical movement, the Notre Dame experience opened the door to a necessary corrective to the liturgical movement. The kerygmatic appeal to "a profound change to catechizing by bringing content more in line with scripture and liturgy" and "a pastoral renewal that would overcome the ineffectiveness of current approaches" resonated with Ryan (Moran 1966, 36). Ryan discovered in the kerygmatic approach what had been lacking in liturgical reform efforts, namely, a theology of progressive revelation integrated into an educational schema. In the context of a salvation history framework of revelation, the message and method enhanced the response of the learner by paying attention to the psychosocial stages of development that informed both learner readiness and style of learning. For Ryan, Hofinger's approach provided the much needed link between liturgy and catechesis and a more systematic understanding of how the liturgy educates. Concomitantly, the pedagogical principle espoused by John Dewey and the experiential movement in general education–the concept of "learning by doing"–was elucidated in the formative role of active liturgical participation. In describing how the liturgy educates,

Hofinger said: "*The liturgy gives what it teaches.* It not only presents the Mystery of Christ concretely, it also lets us immediately participate in this mystery" (Hofinger 1957, 34).

The Changing Relationship of Church and Culture

With the publication of *Perspective for Renewal* (1960), Ryan framed her proposals for a more kerygmatic orientation to educating in the faith within a broader critique of older Catholic ecclesiology. In her view, the strictly institutional bound ecclesiology had created an ambivalent and harmful relationship between faith and culture. Ryan argued that full participation in the life of the liturgy was limited by the Church's own failure to act as a transformative agency in culture. She judged this truncated vision of the Church in the world to be the chief obstacle to formation in a religious way of life based on the Catholic sacramental principle of God's grace mediated through history. Ryan advocated that a more thorough theology of the Christian lay vocation demanded the traditional stance *vis-à-vis* culture be reoriented. Educating in faith, urged Ryan, must be understood as educating to "a religious way of life" rather than merely "teaching about religion." Ryan averred:

> It is this outlook which, it seems, is ultimately responsible–
> beneath the various sociological and economic causes–for the
> dearth of Catholic intellectuals and artists, for the continuation
> of the ghetto-mentality among so many groups, for our lack of
> a positive impact on society. And it is this outlook also which
> is responsible for a great deal of the indifference and "leakage,"
> not only among those whose religious instruction has been
> received in weekly classes more or less faithfully attended, but
> also among those who have received their whole education
> under Catholic auspices. (Ryan 1960, 14)

In the immediate preconciliar period, the changing character of American Catholicism was the result of greater assimilation of Catholics into mainstream society and the spirit of Americanism. In the late-1950s, the themes of Catholic mobilization and anti-ghettoism focused primarily on the question of Catholic intellectual life.

Burgeoning Catholic liberalism's message was often accompanied by praise for American pluralism and "the call that Catholics should abandon separatism, outgrow their siege mentality and break out of their Catholic ghetto" (Gleason 1981, 3). Matters came to a head in 1955 with John Tracey Ellis's essay, "American Catholics and Intellectual Life". Ellis's critique of the miniscule contributions among Catholics to American science, scholarship, and literature argued that this "intellectual backwardness" was predisposed by a Catholic "self-imposed ghetto-attitude."

Ryan joined the debate on Catholic intellectual life in her classic work, *Are Parochial Schools the Answer?: Catholic Education in Light of the Council* (1964). Gleason observed that Ryan's book made "parochial schools a major focus of the controversy" (1981, 7). *Parochial Schools* was foremost a sociological critique of the ethos of separatism that the schools fostered and which Ryan deemed inconsistent with the new and open spirit of the Second Vatican Council. Both *Lumen Gentium* and *Gaudium et Spes* encouraged the Church to dialogue with the modern world. In his opening address to Vatican II, Pope John XXIII ushered in a new era in the life of the Church with this pivotal question: "What does it mean to be a believer, to be a Christian in the modern world?" Ryan's *Parochial Schools* in no small way tried to answer that question. Ryan sensed that the Catholic schools fed off of and into an institutionalism that could not serve the Council's call for renewal. Her work affirmed the call of the Council for "forcing our reasoning process out of worn paths" as well as its mandate to "find fresh expressions." Further, Ryan urged a serious reappraisal of the schools in light of the forms of education that best served the needs of the modern Church.

Ryan's Vision for Educating in the Faith

The publication of *Are Parochial Schools the Answer?* stirred great debate at the annual meeting of the National Catholic Educational Association in 1964. Commenting on the book, Gerard Sloyan astutely observed that its title and content were largely misunderstood in Catholic circles. He opined that Ryan was neither concerned with the issue of parish schools not being a good thing for the Church nor with the question of whether they are perfectible. Sloyan cleared the air by writing, "Mrs. Ryan asks whether parochial schools will be part of the answer when a total pastoral care is undertaken, and she answers in the negative" (Sloyan 1964, 52).

The question that Ryan raised concerned the prospect of Church reforms initiated by the Second Vatican Council. It is in the context of urgent reform and renewal that Ryan argued against the schools as the normative basis for total religious education. She explained:

> But if the outlook and directives of the Council indicate the need for a new approach to the problem of religious formation–it seems likely that in five, ten or twenty years a Catholic school system will neither be necessary nor as desirable as it has been in the past–then much of our current effort is misdirected, quite apart from the considerable ill will it is producing towards the Church. If there is even a possibility that such waste of effort and slowing down of ecumenical progress might be prevented, surely that possibility should be seriously examined. (Ryan 1964, 5)

The "ecumenical progress" that Ryan considered at-risk was situated in the political climate of the time. The prospect of public aid to Catholic schools in the form of a voucher program placed the Church at the center of a national and constitutional debate over the separation of church and state. Ryan's proposal that Catholic schools should be reevaluated cast doubt over the educational value of these schools which Catholic supporters and lobbyists for public support had successfully defended in order to garner public support. The official Church position was that Catholic schools aided the wider public by educating children who would otherwise be an added cost to the public school system. The Catholic educational enterprise in the general education of children was the basis for the position that these schools (like their public counterparts) should be eligible for assistance.

Ryan dismissed the public assistance solution for revitalizing Catholic schools as a stopgap measure that only delayed the inevitable reality that parochial schools were not financially sustainable. She had done the math. Her calculations projected a school system that would become less viable over time due to decreasing student enrollment, rising personnel costs associated with an increasingly lay-dominant school faculty, and the bricks and mortar expenses of building new schools as Catholics followed the general migration from the cities to the suburbs. If Ryan's analysis was correct, a main symbol of American Catholic identity–the parish school–hung in the balance. Since the turn of the century, the rally cry of "every Catholic child in a Catholic school" had become a quasi-article of the Catholic faith. By emphasizing its diminishing financial stability and pointing to the growing numbers of Catholic parents choosing public schools over parochial ones, Ryan advocated a new model for Catholic religious education. She questioned

> whether it would be more realistic, even for the sake of our children, to plan our educational efforts to reach the whole Christian community, in accord with the new mentality now taking shape in the Church and diffused by the Council. (Ryan 1964, 7)

Ryan's vision for total parish religious education placed adults at the center of its activity. Because most parochial schools were already operating at a deficit and surviving on the subsidies from the parish, Ryan called into question the fairness of this strategy for the growing numbers of families who did not use the schools. More important, Ryan queried whether this investment might not be better directed toward educational efforts benefiting the whole faith community.

For those critics who declared Ryan's proposal in *Parochial Schools* as "anti-Catholic," history has proven them short-sighted. However, there were other naysayers who dismissed her idea that the liturgy should become "the central formative force in Catholic life" as "astonishingly naïve." One reviewer characterized Ryan as creating a "post-Council Utopia . . . a dreamland where clergy, without the worry about parish schools, must rely mainly upon the recently updated liturgy to form parishioners, young and adult, into dynamic, fruitful Christians" (McManus 1964, 53). Catholic University of America professor, Roy Deferrari, in his *A Complete System of Catholic Education is Necessary* (1964), charged that Ryan failed to understand the philosophical principles of Catholic education. Deferrari recalled the words of Pope Pius XI in "The Christian Education of Youth" (1939):

The true Christian, the product of Catholic education, is the supernatural man who thinks, justifies and acts consistently in accordance with the example and teaching of Christ; in other words, to use the current term, the true and finished man of character. (Deferrari 1964, 10)

Despite Deferrari's attempt to undermine Ryan's position on the value of the schools, she outflanked his attack. In response, Ryan claimed that the historical conditions that gave rise to parochial schools in the previous century were invalid assumptions for twentieth-century Catholic life. Modern Catholics, argued Ryan, had not only assimilated into a fundamentally pluralistic society but had achieved leadership roles. The renewal of the Second Vatican Council affirmed this new sense of Catholic public identity and the profound shift in the relationship of the faithful to culture. This was the spirit that now urged a new role for the church in dialogue with the universal human community. Arguing from the tradition of the Church, Ryan asserted the more appropriate model of formation for the modern Christian life was to be found in the first and not the nineteenth century's concept of the Church. The catechumenate, remarked Ryan, was the more viable historical precedent for our present educational aims. She contended:

The time has come to examine afresh the way in which the early Church formed Christians both old and young, with a view to its possible application. Already, there has been a convergence of many lines of though–theological, scriptural, catechetical, pastoral–toward a belief that participation in the sacramental rites of the Church is, by the very nature of Catholic faith, the focus of Catholic life and of formation of that life. With the example of the early Church in mind, we cannot dismiss as wild fancy the idea that participation in the worship of the Church–understood in a far fuller sense than has been possible in recent centuries–could once more become the central and most important formative force affecting all member of Christian community, and that around this focus other means of religious formation could be organized to supplement and extend it–without the need for providing young people with a general education. (Ryan 1964, 43-44)

Ryan envisioned "parish schools of education" as adult centers of religious formation within the context of the whole community. With the reformed liturgy as the axis "of Christian community in which everyone present has an active part both inwardly and outwardly," there would be full, conscious and active participation in the liturgy as called for by the "Constitution on the Sacred Liturgy" (Ryan 1964, 108). In Ryan's view, the restoration of the ancient catechumenate that fostered participation in the sacred rites, study of Scripture, and the mystagogy would reorient worship towards service of the wider human community. In short, religious education and the practice of religion could no longer "be kept tidily apart from life".

In Ryan's judgment, Catholic worship as merely a "Sunday affair" or "conformity to private devotions" was a dead end: "One cannot help wondering how long, if the old mentality should continue to dominate, the practice of religion would continue among the intelligent and truly religious members of the coming generation" (1964, 101). In her essay "Liturgical Piety for American Catholics?" Ryan's view of the liturgy pointed to a mode of liturgical catechesis that moved beyond a catechesis *for* the liturgy to the role of the liturgy *as* a catechesis for life that "makes possible and fructifies further personal encounter with Him both in prayer and in the service of our neighbor" (1963, 239). In this way, to educate in the faith "is not to teach people to know their religion in such a way that at the end of grade school or high school or college . . . they feel they know everything they need to know for life" (1963, 238). A catechesis centered on the experience of the liturgy, maintained Ryan, creates a lifelong adventure of love and response to God. She stated:

> A catechesis centered on the liturgy will thus be completely realistic leaving out of account none of the realities of human experience and, as such, will correspond to the best desires both of young people and their elders today—the desire for reality, for vital experience, for meaning-fullness in life. (Ryan 1963, 240)

The Living Light Years

In 1964, the United States bishops launched the catechetical journal, *The Living Light*. Ryan worked alongside of Father Russell Neighbor, who served as editor. Father Neighbor was a veteran advocate of adult education and alternative models to the school-based approach. The journal was intended to promote dialogue between practitioners and scholars on the theological relationship of revelation and catechesis based on the Second Vatican Council and the ways that new learning from the social sciences might inform new models of educating in the faith. However, only two years into the appearance of *The Living Light*, Gabriel Moran's *Theology of Revelation* (1966) effectively reopened the discussion on revelation and its relationship to catechesis. Moran argued, and modern biblical scholarship agreed with him, that the kerygmatic approach to catechetics was based on an inadequate theology of revelation. In his proposal for the continuing revelation of the risen Christ, Moran contended that catechesis began in the experience of the believer and not in the isolated facts of God's intervention in history, as formulated by the salvation history model. In Moran's view, the graced response of each individual must be informed by Scripture and tradition, but it can only be experienced as a free and personal response to God's initiative.

It was during this phase of catechetical debate that Ryan collaborated with Gabriel Moran, Raymond Lucker, Gerard Sloyan, and Gerald Pottebaum, among others, who referred to themselves as the Catechetical Forum (1966-72). Serving as a think-tank for leading religious educators in the United States, the forum "was a loosely structured group which brought together leaders in the field–authors, publishers, academicians, administrators–together with successful practitioners for the discussion and exchange of ideas" (Bryce, *The Living Light* 1975, 281). Bishop Lucker provided the unofficial episcopal presence and was already an established advocate of the new experiential catechesis and the renewal of parish education. He spearheaded the national acceptance of the Confraternity of Christian Doctrine in 1966, serving as its director between 1958 and 1969. The Catechetical Forum published only one article in its history that was jointly penned by its members, "Catechesis for Our Time," which appeared in *Bible Today* and identified its contributing writers as Moran, Ryan, Lucker, and William Reedy. It appealed to an audience of biblical scholars, many of whom were already critical of the salvation history hermeneutic in catechesis for its limited understanding of the relationship between Hebrew and Christian Scriptures with serious implications for Christianity's identity *vis-à-vis*

Judaism (Boys 1980). The authors defended the fundamental relation of biblical theology to catechesis grounded on more existential categories. They wrote:

> [Freedom is] the full development of persons in society with the freedom to love as Christ loves [by] taking account and reflecting [on God's self-revelation] that has been done in the past as the new needs and possibilities for reflecting in the present and the future are opened up by new human thought patterns, new human questions, vocabularies, cultures, etc. (Ryan et al. 1967, 1972)

Ryan's tenure as executive editor of *The Living Light* extended over eight tumultuous years (1964-72) in the ongoing development of catechetical theory following Vatican II. As early as 1966, Ryan redirected the editorial expanse of the journal to explore dimensions of theory and practice in experiential catechesis and the new theology of continuing revelation.

During the same period, Ryan guided *The Living Light* in examining new theories from the social sciences that informed a more enlightened pedagogy. Likewise, the work of feminist scholars had a voice in the journal's pages, thereby contributing to a more critical understanding of biblical knowledge and the cultural conditioning of human ways of knowing. All the while, Ryan held steady the organizing vision of the journal for adult-centered religious education over the lifetime of the believer. Ryan remained firm in her conviction that adult catechesis was not optional but fundamental to the nature of the Christian faith. In 1967, she co-authored with Russell Neighbor, *There's More Than One Way: New Programs and Possibilities in Out-of-School Religious Education*. The work was a collection of previously published *The Living Light* articles that dealt with innovative approaches to adult education. Ryan defined Christianity as a religion for adults, based on its mandate for both personal and social transformation in accordance with gospel values. Adult catechesis, claimed Ryan, is precipitated by "an awareness that Christianity is a religion for adults and the summoning of each Christian to a fuller responsibility for himself and his world" (Ryan and Neighbor 1967, 5).

The Identity Crisis in Religious Education

The aims of religious education expanded a third time to include the social dimension of catechesis. Under the influence of the International Study Weeks (in particular, the 1968 session in Medellin, Colombia) and the appearance of the Synod of Bishops document "Justice in the World" (1971), justice was now considered a constitutive element of the faith, with implications for systematically linking love of God with love of neighbor in all catechetical endeavors. The rapid pace of the changes in catechetical theory since Vatican II was the basis of Ryan's article "Identity Crisis for Religious Education" (1968-69).

Ryan observed that the confusion in parish religious education (an issue familiar to the editors at *The Living Light* through article submissions, letters to the editor, and subscriber research) was the fuzzy identity produced by multiple approaches to catechesis (traditional, kerygmatic, and experiential/social) that were simul- taneously in use in parishes across the country. Even within a particular parish, there were often sharp divisions over the orthodoxy of different catechetical approaches.

Ryan viewed the growing support for a return to the traditional *Baltimore Catechism* model as retrenchment. She urged patience: "We need to appreciate the kind of security it offers adherents [and that] many people still find this a very comforting approach to life's complexities, especially in today's rapidly changing world" (Ryan 1969, 8). Regarding the yielding of the kerygmatic to a more anthropological approach, she explained:

> In this new [experiential] approach then, one might say that the elements of the kerygmatic approach are "changed, not taken away." We find Christ's presence not only in the assembled Christian community, the scriptural word, and in the liturgical celebrations, but also wherever love is present and active and where there is a need of love–and His "sacral" modes of presence are to help us celebrate and discern and respond to his "secular" ones, not the other way around. (1968-69, 11-12)

Ryan acknowledged that the experiential approach might appear to some as inconsistent with Church teaching because it did not lend itself to the traditional method of teaching from the text or the usual separation of content and method. But the major shift, Ryan noted, was the role of the religious educator from the task "to teach people religion to help people think and react as Christian persons" (1968-1969, 13). Ryan made the strong case that the identity problem in religious education was both a cause and a symptom of the lack of professionalism in the field of parish religious education. In her mind, the urgent need for professional standards was stymied by the absence of a more general consensus on the purposes and aims of religious education.

Ryan's most formidable work in consolidating the new directions in Catholic religious education since the time of the Second Vatican Council was *We're All in This Together: Issues and Options in the Education of Catholics* (1972). Ryan's editorial and professional agenda was to identify those educational needs that were still largely unmet by the Church. This dual thrust influenced the continuing trend of Catholic children served by out-of-school religious programs that required more equitable increases in parish funding. The needs of adult religious education were also paramount. Ryan argued that this concern included not only specific education offerings but also the range of parish ministries that were now recognized as formative for adults (e.g,, social justice). To her experienced eye, these ministries must be seen and appreciated as intentional educative forms of parish life and receive adequate financial and personnel support.

Finally, there was Ryan's assessment of the role of the Catholic school. Ryan did not retreat from her original position in *Parochial Schools* that the Church should not be in the business of general education at the primary and secondary levels. However, she did find new life in the old schools' system. In particular, Ryan observed a viable model for Church schools of the future among those urban-based Catholic schools serving the poor in traditionally under-funded public school districts. This model of the Catholic school, Ryan advanced, fulfills a critical mission of the Church in the preferential option for the poor rather than one that merely replicates the public school.

Ryan's Leadership at *PACE*

Ryan's pioneering work on behalf of adult parish education continued after she resigned from *The Living Light* to become editor-in-chief of St. Mary's Press's *Professional Approaches for Christian Educators (PACE)* in 1974. A market large enough to sustain two journals of religious education was indicative of the vibrancy of the field at the time. In this endeavor Ryan rejoined many of her former colleagues, including Moran, Sloyan, Harris, and Groome. Her editorial mission for the journal was to be a leading voice on issues in Christian religious education. Ryan shaped the journal as a hands-on scholarly reference guide for the religious educator.

The catechetical climate of the time had markedly changed since Vatican II. A spate of catechetical documents appeared between the first *General Directory for Catechesis* (GDC) (1971) and the revised *Catechism of the Catholic Church* (1994). During the time of Ryan's leadership at *PACE* (1974-88), the centrality of the adult in faith formation had evolved from its minor status in the *GDC* as a "form of catechesis" to a major focus of Church educational ministry. In the document, *To Teach as Jesus Did* (1972), the U.S. bishops asserted that, "the continuing education of adults is situated not at the periphery of the Church's educational mission but at its center" (43). Other catechetical documents sought to balance life experience and inductive learning with a more systematic presentation of the Christian message. Pope John Paul II's *On Catechesis in Our Time* (1979) affirmed the full integration of method and message: "Nor is any opposition to be set up between a catechesis taking life as the point of departure and a traditional, doctrinal and systematic catechesis" (22).

In 1979, the first national catechetical directory, *Sharing the Light of Faith,* was a watershed document and a model of in-depth conversation within the entire Church. Although the document failed to address significant social issues (i.e., concerning women, cultural diversity, and sexuality), its strengths were found in its holistic approach to catechesis that endorsed the importance of adult lifelong formation in the faith and the need for adaptation of message and method to different ages, experiences, and cultures. *Sharing the Light of Faith* called for a "total catechetical program" comprised of multiple

educational ministries (adults, youth, children, the schools). This
vision resonated with Ryan's editorial direction for *PACE*. Ryan stated:

> [Total religious education] ranges from courses in theology
> and scripture to encounter-type sessions to help persons
> discover their own potentialities and relate to others. To these
> should be added the various encounter movements–Teen
> Encounter groups, Marriage Encounter groups, and others.
> All these, could be designed to foster participants' total
> religious education while achieving their particular objectives.
> (Ryan 1974, 5, 3)

That Ryan guided *PACE* in step with the catechetical
developments in the Church does not mean that she was restricted by
them. Ryan was always open to exploring social/political issues that had
not yet been given adequate coverage in Church teachings. *PACE*
regularly treated the often neglected topics of gender, race, and inter-
religious dialogue. In addition, PACE covered issues concerning
divorced Catholics, single parents, teenage mothers, abortion,
homosexuality and conscientious objection to war. Ryan vigorously
molded *PACE* to communicate an understanding of justice by means
of a hermeneutic of suspicion, critically examining conventional social
and Church wisdom. In her editorial preface to "The Bible, Liberation
and Women," Ryan remarked:

> Today, Catholics with and without a degree in theology need to
> understand what is meant by the historical conditioning of the
> Bible, of doctrinal formulations, and of interpretations of both.
> Agreement on the historical conditioning of our theological
> truths is perhaps the key issue of all the debates that have
> become obvious in the Church today. (Ryan 1987, 18, 4-5)

For Ryan, the professionalism of the religious educator was likewise a
justice issue. The traditional role of lay women volunteers in parish
religious education was radically altered following the Second Vatican
Council and the dramatic decline in vowed women religious as well as
their shift to new apostolic vocations outside of the schools. While lay
women educators increasingly filled the gap, the rapid rise of

professional lay women in religious education occurred without the fleshing out of a new model of the profession. Certification programs, higher education studies, and attendance at regional and national catechetical congresses had yet to draw attention to national standards for intellectual, spiritual and human formation. Likewise, pay scales were at the discretion of pastors, and benefits were often not transferable when a director or coordinator changed employers.

By the late 1980s, Ryan had developed the issue of professionalism for the parish religious education beyond organizational theory. Incisive articles by Thomas Groome, Padraic O'Hare, Maria Harris, Joan Marie Smith, and Gloria Durka reconceptualized the role of the religious educator as a form of lay ministry. While Vatican II had supported the apostolate of the laity in the work of the Church (*Decree on the Apostolate of the Laity*, 1965),   the language of ministry was confined to the ordained of the Church. The seeds of the recognition of lay ministry were planted presciently by Ryan and others at *PACE*. It would be another twenty-five years before the United States bishops acknowledged both the validity of lay ecclesial ministry and the professional formation it required in *Co-Workers in the Vineyard of the Lord* (2005).

Conclusion

The identity of religious education in the Catholic faith tradition of the twentieth century remains incomplete without reference to the full life story of Mary Perkins Ryan. As a Catholic lay woman born into the pre-Vatican II Church, Ryan did not look back nostalgically to times of the past but rather looked forward to a new form of Catholicism that had yet to materialize. She figured prominently in this transformation as a leading voice in the three major Christian religious education movements of the past century. There is perhaps no other figure in American Catholic history who bridged all three movements—liturgical, kerygmatic, and experiential/social. In this way, Ryan stands tall. But she also stood in the company of giants—Gabriel Moran, Gerard Sloyan, Johannes Hofinger, Maria Harris, Gloria Durka, and Thomas Groome. It is true that Ryan lacked the advanced academic and scholarly credentials of her contemporaries, but these missing tassels arguably make her achievements all the more exemplary. In 1985, Ryan was presented with the prestigious Mathis Award from Notre Dame

University for her contributions to modern liturgical reforms of the Church. But it was Ryan's most debated work, *Parochial Schools*, which established her as an educational leader and visionary.

It is common among those who have written about Ryan to commend her prescient prediction that the traditional model of the Catholic school faced a future of struggle (Reidy 2004). But a more balanced evaluation of Ryan's contributions would place emphasis not on her role as critic but rather on her envisioning new forms of Catholic educational life. Old Testament scholar Walter Bruggemann describes it as the capacity of the prophet to "bring the community to fresh forms of faithfulness and vitality" (Bruggemann 1978, 62). When Ryan cried out against the self-perpetuating mindset of Catholic schools that no longer served a post-Vatican II Church, she offered an alternative vision. Ryan envisioned the energized life of the parish community as the center of ongoing adult faith formation. Later, Maria Harris would articulate with even greater precision this idea in *Fashion Me a People: Curriculum in the Church* (1989). Ryan's assertion that the liturgy, and not the schools, should be the central axis of parish education forged the link between instruction and sacramental rites as promulgated in the restored model of the catechumenate (Rite of Christian Initiation for Adults [RCIA]). Since its restoration at Vatican II, this catechetical model has been recognized by the Church as the normative model of all catechesis. Ryan also called for alternative models to Catholic primary and secondary schools. Today, one such alternative model would be the Jesuit program of the Nativity Schools.

Throughout her career, Ryan amplified the voice of women in the twentieth century Church. She did so most directly in her leadership at *The Living Light* and *PACE*. In the pages of these journals, Ryan welcomed women like her, who held no advanced academic credential, into the community of religious educators by giving them a model in her own life's work. In an article eulogizing Ryan, Maria Harris recalled a letter of acceptance from Ryan for her first article in *The Living Light*. Harris wrote, "Ryan put me in touch with the giants of the field" (Harris 1993, 24, 3).

In reclaiming Ryan's rightful place in religious education, we not only restore a critical link to the past but create the means to empower the future. Ryan educated to a new vision of Church that would liberate the role of Catholic education in making accessible a religious way of life in the world. Padraic O'Hare wrote that Ryan, "like so many distinguished Catholics of her time, refused to separate her yearning to live a Christ-life from her allegiance to the Church" (O'Hare 1994, 5). He recalls the words of Godfrey Diekmann, who once characterized Ryan as *mulier fortis*, strong woman. The story of Mary Perkins Ryan tells of the strength of the visionary: one who lives into a new future and transforms the impossible into the inevitable.

Shaping the Christian Century:
The Vision of Gerard Sloyan

PHILIP A. FRANCO

Prominent among the most significant American contributors to Christian education and theology in the last century stands Gerard Stephen Sloyan. Born in 1919 and once proudly proclaiming himself, "a Catholic longer than Pope John Paul II" (Efroymson and Raines 1997, 5), Sloyan is among those few scholars whose progressive work throughout the 1950s and the 1960s, although considered by some to be suspect at first, "contributed to rather than derived from" the Second Vatican Council (Efroymson and Raines 1997, 6). This is a fact Gerard Sloyan himself proudly recounts and boasts as quite accurate.

A prolific writer, Sloyan has made enormous contributions to the fields of religious education, liturgy, scripture studies, moral theology, and other areas over the course of his distinguished and continuing career. Involved in various capacities with ecumenical and interreligious dialogue since their infancy, Sloyan's influence transcends the boundaries of his beloved Catholic Tradition. This chapter attempts to frame a portrait of this highly respected educator and theologian and to assist the reader in appreciating his influence over contemporary Christian education and practice.

Context: The Catholic Church of Sloyan's Youth

As a priest and scholar, Sloyan came of age in the 1940s and grew to prominence in the 1950s, an era notably different from the one experienced by the Church—and surely the whole world—today. Few at the time, particularly in the Catholic Church in America, could have foreseen the profound change waiting on the ecclesial horizon. At the time, Pope Pius XII was reigning in Rome and Catholicism was booming in the United States, with John F. Kennedy poised to carry Catholics into the mainstream of American life.

Many sincerely devout Catholics went about their days "hearing" the Tridentine Mass and offering prayers with myriad indulgences attached. In the classroom, young people dutifully memorized essential passages from their Baltimore Catechisms and worked hard to master basic Catholic doctrines so that they might, in effect, graduate from catechism class and move on to adult Catholic life.

This catechetical climate in which Sloyan found himself coming of age had deep roots in the Tridentine period, influenced by a number of significant factors. Most significant of these factors was the Counter-Reformation emphasis on the teaching of doctrine, usually with an apologetic or even polemic slant. In his work on Catholic educational philosophy, James T. Byrnes outlines this situation:

> From the foundation of the first European universities until the close of the nineteenth century, Catholic educational philosophy (indeed, all Catholic teaching) had rested securely upon Scholastic thought, particularly that of Thomas Aquinas. Spurred on by the "siege mentality" of the Counter-Reformation, the Church saw no need to engage Enlightenment thinkers in debate, nor was it thought that these thinkers had anything to add to the work of the Angelic Doctor, as Aquinas was referred to, or to the Divine Revelation of which the Church was custodian. It was only after observing the major social and intellectual changes of the later nineteenth century that some Catholic intellectuals began to look toward some aspects of Enlightenment thought for answers. (2002, 10)

As these select few intellectuals began exploring Enlightenment ideas, the ordinary magisterium of the Church was seeking to revive and reinforce the use of the scholastic philosophy and theology. Thus, the revival of a Thomistic approach, spurred by Pope Leo XIII's 1879 encyclical, *Aeterni Patris*, which successfully sought a return to scholastic methods according to the mind and method of Saint

Thomas Aquinas, also contributed significantly to the situation in which Sloyan found himself. This Thomistic turn, not without its merits, led to what some would label an arid, overly systematized catechesis, with almost exclusive emphasis on the classroom teaching of doctrine. A certain level of suspicion toward non–Thomistic methods and approaches often accompanied this emphasis, as if somehow Thomism was not only the favored approach to theology but the sole approach for Catholics.

During the twentieth century, as Sloyan was first appearing on the ecclesial scene, theologians around the world, but particularly in France and Germany, were exploring newer ways to engage in theological discourse and to teach the faith. Some theologians were now more willing to entertain different approaches and dialogue with the contemporary sciences in their theological investigations and pedagogical work. They were also willing to dialogue with contemporary philosophical approaches, some of which had been given blanket condemnations by the ordinary magisterium as "modernist errors." The average Catholic in the pew, and not a few clerics as well, were largely unaware of this phenomenon. They assumed that every aspect of the Catholic faith, its practice and transmission, was sacrosanct and immutable.

There were some, however, who possessed the unique ability to read the signs of the times and, in light of these signs, work for changes and adaptations in the way the Church lived and the way the Church educated. Suspect at first, many of these brave and visionary souls would eventually be numbered among the heroes and giants of nineteenth and twentieth century Catholicism. Sloyan himself would eventually note, with a hint of playful sarcasm, that it was these visionaries who were truly responsible for the changes of the Vatican II Council, not the bishops who seemed to think they were the ones accomplishing reform. This is the situation in which Gerard Sloyan found himself as a priest and educator.

Biographical Background

Gerard Stephen Sloyan is a second generation American of Irish decent. He was born into a relatively comfortable family in the Fordham section of the Bronx in New York City. Eventually, after some moves in between, the family settled in Central New Jersey when young Gerard was seven (Efroymson and Raines 1997, 1). Financially, the Sloyans enjoyed the roar of the twenties and endured the depression of the thirties. Like each of us, Sloyan's personal experiences as a child and young adult would have an enormous influence over his later work and philosophical approach.

Sloyan's parents were both educated and professional people. His mother, Marie Virginia Kelley, was particularly influential, as she received a solid education in an age when most women were not permitted a voice in society. She was a graduate of the New York Training School for Teachers, but "her classroom career was brief because in those days at marriage you resigned" (Efroymson and Raines 1997, 1).

Sloyan's father, Jerome James Sloyan, was an engineer who had attended the prestigious Stuyvesant High School in New York City, an alma mater to which he remained dedicated throughout his life. After graduating from Stuyvesant, Jerome Sloyan received a degree from Cornell University and went on to specialize in what was called "scientific dairy farming" in various locations throughout the United States, both before and after World War I. After several other jobs and varying degrees of accomplishment and struggle, the elder Sloyan eventually found success as the owner of Automatic Motor Base Company. During this time, Jerome was successful in building, developing, and marketing "an oil burning unit designed after the jet principle and after that an automatic coal furnace" (Pelletier and Panganiban 2006, 1). Sloyan would later recount, with a strong hint of lament, that his mother never lived to see these more comfortable days for the family (Efroymson and Raines 1997, 2).

Having educated and industrious parents, as well as a financially and geographically mobile childhood, helped to form Gerard Sloyan into a disciplined and studious young man. He and his three sisters, Jean, Elizabeth, and Virginia, were given an education in their younger years by the Sisters of Mercy, who staffed both the grammar and high school that Sloyan attended. Later commenting on the quality of education afforded him by the good sisters in his parish's Saint James Grammar School and Red Bank Catholic High School, Sloyan recalled that the sisters ran "an intelligent, no nonsense operation" (Pelletier and Panganiban 2006, 1).

In retrospect, it was in his family life, centered on schooling and his parish of Saint James, that the seeds for Gerard's vocation to the priesthood were planted and nurtured. The liturgy, in particular, which would remain a love of Gerard's life, was particularly formative. Years later, Sloyan wrote,

> If I were ever to write an autobiography it would mention, somewhat incidentally, that I got an elementary and secondary education, played all the sports indifferently and got to be an Eagle Scout, but mostly was an altar boy. I was so deeply in the Church's offices in my youth that they all but defined me. . . . The only thought that came to me and stayed was: "This is pretty serious business. Some priests do it better than others. I think I'd like to be in group A." (Sloyan 1986, 312)

After these many years of being formed in the context of the lived Christian experience, centered on the Church's public worship that mesmerized him, Sloyan then matriculated at Seton Hall College in South Orange, New Jersey, in 1936 (Pelletier and Panganiban 2006, 2). He looks back on these years of schooling happily as well. It was during these equally impressionable years that Sloyan discerned his vocation to the priesthood and the seeds nurtured earlier by his family and parish life came to bear fruit. It was here that he began to seriously consider joining the seminary, as he encountered more "men like the genial, athletic priests of my parish devoting their lives to study and teaching. This bore looking into" (Efroymson and Raines 1997, 3).

Sloyan has also noted, however, that the curriculum adopted by the institutions he attended was "unimaginative," an insight that was most likely formed retrospectively, in a manner of speaking, by his many years of studying and living the Christian life and being exposed to Christian scholars and their writings. Soon after receiving his education, in fact, Sloyan would begin imaginatively rethinking the manner in which the Church educated its members.

In his second year of college, Sloyan applied and was accepted as a candidate for the priesthood in the Diocese of Trenton, which sent him to the seminary of the Archdiocese of Newark, Immaculate Conception Seminary, located in Darlington, New Jersey (Pelletier and Panganiban, 2006). Sloyan then spent six years in the seminary studying theology, another phase of his education that he describes as "earnest but uninspired, as had been the two years of philosophical study before them" (Efroymson and Raines 1997, 3).

Sloyan was afforded around this same time the unique experience of spending his summer vacations working as both a checker in the local hotel and a cashier behind the bar of a nightclub. This was not typical work for the average young man of his day who was preparing for ordination to the priesthood. Sloyan himself described these jobs as "different worlds" from the seminary (Efroymson and Raines 1997, 3). This, perhaps, gave Sloyan a unique view of the "real world" not often afforded to aspiring clerics of his day. As it was for Karol Wojtyla, the only modern pope to have been a laborer prior to his priestly ordination, these distinctive and formative experiences would soon find their way into Sloyan's thought and approach to ministry.

His summers, however, were not all labor and bartending. They were, in fact, quite significant in the development of his thought. Often, he would spend time during the summers absorbing what was new and cutting edge in the world of theology:

> Sloyan devoted his summers to seminars exercising his zealous intellectual energy and acumen for the theological panorama of the initial waves of European *nouvelle theologie* that drifted across the Atlantic through guest lecturers and professors and directed summer seminars in patristics, Hebrew, the theologies of the Orthodox Churches, and *Fundamental theologie.* (Pelletier and Panganiban 2006, 2)

During these years in the seminary, Sloyan attained the traditional pre-conciliar ecclesial offices, rising to subdeacon and then to the penultimate step in his preparation, the diaconate, in 1943. In 1944, with World War II still raging, Sloyan was ordained a Roman Catholic priest for the Diocese of Trenton, New Jersey (Efroymson and Raines, 1997). A gifted student throughout his academic career, Sloyan was among a small handful of his seminary class chosen to earn the Licentiate in Sacred Theology from the Catholic University of America. Given the University's residency requirements, Sloyan then found himself studying in Washington, D.C., residing in the Theological College of The Catholic University for his last year of formal priestly formation. There, while pursuing the S.T.L., Sloyan met and studied alongside seminarians from around the nation (Pelletier and Panganiban 2006, 3).

Although demonstrating a keen personal interest in education for much of his adult life, as well as a tremendous talent in his studies, Sloyan never sought to study education itself in any formal way. His first official foray into the study of education came, not at his own direct initiative, but when his Ordinary, Bishop William A. Griffin, requested that Sloyan earn a Ph.D. in Education in order to be eventually appointed the diocesan superintendent of schools. As Sloyan suggests in his own personal reflections, those were the days when an episcopal request was synonymous with a binding demand, and so it came to pass exactly as his bishop requested. Sloyan began his studies for the doctorate in Education at The Catholic University of America and would become superintendent over his diocese's twelve high schools and forty elementary schools, all located in central New Jersey (Efroymson and Raines 1997, 4).

Father Sloyan successfully completed his doctorate in Education in 1948, writing a dissertation entitled *Christian Concepts in Social Studies in Catholic Education*. In many ways, this work was an indictment of the state of Catholic education in most traditionally operated Catholic elementary schools, with his diocese of Trenton very clearly included. In his dissertation, Sloyan demonstrated that significant Catholic social values and teachings did not permeate the social studies curriculum. This was the first significant step in Sloyan's call for a new vision of education in the Church. The dissertation, later published under a similar name, offered some significant challenges in regard to social studies teaching in Catholic schools:

> Sloyan drew seven conclusions that challenged the status quo of social studies curriculum on the 1940's. His research revealed that only two of the twenty five elementary social studies curricula integrated Catholic social doctrine. . . . Catholic courses in geography contribute almost nothing to the socialization of the child, . . . history courses seldom include a religious vision of history, . . . [and] racism, as a social reality was not addressed; hence, there was no serious application of the theology of the Mystical Body. . . . Catholic mission activity was presented in isolation from the growth of Christianity. Christianity's contribution to the alleviation of social, cultural and economic ills was not linked to the mission

of the church. . . . Catholic teachers lacked an informed understanding of Catholic social teaching. And, the curriculum guidelines were inadequate. (Pelletier and Panganiban 2006, 5)

Sloyan acknowledged within the dissertation that his criticisms may have seemed harsh or difficult to accept for those in Catholic education, but he saw the criticism as necessary and called for much needed change. In this regard, he noted, "The writer sincerely trusts that such remarks will be taken as merely antiseptic" (Sloyan 1948, 180).

Despite being the original purpose for his pursuing the doctorate, Sloyan's appointment as superintendent of schools for the diocese of Trenton never actually came to pass. After he spent some time in pastoral work as well as in the diocesan schools' office as assistant superintendent, Bishop Griffin died. In 1950, Trenton's new bishop George Ahr acquiesced to the petition of The Catholic University of America to have Sloyan released from diocesan assignment so that he might join their ranks in the Department of Religious Education. It seems Sloyan had left quite an impression on his professors and colleagues while earning his doctorate. Rather than heading a diocesan school system, Sloyan was granted a larger forum in which to work, with the opportunity to share and develop ideas with fellow scholars and students from around the nation and the world. Theoretically at least, this also meant more freedom in which to conduct his work. It was in this capacity as professor and respected author that Sloyan would begin to make his mark in various theological and ecclesial fields, especially the field of religious education.

Sloyan spent seventeen years in his first stint at The Catholic University of America. Upon joining the faculty, Sloyan became part of a groundbreaking and innovative project that offered Religious Studies to non-clerics (Pelletier and Panganiban 2006, 4). He began humbly enough, with the rank of instructor despite his doctorate and a salary of $2,625 per year, plus laundry, room,and board (Efroymson and Raines 1997, 5). At first he taught undergraduate courses in the faith of the Church and Christian Morality, and then only biblical theology. Later, he taught graduate courses on the Gospels (Efroymson and Raines 1997, 5). Sloyan achieved the rank of full professor and was eventually named chairperson of the Department of Religious

Education in 1957. In this capacity he had the good fortune to work with such noted religious education scholars as Mary Charles Bryce, Joseph Jensen, and Berard Marthaler (Swartz 1997, 46). It was during this time that Sloyan became quite influential in his work and writing on religious education:

> In his headship, he actively promoted graduate and undergraduate courses in religion and theology for religious sisters, laymen and women. During his tenure the department progressively became a center for research in the history of religious education and for the preparation of professors and teachers in Catholic schools and religious education programs throughout the United States and the world through missionaries earning graduate degrees. (Pelletier and Panganiban 2006, 6)

In all, during his time at Catholic University "Sloyan produced two books and fifty-three essays and articles in a variety of professional periodicals dealing with religious education and related fields" (Swartz 1997, 55).

In 1967, Sloyan accepted an appointment in the Department of Religion at Temple University in Philadelphia, Pennsylvania. (It is interesting to note that Sloyan's successor at the Catholic University of America was Berard Marthaler, an influential religious educator in his own right. Sloyan brought Marthaler into the Catholic University fold a few years earlier, after a meeting of the two at a convention of the College Theology Society.) Despite his prominence in the field of religious education, Sloyan was apparently unhappy with his work output and sought to leave the administrative dimension of academia behind. Concerning this particular career move, Sloyan wrote,

> My chief motivation was the desire to return to full time teaching and research. I had never left the classroom, despite the demands of ten years in the department's headship; the work of serious scholarship had suffered badly, however. Two extended entries in an encyclopedia and a half dozen journal articles, the bare minimum for academic promotion, were all I had to show for that decade. (Sloyan 1968, 7)

Although his love for Scripture predates this appointment, it was during (and immediately prior to) these years at Temple University that Sloyan would turn his interest, as well as his teaching and writing talents, primarily toward biblical theology and liturgical studies. During this time, he contributed to the development of liturgical practice and understanding emanating from the reforms of the Second Vatican Council. He also immersed himself in contemporary exegesis of Scripture.

Sloyan published *Worship in a New Key: What the Council Says about the Liturgy* in 1966. In this volume he combined his passion for education with his love for liturgy, as well as his desire to educate the average reader about the post-conciliar liturgy and its significance. Sloyan also wrote many works on the importance and meaning of preaching and even tried his hand, successfully, in the area of moral theology, publishing several pieces in this field, most notably *How Do I Know I'm Doing Right? Toward the Formation of a Christian Conscience* (1976). A man of many interests and gifts, he even delved into the realm of Christology, publishing *Jesus in Focus: a Life in its Setting* in 1983. This work examined biblical Christology from the point of view of the ancient culture in which Jesus lived. All these works, although not written specifically on the topic of Christian education, flowed from Sloyan's vision of religious education and his gift of presenting the Christian Faith to the modern person without clinging to outdated methods.

In 1997, as a means of honoring the significant work and contributions of Sloyan, some noteworthy scholars within different branches of Theology and Religious Education penned essays in his honor. The work, entitled *Open Catholicism, The Tradition at Its Best: Essays in Honor of Gerard S. Sloyan* (1997), contains ten essays on various subjects, and lists the various awards and honors afforded to Sloyan throughout his life, such as the *Pro Ecclesia et Pontifice* Medal in 1970, the John Courtney Murray Award in 1981, the *Berakah* Award from the North American Academy of Liturgy in 1986, and the presidency of the College Theology Society, the Catholic Theological Society of America, and the Liturgical Conference (Efroymson and Raines 1997). The collection also includes an extensive bibliography of Sloyan's writings and an introductory chapter by Sloyan himself, entitled "I Was There When Some of It Happened" (1997). This essay recalls his long and continuing career with much humility, occasional hints of well-earned pride and a great deal of happiness and satisfaction in a still active life that has been given over entirely to service of God and the advancement of scholarship.

Contributors to this Festschrift include prominent systematic theologian Elizabeth Johnson and religious educator Gabriel Moran. Topics range from the nature of God to Pope John Paul II's relationship with Islam. Each general topic covered is an area into which Sloyan has, at one time or another, delved. The breadth and depth of the topics covered in the collection are a tribute to the scope and significance of Sloyan's widely respected scholarly work.

Now in his eighties, Sloyan celebrated the sixtieth anniversary of his ordination to the priesthood along with members of his ordination class. Although semi-retired, the indefatigable Sloyan is by no means idle. He continues to write on various issues and has returned to The Catholic University of America with the title of distinguished professorial lecturer. He also teaches courses at Georgetown University.

Formative Influences

As we examine the work and impact of Gerard Sloyan in the field of religious education, it is important to note three distinct and basically contemporaneous movements within the Church, with their roots in the nineteenth century, which greatly influenced Church thinkers and heavily influenced his vision and work. In her dissertation on the work of Sloyan, Alice Marie Swartz notes that these movements or periods were the liturgical movement (1830-1969), the catechetical movement (beginning about 1900), and the modern Catholic biblical movement (beginning about 1940) (Swartz 1997, 4). In order to better understand the context in which he began his work and the motivations behind it, it is necessary to briefly examine each of these movements.

The first movement to influence Sloyan was the liturgical movement. His work in this area has interwoven liturgy and education basically from the beginning, making the liturgy not simply an optional adjunct in the work of Christian education, but an indispensable component of its practice. This is due in great part to the fact that, as mentioned previously, Sloyan himself was socialized into Catholic life primarily through his joyful experiences of the Church's sacred liturgy. It was and remains his firm conviction that one simply cannot engage in true Catholic religious education without putting the students, whoever they may be, in touch with the liturgy. In regard to the educational power of the liturgy, he wrote:

> The Council Fathers of Vatican II have proposed a worldwide program of popular education in the deeper meaning of the Mass. The Mass is of course, at the center of the prayer life of the Church, like the sun in the universe. (Sloyan 1966, 22)

Additionally, Sloyan held that

> Preaching within the liturgy is liturgy. This means that it is not only worship proceeding from man upward; it is also God's incorporative and formative action making the hearers into the living Christ who is forever at work in Glory redeeming us. (Sloyan 1968, 150-51)

With this love for liturgy and his interest in the field of theology, Sloyan was deeply involved in the liturgical movement.

The liturgical reforms of the Second Vatican Council did not suddenly materialize in the minds of the Council bishops. Rather, beginning in the earlier part of the nineteenth century, there was a gradual movement within Catholic circles toward a renewal of liturgy, an appreciation of its history, and a realization of the importance of active participation on the part of the laity. The eventual reforms decreed by the Council were influenced by decades of research and writing by various scholars, many of them Benedictines, such as Abbot Dom Prosper Gueranger, Archabbot Maurus, Abbot Placidus Wolter, and Abbot Idlefons Herwegen (Swartz 1997, 6).

While these monks were attempting to incorporate the Benedictine understanding and rich history of profound liturgical worship and sacred music once again into the Church at large, biblical and patristic scholars were busy reviewing the history and development of the Church's public worship and the manner in which this worship has been practiced and understood over the centuries (Swartz 1997, 6). Of this scholarly academic component to the liturgical movement, the centerpiece was Josef Jungmann's *Missarum Solemnia* (1948), translated into English as *Mass of the Roman Rite*. This highly influential two-volume work traced the development and meaning of the Mass of the Roman Rite (Swartz 1997, 7).

As the twentieth century wore on, scholars began to bring liturgical research and findings to the people, although to be sure this occurred gradually and not without some moments of suspicion. Lambert Beauduin, for example, was a monk who advocated the use of the vernacular language and active participation of the people in the liturgical celebrations. Romano Guardini published *The Spirit of the Liturgy* in 1918, which became a staple of liturgical study. Pope Benedict XVI, prior to his election as pope, published a work that bore the same name in its English translation. He offered this book as a type of homage to Guardini's work, which "inaugurated the liturgical movement in Germany" (Ratzinger 2000, 7). These liturgical ideas, essentially one movement with three distinct components, eventually began to find their way to the United States, where influential journals such as *Orate Fratres* (later called *Worship*) became means through which scholars and clergy in the United States could remain in touch with the liturgical movement throughout the world. Sloyan would be among those who helped to keep such lines of communication open. (For a more detailed look at the manner in which these movements influenced the work of Sloyan, see Swartz 1997.)

All of these efforts began to slowly but surely bear fruit, as the Catholic Church eventually responded with some reforms at the official level. In the early twentieth century various decrees were promulgated by Popes Pius IX and Pius X regarding the renewal of sacred music as well as initiatives for more frequent reception of Holy Communion on the part of the faithful, a practice from which many well-meaning Catholics often felt they needed to abstain. This even included moving the reception of first Holy Communion to the age of reason. Pope Pius XII would continue this trend with the groundbreaking liturgical encyclical, *Mediator Dei* (1947). This was the first encyclical written on the topic of liturgy and certainly the most serious signal from Rome that serious reform was possible and imminent. Many, in fact, would consider this the key that opened the gates for the reforms of the Second Vatican Council. The Council would embrace active participation for the laity and a vernacular celebration, which for years had been considered suspect proposals for reform.

Sloyan was heavily influenced by the liturgical movement. Especially noteworthy, however, was a formative moment that occurred in 1947 shortly after he completed his doctoral studies and was preparing his dissertation. It was then that

> Sloyan had the unforgettable opportunity to attend six weeks of lectures at Catholic University in Washington under the Benedictine, Dom Godfrey Diekmann. For the new Doctor of Philosophy, this was the beginning of a special friendship and a lifelong dedication to the pursuit of liturgy as an essential element permeating and giving scope to Sloyan's various primary foci. (Swartz 1997, 46)

From that moment on, liturgy became essential in all of Sloyan's endeavors. It would be fair to state that among Sloyan's most significant contributions to religious education was his insistence, along with that of other scholars, upon the essential place of liturgy in the work of religious education. Eventually, he was granted the prestigious Berekah Award in 1986, bestowed by the North American Liturgical Conference. Self-taught yet characteristically humble, Sloyan noted that he felt himself to be, " a little bit of a goose among swans, namely, a practicer of the art of public worship without any formal training in its history or theory" (Sloyan 1986, 305).

The second movement to directly influence Sloyan's vision and work was the catechetical movement, which both historically and in the thought of Sloyan was intimately connected to the liturgical movement (Swartz 1997, 19). An increased emphasis on Church history and knowledge of the development of doctrine and its transmission led many scholars of Christian education to become increasingly dissatisfied with the question-and-answer catechism methods so prevalent in the Church (Swartz 1997, 19). Influential thinkers such as Jungmann and Hofinger began to propose newer, creative ways of passing on the faith, such as the kerygmatic approach. Many educators were turning to psychology for assistance in developing more appropriate student-centered, effective catechetical methods (Swartz 1997, 18-19). Sloyan himself would become a major player in this movement that had a significant influence upon the field of religious education.

Finally, Sloyan was influenced by the modern Catholic biblical movement, which opened the doors for Catholic scholars to examine Scripture in the light of modern historical and literary means and methods. Throughout the theological world, particularly in non-Catholic circles, scholars were examining the Bible in light of contemporary understandings and approaches to history, textual criticism, interpretation and translation. This led to newer and deeper understandings of the historical context of Scripture. In particular, it brought about numerous questions regarding the historicity of certain aspects of the Bible as well as the dating and purported authorship of its books.

Although at first very suspicious of scientific techniques of studying and interpreting sacred Scripture, the magisterium of the Catholic Church eventually, particularly under Pope Pius XII, became more accepting of modern scholarship. With the promulgation of the encyclical, *Divino Afflante Spiritu* (1947), Pius XII definitively offered scholars the possibility of engaging in scientific examination of the Scriptures in order to better understand their historical context:

> Pius XII announced that the time for fear was over and that Catholic scholars should use modern critical methods in their exegesis. This permission along with the permission to translate the Bible from the original languages was an invitation to Catholic scholars to begin to write freely and catch up with Protestant scholarship. (Swartz 1997, 28-29)

The biblical movement led the way for a greater emphasis on Scripture and renewed interest in its study, as endorsed by the decrees of Second Vatican Council.

The biblical movement helped to shape Sloyan's vision of religious education, as he advocated increased incorporation of sacred Scripture into religious education at all levels. Rather than a simple "add on" to catechetical endeavors, Scripture in Sloyan's view and that of an increasing number of religious educators had to be foundational for authentic religious education to take place.

These three movements, distinct but certainly connected, are essential in understanding the "movements," in a manner of speaking, of Gerard Sloyan's career and writings. In many ways his work in the areas of liturgy and scripture continued his profound educational work. Sloyan envisioned true Christian education as essentially encompassing each of these areas. He truly believes and continues to live his oft-repeated contention that "liturgical, educational, biblical, spiritual and ecumenical apostolates are interrelated" (Swartz 1997, 47).

Contributions to Religious Education

Few could doubt that Sloyan is one of the most significant contributors to religious education of the twentieth century and that his efforts continue to influence religious education at the present time. While his work eventually grew beyond education in the faith, the focus in this section will be on what can be called his fundamental contributions to religious education and catechesis, both within the Catholic Church and within the Christian community at large. In the outline of Sloyan's contributions that follows several prominent themes will be highlighted.

Reading the Signs of the Times

During the 1950s and 1960s, Sloyan was at the forefront of major developments in the field of catechetics and religious education. He advocated and worked for reforms and improvements in theory and praxis before these were widely accepted, particularly in the United States. In the Foreword to one of Sloyan's early books, Sloyan is described as

> The man who presides over the Department of Religious Education at Catholic University in Washington, D.C., and who has been largely instrumental in changing the entire approach of teaching religion in the United States is Father Gerard S. Sloyan. His one goal is to renovate for U.S. Catholics an outdated, inadequate, often defeatist approach to the teaching of religion. (Sloyan, 1966)

From the earliest days of his career, therefore, Sloyan was seen as a ground-breaking educator who was introducing significant changes into the Church.

Sloyan was inspired in this crusade by his keen interest in and familiarity with the catechetical movement and by the work of his counterparts in European religious education who were the heirs to the founders of this movement, such as Jungmann and Hofinger. Sloyan was one of the people through whom the United States caught up with the rest of the catechetical world. In various articles such as "Catechetical Roundup" and "The International Study Week on Mission Catechetics," Sloyan kept American religious educators abreast of significant trends and writings. His first major contribution to the field, *Shaping the Christian Message: Essays in Religious Education* (1950), is further evidence of this fact. It is filled with essays from influential European religious educators whose ideas and concepts Sloyan was introducing to American readers. A decade after its publication, in reflecting on its significance in the changing approach to religious education, Sloyan wrote:

> At the time of its appearance a few of its contributors were already known in this country–Hoffinger, Jungmann, Drinkwater and Weigel–the greater number like Colomb, Coudreau, Boyer, Decluve, Ranwez and Crichton were new names to an American readership. (1968, 7)

Furthermore, the work was significant in its use of the term "religious education," not yet widely used among Roman Catholics. In a testimony to Sloyan's foresight and influence, the term appeared prominently in the title of this volume. In regard to the late arrival of educational progress in the United States at the time, Sloyan observed:

> At the time of its appearance . . . the term, 'religious education' was not widely used in the Roman Catholic community. Few were acquainted with the fifty-five-year-old interconfessional association and its journal of that title, whereas only a slightly larger number had heard of an academic department of that name in Washington associated with educators like Russell and Sheehy, Cooper, Kirsch and Dowd. . . . "Catechetics" was still largely a seminary word ten years ago. (1968, 8)

In the pioneering collection, Sloyan, along with his colleagues, advocated a broader approach to Christian education and sought to achieve much of what would eventually come to fruition during and after the Second Vatican Council. This broader approach had not yet found favor in Catholic circles. Nevertheless, Sloyan held that "every Christian has the freedom to work for the improvement of a situation in the Church provided he has the needed knowledge and can bring his reform to the attention of those who have jurisdiction" (Sloyan 1958, 9). Sloyan did just that. He used his vast knowledge to advocate reforms and bring these needs to those with "jurisdiction," and eventually saw positive results. His concern in this endeavor was not to demean all that had gone before, but rather, in light of his knowledge of Church history, to demonstrate that the older methods were no longer relevant or effective in the modern experience of Catholic Christians. His purpose was to examine "not how right was what went before, but how right is it in the present, and [how right] will it be in the immediate future" (Sloyan 1968, 8-9).

Christ-Centered Religious Education: The Kerygmatic Approach

Sloyan argued for a more person-centered, humanistic approach to the ministry of Christian education. Rather than assuming that all modern modes of thought were heretical and to be avoided, Sloyan warmly embraced humanistic thought. Concerning the importance of understanding the students being taught, Sloyan wrote that "We are hampered from clear thought in catechetics, however, until we have got some notion of the complexity of the child's nature" (Sloyan 1958, 10).

Influenced in great part by the ideas of Johannes Hofinger, Sloyan was therefore among those who moved from a very traditional method of doctrinally based, question-and-answer catechesis to what is commonly called the kerygmatic approach. *Kerygma* in Greek means, "proclaiming the message" (Buchanan 2005, 23). This method of catechesis is a Christ-centered approach, and Sloyan was among its most effective and passionate promoters, particularly in the United States. The kerygmatic approach does not deny the importance of having students come to know doctrine, but its primary focus is putting the student into contact with Christ, stressing the importance of knowing the core message of Christianity (Buchanan 2005, 23). Much greater emphasis is therefore placed upon liturgical and sacramental catechesis than on memorization of doctrinal formulas found in the catechism.

Sloyan discussed the kerygmatic approach in the journal *The Living Light*, saying, "Kerygma is an 'address,' a 'speaking to,' not primarily a matter of communicating religious doctrine or providing information about historical events concerned with salvation" (Sloyan 1965, 103). For Sloyan and others who shared his passion for this particular approach to religious education, the Church's efforts to pass on the faith had become bogged down in poor methodology, theological non-essentials, and a profoundly inadequate vision of the Church in the modern world. In 1962, standing at the threshold of conciliar change, Sloyan boldly stated:

> The basic problem is that the clear lineaments of our biblical and Catholic faith have been blurred somewhat by uncertain unintended omissions and stresses on the accidental. At times, human language has been substituted for the divine speech of the Scriptures, in speaking of the mighty works of God. We have made available in the Church, again unwittingly, a view of the mystery of salvation that is a pale and bloodless copy of the actual deed of God. The Church has been faithful to her master of course; by definition she must be or she is not his Church. But this fidelity, which is undeniable, has not always been paralleled by a concern to go direct to hearts with the challenge comprised by the person of Christ in his redemptive and mediatory role. (1962, 332)

In light of this view, Sloyan felt it necessary and beneficial to encourage the use of the kerygmatic approach. Sloyan then went on,

> (1) Search for the form in which the Apostles first preached faith in Jesus in the "Acts of the Apostles" but also in the writings of Paul. (2) Read Paul's letters to learn what he has to say about God's eternal plan to bring all of us to Himself in Christ. (3) Study all that it means to Paul to be a new man in Christ. This is the heart of Christian morality. (4) Master the teachings of Jesus by turning to the Gospels. Deliberate often on Jesus as the fulfillment of all prophecy, His stance on the relation to the Law, the Prophets and the Writings. (5) Read all of sacred history itself. (Swartz 1997, 58)

This thoroughly Christocentric and biblical approach was clearly a shift from the established methods and theories of catechesis in the Roman Catholic tradition, particularly the traditional catechism that had become such a staple of the American Catholic experience.

This method of engaging in religious education did indeed become influential and popular among religious educators. In 1962,

> The editors of the symposium on "Kerygmatic Catechetics" in the journal, *Religious Education* pointed out to its readers that, "We can see the fruits of a revolution in religious education within the Roman Catholic Church. . . . Partly it is a change in educational theory and methods, but chiefly it is a new emphasis on the place of *kerygma* or proclamation. The Bible tells a story in such a way that the one who hears the story also hears the Word of God for him." (Swartz 1997, 56)

Sloyan himself wrote the lead article for the symposium and spent considerable time justifying and further explaining the recent acceptance of the kerygmatic approach by many Roman Catholics of the day.

Although quite influential at the time, it was not long before other prominent religious educators, including Sloyan's own student Gabriel Moran, would sharply critique this kerygmatic approach (Elias 2002, 211). Even Sloyan himself eventually became ambivalent toward the approach, without altogether rejecting it or changing his views: "He was concerned about its becoming a fad. He had a fear of the lack of length and breath of study, and its claims of newness" (Swartz 1997, 58).

A Forward Thinking Knowledge of the Past

As far as the practical means of achieving the goals of Christian education, Sloyan, in light of the methods he endorsed, clearly argued against the traditional use of question-and-answer catechisms that had become so closely associated with Catholic religious education in the United States. For Sloyan, such catechisms were part and parcel of the myopic view of religious education and obviously incompatible with the kerygmatic approach. He referred to the revered *Baltimore Catechism*, used in Roman Catholic catechetical work throughout the

United States up to and beyond the Second Vatican Council, as a, "painfully inadequate book" (Sloyan 1968, 19). He consistently and loudly proclaimed that the, "exclusive use of the question and answer method is a pedagogical straight jacket" (Sloyan 1968, 16).

While many educators may have assumed that the catechism was the sole acceptable method of passing on the faith, Sloyan knew that this method was neither ancient nor was it being used as originally intended. In *Shaping the Christian Message*, Sloyan wrote:

> In concept, the catechism is a doctrinal handbook prescribed by bishops as a guide to their clergy in providing a pulpit catechesis. It has inevitably made its way into the hands of children as both the first outline of faith presented to them . . . and the last summary many of them see of religious knowledge. This is a development no more than four centuries old, that each child should have a summary of doctrine in the form of a handbook for his own use. (Sloyan 1958, 11)

Armed with this knowledge of Church history, Sloyan avoided ahistorical conservatism, and argued that the catechism was by no means synonymous with religious education. There was, therefore, the possibility of change and a broader, less academic approach.

For Sloyan, what was necessary was an approach to the passing on the faith that did not confine Christianity to a mere intellectual pursuit, and certainly not to a question-and-answer catechism. He said, "Nothing is worse than telling someone that something is joyful when you have not put him in contact with the source of that joy" (Sloyan 1968, 16). What then, should be used instead of the Catechism? Sloyan advocated books and methods that utilized the kerygmatic approach which would

> highlight the love of God who created us and sent his Son to save us and who sent the Spirit to remain with us in the living Church. Such a volume would bring out the nature of Christian life as a loving response to the love of God." (Sloyan 1968, 19)

He was seeking to take Christian education from the arid exercise of memorization to a context of lived Christian experience. Sloyan advocated religious education that was faithful to the Tradition of the

Church, rooted firmly in Scripture, and proclaimed in a manner understandable by a contemporary audience.

As a student of Church history, particularly the history of the Church's educational mission, Sloyan understood clearly that what was often canonized as the one and only method of passing on the faith was in fact a method very much influenced and changed by different periods in Church history. He consistently reiterated that the catechism method, as it was practiced in the mid-twentieth century, was by no means one that dated back to the early Church:

> It is simply false to say that there are no substantial changes required by modern catechetics, merely an updating of catechisms long in use by the addition of biblical and liturgical elements. In many cases the shape imposed on the Christian message by these handbooks in question and answer form is quite foreign to the spirit of the Bible and the liturgy. Hence the work of the whole Church is to make the Gospel in all its purity available to children and adults on optimum pedagogical terms, so that when they gather in liturgical assembly they will know the holiness of all they do there. (Sloyan 1958, 45)

This was in response to those who sought to maintain the use of catechisms and simply "add on" a biblical and liturgical dimension.

Sloyan believed that Christian education could no longer rely on medieval and Tridentine modes of teaching and learning, because the Christian world was no longer functioning in such a manner. Whereas former modes of imparting the Christian message may have had their value in their day, the seeds of secularization, which had already begun to take root in the 1950s, made it clear that newer and more comprehensive approaches were necessary. Sloyan charged, "A further hindrance to fruitful catechetical action is ignorance of the profound inroads made by 'dechristianized' modes of thought" (Sloyan 1958, 10). Catechesis that took place exclusively in the confines of the conventional classroom assumed that the young person's life was being lived in a thoroughly Christian context. Therefore, catechesis was envisioned narrowly as a means of imparting the doctrines in a total Christian atmosphere. Sloyan realized this assumption was simply not the case and therefore different educational approaches were necessary.

Sloyan and Higher Education

Gerard Sloyan did not limit his work and ideas to commentary upon the teaching of religion in the classroom or in parish situations. Always aware of the bigger picture, he clearly understood that if Christian education was to change and improve in his day, the manner in which the educators themselves were educated also needed to be updated and improved. Moreover, the manner in which educators were educated needed not only to improve in quality, but had to be made available for an increasing number of laypersons who were accepting a call to catechetical ministry. If Catholic Christians were to be formed in various ways through the liturgical, sacramental, and catechetical experiences, then those who were planning and facilitating these experiences needed also to be familiar with modern means of education and catechesis. This kind of education meant quality theological and catechetical courses for students besides ordained clergy and the occasional religious sister or brother. While there is little difficulty in finding such programs marketed to laypersons today, such courses were quite scarce before and immediately after the Council.

In advocating for greater academic freedom within Catholic institutions, Sloyan lamented:

> The largest number of those who teach theology in Catholic college continue to be priests with seminary educations who have not had the opportunity to do further study. It is sometimes remarked that the seminary was not helpful in making them pedagogues, but this does not comprise nearly the weakness afforded by the inferior quality of theological education in certain seminaries. Some of the best theology teachers in the Catholic colleges are priests with only seminary education and non-clerics who hold Master's degrees in this discipline by the summer route. . . . The fact remains after thirteen years of the existence of SCCTSD (which changed its name to the College Theology Society in March, 1967) the profession of college theology teaching in Roman Catholic circles is not one that is at ease. Its inadequate preparation continues almost undiminished. (Sloyan 1968, 97)

Probing this problem more deeply, Sloyan discussed the level of academic freedom existing within the Church. The reader cannot help but notice throughout Sloyan's comments on the subject a hint of personal frustration: "There is still nothing resembling full academic freedom in Catholic theological circles except under such an umbrella as the concept 'university' can provide" (Sloyan 1968, 103).

Sloyan's Personal Faith

While Sloyan was and remains a progressive thinker and a groundbreaking reformer in the field of religious education and beyond, his work has never failed to radiate a deep and abiding love for the Church and the Catholic Tradition. In fact, Sloyan has never failed to admit that "It was the Catholic Church that made me, through its incarnation in this country over the present century" (Efroymson and Raines 1997). His work, like the methodology of religious education he championed, is centered firmly on faith in Jesus Christ. This faith, far from being closed or defensive, has led him to collaborate with and appreciate various faiths through his involvement in the ecumenical and interreligious movements.

Even before and after Vatican II, Sloyan has seen himself not as a radical in some negative or anti-institutional sense, but as a reformer who was seeking to assist the Church, particularly with regard to the Church's educational mission, in becoming what it was (and is) meant to be. A perusal of Sloyan's work reveals that he never lost sight of the understanding of the role of religious education within the Church as a form of ministry and that he always maintained an intellectual and experiential balance in describing its essence.

In a pre-conciliar article published in *Worship*, entitled "The International Study Week on Mission Catechetics," for example, Sloyan identified what he describes as the first principle of modern catechetics, namely, that "Catechesis carries out the command of Christ to proclaim God's message of salvation to all men" (Sloyan 1960, 49). Furthermore, in a 1957 article in *Worship* entitled, "The Eucharist and the Aims of Christian Education," Sloyan emphasized that the Eucharist is essential in the work of religious education. This should be the focus of those being educated as well as those who are the educators. He counseled that the Eucharist should be the very center of academic life and teaching: "The Eucharist worthily taken results in a gradual transforming union, imperceptible to the bodily senses, by which Christ is formed in us, in our ideas and thoughts, our ideals and convictions, our desires and choices" (Sloyan 1957, 313). While this Eucharistic teaching is by no means novel, it does clearly demonstrate Sloyan's firm belief in the importance of Christ-centered Christian education that leads the student not merely to intellectual knowledge or understanding of doctrines, but to Christ himself.

Perhaps one of the greatest insights into Sloyan's understanding of religious education–his understanding of all human endeavors–is his expression of this unambiguous faith and belief in religious education, one that is guided not merely by men and women but by the Lord. Sloyan reminds us, "The supreme blunder would be to forget that all religious education is primarily the work of the Holy Spirit, the 'interior master.' Consequently, His is the final word, as it was the first on Pentecost Day" (Sloyan 1958, 10).

Sloyan's Legacy

The contributions of Gerard Sloyan to religious education and catechetics have been as follows: 1) Sloyan possessed the ability to read the signs of the times and engage in dialogue with the modern world and modern modes of thought in the areas of philosophy, theology and the sciences; 2) Sloyan understood and advocated for a truly Christ-centered religious education, as opposed to the various emphases of counter-reformation catechesis. He championed the "kerygmatic approach"; 3) he was among the champions of the proper integration of liturgy and scripture into religious education; 4) he contributed his forward-thinking approaches to religious education praxis; and 5) he understood that religious education seeks to put the person into contact with Jesus Christ. He was and remains motivated by a love for Christ and the Church and a sincere concern for the faithful and intellectual transmission of the Gospel in the modern world.

In all fields of human endeavor there arise from time to time those who, despite opposition or suspicion, recognized and faced the challenges of their day, leaving the world a better place than the one they entered. Gerard Stephen Sloyan, still active and vibrant more than six decades after his ordination as a priest, is one of those rare few.

Sloyan was among the voices of reform in the field of religious education, and his voice resonated throughout the areas of liturgy, Scripture, and ecumenism. It still can be heard today.

Sloyan, along with other reformers, can rightly claim that their contributions to Vatican II helped to redefine the Church in the twentieth century. He spent much of his career helping to articulate and implement these reforms. For this, all those in the work of religious education, regardless of the perspective from which they operate, owe him a debt of gratitude.

Sloyan describes himself as being simply, "a guy who was around. . . . My sole distinction is that I have been 'around' with some splendid men and women, discussing the most important things imaginable in our short life" (Efroymson and Raines 1997, 8). In many ways, the world of religious education today is profoundly altered from the one he entered six decades ago. Many may argue that what remains is an entirely different world. Sloyan, despite his modest regard of his own impact, certainly deserves to be counted among those pedagogical and theological architects who skillfully constructed this new world, with Christ, rather than a catechism, as the center around which it revolves.

Today's Catholic educators widely accept an encompassing vision of religious education which invites the person into the Christian community through the intimate experience of Christ's people. Even official documents of the Catholic Church advocate an approach to religious education that is Christ-centered and transcends the once stifling boundaries of a traditional catechesis. *The Baltimore Catechism*, while remaining an important sacred symbol for some, has in most cases taken been relegated to the annals of educational history. Even with the promulgation of the new universal Catechism in the 1990s, most classrooms remain devoid of a question-and-answer system of memorization. All Christians are indebted to Father Sloyan for his singular ability to read the signs of the times and to move others to do likewise.

References

Allard, Jean-Louis. 1982. *Education for freedom: The philosophy of education of Jacques Maritain.* Ottawa, Canada: University of Ottawa Press.

_____. 1995. La presence et le rayonnement de Maritain au Canada Français. *Cahiers Jacques Maritain* 31: 41-50.

AMHSH. The Archives of the Mission Helpers of the Sacred Heart, Towson, MD.

Appleby, R. Scott, Patricia Byrne and William L. Portier, eds. 2004. *Creative fidelity: American Catholic intellectual traditions.* New York: Orbis Books.

Augustine of Hippo. 1946. *The first catechetical instruction (De catechizandis rudibus).* Trans. Joseph P. Christopher. Westminster, MD: Newman Press.

_____. 1995a. *Against the academicians and the teacher.* Trans. Peter King. Indianapolis, IN: Hackett Publishing.

_____. 1995b. *Teaching Christianity (De doctrina Christiana): Works of Saint Augustine,* vol. 11. Trans. Edmund Hill. Hyde Park, NY: New City Press.

_____. 2007. *Confessions of Augustine.* Ed. Michael P. Foley. Introduction by Peter Brown. Trans. F.J. Sheed. Indianapolis: Hackett Publishing.

Avanzini, Guy. 1978. *Des finalités introuvables in la pédagogie au XXe siècle.* Toulouse: Privat.

_____. 1996. *Unitè et diversitè de la pédagogie chrétiene, in pédagogies chrétiennes, pedagogues chrétiens.* Actes du colloque d'Angers–septembre 1995. Paris: Éd. Don Bosco.

Bandas, Rudolph G. 1935. *Religion teaching and practice.* New York: Joseph F. Wagner.

Barger, Robert Newton. 1976. John Lancaster Spalding: Catholic educator and social emissary. Ph.D. diss., University of Illinois at Urbana-Champaign.

Basil of Caesarea. 1933. *Address to young men on reading Greek literature*. Ed. Roy De Ferrari. Cambridge, MA: Classical Library.

Beaudoin, David M. 1988. A personalist approach to catechetics. *Worship* 62, 237-49.

_____. 1989. Dom Virgil Michel on liturgy, catechesis and social reconstruction: Implications for Catholic education. *Living Light* 25: 232-42.

Beauduin, Lambert. 1926. *Liturgy the life of the church*. Trans. Virgil Michel. Collegeville, MN: Liturgical Press.

Blanshard, Paul. 1949. *American freedom and Catholic power*. Boston: Beacon Press.

Borgatta, E. F. and Neil G. McCluskey, eds. 1980. *Aging and society: Current research and policy perspectives*. Thousand Oaks, CA: Sage Publications.

Boys, Mary C. 1980. *Biblical interpretation in religious education: A study of the kerygmatic era*. Birmingham, AL: Religious Education Press.

_____. 1989. *Maps and visions: Educating in the faith*. Lima, OH: Academic Renewal.

Braun, William P. 1969. Monsignor Edward A. Pace: Educator and philosopher. Ph.D. diss., The Catholic University of America.

Bréhier, Émile. 1932. *Histoire de la philosophie. Tome premier: L'antiquité et le moyen age*. Paris.

Bressolette, Michel et Mougel, René. 1995. *Jacques Maritain face à la modernité*, Colloque de Cerisy. Toulousse: Presses Universitaires du Mirail.

Bruggemann, Walter. 1978. *The prophetic imagination*. Minneapolis, MN: Fortress Press.

Brunner, Fernand. Chairman. 1975. Opening Address in Actes du XVI ᵃ *Congrès des sociétés de philosophie de langue Français*. Reims, September 3-6, 1974, *La Culture*, VanderNauwelaerts, 5.

Bryce, Mary Charles. 1970. The influence of the catechism of the third plenary council of Baltimore on widely used elementary religion textbooks from its composition in 1885 to its 1941 revision. Ph.D. diss., The Catholic University of America.

_____. 1975. Mary Perkins Ryan. *The Living Light* 9: 276-81.

_____. 1978. Four decades of Roman Catholic innovators. Special issue, *Religious Education* 73: S-36-S-57.

_____. 1985-86. Pioneer women in catechetics. *The Living Light* 22: 313-24.

Bryk, Anthony S., Valerie E. Lee, and Peter B. Holland. 1993. *Catholic schools and the common good.* Cambridge, MA: Harvard University Press.

Buchanan, Michael. 2005. Pedagogical drift: The evolution of new approaches and paradigms in religious education. *Religious Education* 100: 20-37.

Buetow, Harold A. 1970. *Of singular benefit: The story of Catholic education in the United States.* New York: Macmillan.

Byrnes, James Thomas. 2002. *John Paul II & educating for life: Moving toward a renewal of Catholic educational philosophy* New York: Peter Lang.

Cantor, Nicholas. 1993. *The civilization of the middle Ages.* New York: Harper Collins.

Cantwell, Thomas S. 1949. A comparative study of the theories of self-activity and religion according to very reverend Thomas E. Shields and Monsignor George W. Johnson. Ph.D. diss., The Catholic University of America.

Caronti, Emmanuele. 1926. *The spirit of the liturgy.* Trans. Virgil Michel. Collegeville, MN: The Liturgical Press.

Cassata, Maria Letizia. 1953. *La pedagogia di Jacques Maritain.* Palermo: Boccone del Povero.

Castle, E. B. 1958. *Educating the good man.* New York: Collier Books.

Catechetics. December 1908. *American Ecclesiastical Review* 39: 705.

Ceremonies of the golden sacerdotal jubilee of his grace John Lancaster Spalding, titular Archbishop of Sciotopolis. 1913. Chicago.

Clanchy, M. T. 1997. *Abelard: A medieval life.* Cambridge, MA: Blackwell.

Clement of Alexandria. 2004. *The instructor.* Whitefish, MT: Kessinger Publishing.

Clement, Carol Dorr. 2000. Catholic foremothers in American catechesis. *The Living Light* 37: 55-68.

Commission on American Citizenship of the Catholic University of America. 1943. *Better men for better times.* Washington, DC: The

Catholic University of America. Acknowledgment is given to George Johnson and Robert Slavins, who collaborated with him in its formulation.

Cosgrove, Rev. J.J. 1960. *Most Reverend John Lancaster Spalding: First bishop of Peoria.* Mendota, IL: The Wayside Press.

Cross, Robert D. 1974. Recent histories of U.S. Catholic education. *History of Education Quarterly* 14: 125-30.

Curti, Merle. 1935. *The social ideas of American educators.* New York: Charles Scriber's Sons.

Cyril of Jerusalem. 1986. *Lectures on the Christian sacraments: The procatechesis and the five mystagogical catecheses.* Ed. Frank L. Cross. Yonkers, NY: St. Vladimir Press.

Deferrari, Roy, J. 1964. *A complete system of Catholic education is necessary.* Boston: Sisters of Saint Paul Press.

De Hovre, Franz. 1934. *Catholicism in education: A positive exposition of the Catholic principles of education with a study of the philosophical theories of some leading Catholic educators.* New York: Benziger Brothers.

De la Salle, Jean Baptiste. 1996. *The conduct of the Christian schools (Lasallian sources).* Landover, MD: Lasallian Publications.

Dewey, John. 1916. *Democracy and education.* New York: Scribner.

_____. 1938. *Experience and education.* New York: Scribner.

Donohoe, John. 1958. *St. Thomas Aquinas and education.* New York: Random House.

Driscoll, Jeremy. 2000. Monastic culture and the Catholic intellectual tradition. In *Examining the Catholic intellectual tradition*, Ed. Anthony J. Cernera and Oliver J. Morgan. Fairfield, CT: Sacred Heart University Press.

Durand, Jean-Dominique. 1998. Le gran attaque de 1956. *Cahiers Jacques Maritain* 30: 2-31.

Efroymson, David & John Raines, eds. 1997. *Open Catholicism: The tradition at its best. Essays in honor of Gerard S. Sloyan.* Collegeville, MN: The Liturgical Press.

Elias, John L. 1976. *Conscientization and deschooling: Freire's and Illich's proposals for reforming society.* Philadelphia: Westminster Press.

_____. 1995. *Philosophy of education: Classical and contemporary.* Malabar, FL: Krieger Publishing Company.

_____. 1999. Whatever happened to Catholic philosophy of education? *Religious Education* 94: 92-110.

_____. 2002. *A history of Christian education: Protestant, Catholic, and Orthodox perspectives.* Malabar, FL: Krieger Publishing Company.

_____. 2004. Catholics in the REA, 1903-1953. *Religious Education* 99: 225-346.

Ellis, John Tracy. 1961. *John Lancaster Spalding: First bishop of Peoria, American educator.* Milwaukee, WI: The Bruce Publishing Company.

Evans, Joseph W. and Leo R. Ward. 1995. *The social and political philosophy of Jacques Maritain.* New York: Charles Scribner's Sons.

Evans, J. W. 2003. Shields, Thomas Edward. *New Catholic Encyclopedia.* Vol. 13, 2nd ed. Detroit, MI: Gale.

Fecher, Charles A. 1953. *The philosophy of Jacques Maritain.* Westminster, MD: The Newman Press.

Fillot, Philippe. 2007. Jacques Maritain: l' éducation à la croisèe des chemins. *Le journal des chercheurs,* (May). (http: www.barbier-rd.nom.fr/journal/article.php3?id_article=559 (accessed May 24, 2007).

Florian, Michel. 2002. Jacques Maritain en Amérique du Nord. *Cahiers Jacques Maritain* 45: 7-28.

Fraile, Guillermo. 1956. *Historia de la filosofia.* Cristianos, vol. 1. Madrid: Biblioteca de Autores.

Franklin, R.W. 1988. Virgil Michel: An introduction. *Worship* 62: 194-201.

_____. and Robert L. Spaeth. 1988. *Virgil Michel: American Catholic.* Collegeville, MN: The Liturgical Press.

Fuller, Edmund, ed. 1957. *The Christian idea of education.* New Haven, CT: Yale University Press.

Galeazzi, Giancarlo. 1999. *Jacques Maritain un filosofo per il nostro tempo.* Milano, Italia: Editrice Massimo.

Gallagher, Donald and Idella Gallagher, eds. 1963. *The education of man: The educational philosophy of Jacques Maritain.* Notre Dame, IN: Notre Dame University Press.

Gallin, Alice. 2000. *Negotiating identity: Catholic higher education since 1960.* Notre Dame, IN: University of Notre Dame Press.

Gatterer, M. and F. Krus. 1924. *Theory and practice of the catechism.* Trans. J.B. Culemans. New York: Frederick Pustet.

Gibbons, James Cardinal. 1916. *Silver jubilee of the Catholic University: A retrospect of fifty years.* Baltimore: John Murphy Company.

Gibreau, Dawn. December 10, 1933. Fr. Virgil Michel, St. John's monks spread idea that liturgy creates community. *National Catholic Reporter*. www.fdle.org/Liturgy_Resources/LITURGICALMOVE MENT-VirgilMichel. htm (accessed on November 26, 2007).

Gillespie, C. Kevin. 2001. *Psychology and American Catholicism: From confession to therapy?* New York: Crossroad Publishing Company.

Gilson, Étienne. 1944. *Le Thomisme: Introduction à la philosophie de Saint Thomas d'Aquin*. Paris.

Gleason, Philip. 1981. A browser's guide to American Catholicism. *Theology Today* 38: 1-14.

———. 1995. *Contending with modernity. Catholic higher education in the twentieth Century*. New York: Oxford University Press.

Grollmes, Eugene E. 1969. The educational theory of John Lancaster Spalding: The ideal of heroism. Ph.D. diss., Boston College.

Hardy, William. 2005. Catholic education in the USA. http://www.dioceseofcheyenne.org/history/WY_Cath_Schools_ Hardy_3_Cheyenne_Deanery.html 2005.

Harris, Maria. 1994. Telling a woman's life. *Professional Approaches for Christian educators* 24: 3-4.

Hellman, John. 1981. *Emmanuel Mounier and the new Catholic left. 1930-1950*. Toronto: University of Toronto Press.

Hellwig, Monica. 2000. The Catholic intellectual tradition in the Catholic university. In *Examining the Catholic intellectual tradition*, ed. Anthony J. Cernera and Oliver J. Morgan. Fairfield, CT: Sacred Heart University Press.

Hirschberger, Johannes. 1958. *The history of philosophy, Vol. 1*. Milwaukee, WI: The Bruce Publishing Company.

Hofinger, Johannes. 1957. *The art of teaching Christian doctrine*. Notre Dame, IN: Notre Dame Press.

Hughes, Thomas. 1894. The growth and spirit of modern psychology. *American Catholic Quarterly Review* 19: 523.

Hughes, Kathleen, ed. 1990. *How firm a foundation: Voices of the early liturgical movement*. Chicago: Liturgy Training Publications.

Hunt, Thomas C., E. A Joseph, Ronald N. Nuzzi, and J.O. Geiger, eds. 2003. *Handbook of research on Catholic higher education*. Greenwich, CT: Information Age Publishing.

John Paul II. 1980. Perennial philosophy of St. Thomas for the youth of our times. *Angelicum* 57.

Johnson, George. 1919a. The curriculum of the Catholic elementary school: Psychological and social foundations. Ph.D. diss., Catholic University of America.

_____. 1919b-1920. The curriculum of the Catholic elementary schools: A discussion of its psychological and social foundations. *The Catholic Educational Review* 17: 528-46, 580-600; 18: 6-27, 98-110, 164-72, 237-46, 275-87, 357-68.

_____. 1920a. The training of the diocesan superintendent. *The Catholic Educational Review* 19: 127-35.

_____. 1920b. A plan for teacher certification. *The Catholic Educational Review* 19: 446-52.

_____. 1921. Secular teachers. *The Catholic Educational Review* 19: 559-64.

_____. 1922. On trying to serve two masters. *The Catholic Educational Review* 20: 457-464.

_____. 1924a. The teacher in the grades. *The Catholic Educational Review* 22: 385-89.

_____. 1924b. The elementary school curriculum. *The Catholic Educational Review* 22: 449-56.

_____. 1925. The aim of Catholic elementary education. *The Catholic Educational Review* 23: 257-68.

_____. 1926a. A fundamental principle in the teaching of religion. *The Catholic Educational Review* 24: 457-63.

_____. 1926b. The liturgy as a form of educational experience. *The Catholic Educational Review* 24: 529-34.

_____. 1927. Notes on the teaching of religion. *The Catholic Educational Review* 25: 562-66.

_____. 1928a. Notes on the teaching of religion: The ascetical element in religious instruction. *The Catholic Educational Review* 26: 41-44.

_____. 1928b. Notes on the teaching of religion: Teaching children how to meditate. *The Catholic Educational Review* 26: 239-45.

_____. 1928c. Notes on the teaching of religion: Lessons from church architecture. *The Catholic Educational Review* 26: 493-97.

_____. 1928d. Notes on the teaching of religion: Education for humility. *The Catholic Educational Review* 26: 553-59.

_____. 1929a. Character education in the Catholic Church. *Religious Education* 24: 54-57.

_____. 1929b. The Goal of Catholic Education. *National Catholic Welfare Conference Bulletin* (hereafter cited as *NCWC Bulletin*) 10: 4.

_____. 1930. Abiding values in inherited religion. *Religious Education* 25: 564-67.

_____. 1932. Consequences of education without religion. *Religious Education* 27: 515-17.

_____. 1935. Noblesse Oblige. *The Catholic Educational Review* 33: 513-20.

_____. 1937a. Render unto Caesar: Render also unto God. *Religious Education* 32: 202-06.

_____. 1937b. Education and social security. *The Catholic Educational Review* 35: 257-63.

_____. 1940a. Progressive education. *The Catholic Educational Review* 38: 257-64.

_____. 1940b. The duties of teachers in the defense of American democracy. *The Catholic Educational Review* 38: 450.

_____. 1941a. The activity curriculum. *The Catholic Educational Review* 37: 65-72.

_____. 1941b. Our task in the present crisis. *The Catholic Educational Review,* 39: 257-64.

_____. 1941c. The practical aspects of patriotism. Washington, DC: National Council of Catholic Men. George Johnson Archives, Catholic University of America.

_____. 1942. Report of the secretary general. *NCEA Bulletin,* 39: 70-79.

_____. 1944a. Catholic education for citizenship. *Religious Education,* 39: 204-09.

_____. 1944b. The unchanging Christian life in a changing society. *The Catholic Educational Review* 42: 407-12.

Jugnet, Louis. 1964. *Pour connaître la pensée de Saint Thomas D'Aquin.* Bordas, France.

Jungmann, Joseph A. 1959. *Handing on the faith: A manual of catechetics.* West Germany: Herder and Herder.

Jungmann, Joseph A. 1962. *The good news yesterday and today.* Trans. and ed. William A. Huesman. New York: W. H. Sadlier.

Kerr, Fergus. 2006. *Twentieth century Catholic theologians.* London: Wiley-Blackwell.

Kilcawley, Margaret P. 1942. The contribution of Very Reverend Doctor Thomas E. Shields to educational sociology. Ph.D. diss., Catholic University of America.

Killen, David P. 1973. Americanism revisited: John Spalding and *Testem Benevolentiae*. *Harvard Theological Review* 66: 413-54.

Kinast, Robert L. 1997. Vatican II and American Catholics. *The encyclopedia of American Catholic history*. Ed. Michael Glazer and John T. Shelly. Collegeville, MN: The Liturgical Press.

Knasas, John. 2003. *Being and some twentieth-century Thomists*. New York: Fordham University Press.

Lacombe, Olivier. 1991. *Jacques Maritain: La générosité de l'intelligence*. Paris: Tequi.

LeClercq, Jean. 1959. *The love of learning and the desire of God: A study of monastic culture*. New York: Fordham University Press.

Lee, James Michael. 1968. *The purpose of Catholic schooling*. Dayton, OH: National Catholic Education Association.

Legault, Michel. 1986. Pour une philosophie de l'éducation. *Cahiers Jacques Maritain* 14, 5-58.

Leo III. 1879. *On the restoration of Christian philosophy (Aeterni Patris)*. http://www.newadvent.org/library/docs_le13ae.htm.

Lonergan, Bernard. 1973. *Method in theology*. New York: Herder and Herder.

Lucker, Raymond. 1966. *The aims of religious education in the early church and in the American catechetical movement*. Rome: Catholic Book Agency.

Maritain, Jacques. 1922. *Antimoderne*. Paris: Editions de la Revue des Jeunes.

_____. 1925. *Trois réformateurs: Luther. Descartes, Rousseau*. Paris: Librarie Plon.

_____. 1930. *An introduction to philosophy*. Westminster, MD: Christian Classics.

_____. 1932-1933. *Sept leçons sur l'etre et les premiers principes de la raison speculative*. Paris: Tequi.

_____. 1933. *Some reflections on culture and liberty*. Chicago: The University of Chicago Press.

_____. 1936. *Freedom in the modern world*. New York: Charles Scribner's Sons.

_____. 1943. *Education at the crossroads.* New Haven, CT: Yale University Press.

_____. 1946. *True humanism.* London: The Centenary Press.

_____. 1947a. *Jacques Maritain, son Oèuvre philosophique,* Bibliotheque de la revue Thomiste. Paris: Desclée de Brouwer éditeurs.

_____. 1947b. *The person and the common good.* New York: Charles Scribner's Sons.

_____. 1955a. *An essay on Christian philosophy.* New York: Philosophical Library.

_____. 1955b. *Reflections on America.* New York: Charles Scribner's Sons.

_____. 1959a. *Distinguish to unite or the degrees of knowledge.* London: Geoffrey Bles.

_____. 1959b. *Pour une philosophie de l' éducation.* Paris: Librairie Arthème Fayard.

_____. 1961. *On the use of philosophy: Three essays.* Princeton, NJ: Princeton University Press.

_____. 1966. The Future of Thomism, presented at a Conference of Philosophy in an Age of Christian Renewal, held at the Center for Continuing Education at Notre Dame University, September 6-10, 1966.

_____. 1968. *The peasant of the Garonne: An old layman questions himself about the present time.* New York: Holt, Rinehart and Winston.

_____. 1973. *Approaches sans entraves.* Paris: Librarie Arthème Fayard.

_____. 1982-2000. *Oèuvres complètes* 16 vols. Paris: Édition Universitaires de Fribourg et Éditions Saint-Paul, 1982-2000.

Marx, Paul. 1957. *Virgil Michel and the liturgical movement.* Collegeville, MN: The Liturgical Press.

Massa, Mark S. 2003. *Anti-Catholicism in America: The last acceptable prejudice.* New York: Crossroad.

Maurelian, Brother. 1894. *Final report of the Catholic education exhibit.* Chicago, Illinois.

Mayer, Helen. 1929. *The philosophy of teaching of St. Thomas Aquinas (De magistro).* Milwaukee, WI: Bruce Publishing Company.

McAvoy, Thomas T. 1957. *The great crisis in American Catholic history, 1895-1900.* Chicago: Regnery.

McCluskey, Neil G. 1950a. *Federal aid to private schools?* St. Louis: Queen's Work (Pius XII Memorial Library, St. Louis University).

_____. 1950b. *Your church is "undemocratic."* St. Louis: Queen's Work Pius XII Memorial Library, St. Louis University.

_____. 1955. Who are Jehovah's Witnesses? *America*, 94: 204-08.

_____. 1958. Public schools and moral education. New York: Columbia University Press.

_____. 1959. *Catholic viewpoint on education.* Garden City, NY: Image Books.

_____. 1963. Public funds for parochial schools? Yes! In *Religion in the schools*, ed. E. Shoben, Jr., 1-8. New York: Teachers College, Columbia University, Bureau of Publications.

_____, ed. 1964. *Catholic education in America: A documentary history: Classics in education.* New York: Teachers College, Columbia University, Bureau of Publications.

_____. 1965. The dinosaur and the Catholic school. In *Catholic education: A book of readings*, ed. W. Kolesnik and E. Power, 111-18. New York: McGraw-Hill Book Company.

_____. 1968. *Catholic education faces its future.* Garden City, NY: Doubleday & Co., Inc.

_____, ed. 1970. *The Catholic university: A modern appraisal.* Notre Dame, IN: University of Notre Dame Press.

_____. 1973. George Johnson. *Dictionary of American Biography.* Supplement 3. New York: Scribner.

_____. 1979. New dimensions of gerontology programs. In *Gerontology in higher education: Developing institutional and community strengths*, ed. H. Stearns, et. al., 14-20. Belmont, CA: Wadsworth.

_____. 1981. Preretirement education and preparation for aging. In *Aging: Prospects and issues*, R. Davis, 362-82. Los Angeles: University of Southern California Press.

_____. and Borgatta, E. F., eds. 1981. *Aging and retirement: Prospects, planning and policy.* Thousand Oaks, CA: Sage Publications.

McCool, Gerald A. 1989; 1977. *Nineteenth century scholasticism: The search for a unitary principle.* New York: Fordham University Press.

_____. 1992. *From unity to pluralism*. New York: Fordham University Press.

_____. 1990. Is Thomas' way of philosophizing still viable today? *Proceedings of the American Catholic Philosophical Association* 64: 1-13.

_____. 2000. The ideal of the Catholic mind. In *Examining the Catholic intellectual tradition*, ed. Anthony J. Cernera and Oliver J. Morgan. Fairfield, CT: Sacred Heart University Press.

McManus, William E. 1964. Are parochial schools the answer? *Critic*: 52-54.

Messmer, Sebastian. 1996. Edward A. Pace Papers, Messmer to Pace, Green Bay, Box 20, 1896.

Metral, Marie-Odile. 1969. Preface to *Pour une philosophie de l' éducation* 2nd ed. by Jacques Maritain. Paris: Libraire Arthème Fayard.

Misiak, H, and V. M. Staudt. 1954. *Catholics in psychology: Historical survey*. New York: McGraw-Hill.

Michel, Virgil. 1919. Brownson's political philosophy and today. *American Catholic Quarterly Review* 44: 193-202.

_____. 1924. A high school course in religion. *The Catholic Educational Review* 22: 400-19, 472-87.

_____. 1925. A religious need for the day. *The Catholic Educational Review* 23: 449-56.

_____. 1926. Participation in the Mass. *Orate Fratres* 1: 17-20.

_____. 1927a. Are we educating moral parasites? The *Catholic Educational Review* 25:147-55.

_____. 1927b. Stimulating intellectual independence in senior college students. *Catholic Educational Review* 25: 524-33.

_____. 1935. Infidelity of the Church. *Orate Fratres* 9: 492-96.

_____. 1936. The scope of the liturgical movement. *Orate Fratres* 10: 485-90.

_____. 1937a. Religious education. *Orate Fratres* 11: 218-20.

_____. 1937b. Liturgical religious education. *Orate Fratres* 11: 267-69.

_____. 1937c. Religious instruction again. *Orate Fratres* 11: 321-22.

_____. 1938a. Adequate preparation for teaching the Mass. *Journal of Religious Instruction* 8: 594-98.

_____. 1938b. Knowledge requirement for teaching the Mass. *Journal of Religious Instruction* 8: 765-70.

_____. 1940. Rediscovering the obvious: Liturgy and the psychology of education. *Orate Fratres* 14: 529-32.

Mitchell, Nathan O.S.B. 1982. *Mission and ministry: History and theology in the sacrament of order.* Collegeville, MN: The Liturgical Press.

Mongoven, Anne Marie. 2000. *The prophetic spirit of catechesis.* Mahwah, NJ: Paulist Press.

Moran, Gabriel. 1966. *Theology of revelation.* New York: Herder & Herder.

_____. 1994. Loyal and steadfast. *Professional Approaches for Christian Educators* 24: 3-4.

Mougel, René. 1988. Les annés de New York, 1940-1945. *Cahiers Jacques Maritain* 16-17: 13-28.

Mougniotte, Alain. 1992. Actualité des idées pédagogiques de Jacques Maritain, *Cahiers Jacques Maritain* 25: 15-29.

_____. 1997. *Maritain et l'éducation.* Paris: Éditions Don Bosco.

Mounier, Emmanuel. 1938. *A personalist manifesto.* New York: Longmans, Green and Co.

Murphy, John Francis. 1971. Thomas Edward Shields: Religious educator. Ph.D. diss., Columbia University.

Murray, Frank S. 1979. Psychology laboratories in the United States prior to 1900. *Teaching Psychology* 6: 19-21.

Murray, John Courtney 1957. The Christian idea of education. In *The Christian idea of education,* ed. Edmund Fuller. New Haven, CT: Yale University Press.

Newman, John Henry. 1982 [1852]. *The idea of a university.* Introduction and notes by Martin J. Svaglic. Notre Dame, IN: Notre Dame Press.

_____. 1957. *Autobiographical writings.* Ed. Henry Tristram. New York: Sheed and Ward.

Nolan, Lucinda A. 2007. Scaling the heights of heaven. *Religious Education* 102: 314-27.

Nuesse, C. Joseph. 1990. *The Catholic University of America: A centennial history.* Washington, DC: The Catholic University Press.

O'Brien, Dennis J. 1994. *Catholic higher education at the crossroads.* Santa Clara, CA: University of Santa Clara Press.

O'Connor, Augustine. 1941. The influence of very reverend doctor Thomas E. Shields on Catholic education in the United States. Ph.D. diss., Catholic University of America.

O'Hare, Padraic. 1994. Mary Perkins Ryan (1912-1993): *Mulier fortis, strong woman. The Living Light* 39: 3-8.

Pace, Edward A. No date. Report to the academic senate. Unpublished manuscript, Catholic University of America Archives, 1-12.

_____. 1894. Growth and spirit of modern psychology. *American Catholic Quarterly Review* 19: 522-44.

_____. 1895a. Relations of experimental psychology. *American Catholic Quarterly Review* 22: 131-62.

_____. 1895b. Our theological seminaries. *The Catholic University Bulletin* 20: 389-400.

_____. 1896-1897. Annual Report of the Rector.

_____. 1898. The college training of the clergy. *The Catholic University Bulletin* 4: 393.

_____. 1899. The world copy according to Saint Thomas. *The Catholic University Bulletin* 4: 205-14.

_____. 1900. The concept of immortality in the philosophy of Saint Thomas. *The Catholic University Bulletin* 6: 13-17.

_____. 1902. Saint Thomas's theory of education. *The Catholic University Bulletin* 8: 290-303.

_____. 1906. Some modern substitutes for the soul. *The New York Review* 1: 541-57.

_____. 1910. Education, development, and soul. *The Catholic World* 91: 812-25.

_____. 1911a. The papacy and education. *The Catholic Educational Review* 1:1-9.

_____. March 1911b. Lessons from the liturgy. *The Catholic Educational Review* 1: 239-46.

_____. 1911c. The seminary and the educational problem. *The Catholic Educational Review* 2: 576-92.

_____. 1911d. Religion in education. *The Catholic Educational Review* 2: 769-76.

_____. 1912a. The seminary and education. *The Catholic Educational Review*, 3: 70-79.

_____. 1912b. The Holy Father's letter. *The Catholic Educational Review* 3, 104-13.

_____. 1912c. The university: Its growth and its needs. *The Catholic Educational Review* 4: 353-58.

_____. 1913a. Education. *The Catholic Encyclopedia*. Second Edition. http://www.newadvent.org/cathen/05295b.htm.

_____. 1913b. The teaching of philosophy in the college. *The Catholic Educational Review* 6: 110-19.

_____. 1915. Education and the constructive aim. *The Constructive Quarterly* 3: 584-602.

_____. 1926. The sense of responsibility. *The Catholic Educational Review* 24: 513-17.

_____. 1928. Assimilari Deo. *New Scholasticism* 2: 342-56.

_____. 1936. The problem of freedom. *The New Scholasticism* 10: 207-25.

Pecklers, Keith. 1998. *Unread vision: The liturgical movement in the United States of America 1926-1955*. Collegeville, MN: The Liturgical Press.

Pelletier, Annette and Patricia Panganiban. 2006. *Gerard S. Sloyan*. In Christian Educators of the Twentieth Century. http://www.talbot.edu/Ce20/ (accessed November 14, 2007).

Pius XI. 1929. *Divini illius magistri (On the Christian education of youth)*. Washington, DC: National Catholic Educational Association.

_____. Christian education of youth. *Five great encyclicals*, ed. Gerald Treacy. New York: The Paulist Press, 35-75.

Power, Edward J. 1953. Progressive education and Bishop Spalding. *The Catholic Educational Review* 51: 671-79.

Power, Edward J. 1972. *Catholic higher education in America: A history*. New York: Meredith Corporation.

Ratzinger, Joseph. 2000. The spirit of the liturgy. San Francisco: Ignatius Press.

Reboul, Olivier. 1989. *La philosophie de l'education*. Paris: Presses Universitaires de France.

Redden, John D. and Francis A. Ryan. 1942. *A Catholic philosophy of education*. Milwaukee, WI: Bruce.

Reeder, Rachel. 1997. The liturgical movement in America. In *The encyclopedia of American Catholic history*, ed. Michael Glazier and Thomas Shelly. Collegeville, MN: The Liturgical Press: 805–11.

Reidy, Timothy. 2004. Needed the vision thing: Rethinking the mission of Catholic primary schools. *Commonweal* 81: 15–18.

Religious Education. 1944. Obituary for George Johnson. *Religious Education* 39: 204.

Religious education in a war-shocked world: A syllabus for local study groups. 1945 *Religious Education* 40: 111-14.

Reports from convention seminar groups. *Religious Education* 39: 282-92.

Roach, John. 1988. Virgil Michel's prophetic vision. *Origins* 18: 13.

Robin, Léon. 1908. *La Théorie platonicienne des idées et des nombres d'après Aristote. Étude historique et critique.* Paris.

Ross, Bruce. 1994. Development of psychology at the Catholic University of America. *Journal of the Washington Academy of Sciences* 82: 133-59.

Rousselot, Pierre. 1924. *L'intellectualisme de Saint Thomas.* Paris.

Rudolph, Frederick. 1962. *The American college and university.* New York: Knopf.

Ryan, John A. 1941. *Social doctrine in action: A personal account.* New York: Harper & Brothers.

Ryan, John H. 1932. Edward Aloysius Pace, philosopher and educator. In *Aspects of the new scholastic philosophy,* ed. Charles A. Hart. By the associates and former pupils of Dr. Edward A. Pace. New York: Benzinger.

Ryan, Mary Perkins. 1937. *At your ease in the Catholic church.* New York: Sheed & Ward.

_____. 1940. *Your Catholic language: Latin from the missal.* New York: Sheed & Ward.

_____. 1944. *Speaking of how to pray.* New York: Sheed & Ward.

_____, ed. 1948. *The sacramental way: The National liturgical conference.* New York: Sheed & Ward.

_____. 1949. *Mind the baby.* New York: Sheed & Ward.

_____. 1952. To sum it all up. *Worship* 26: 497–505.

_____. 1955. *Beginning at home: The challenge of Christian parenthood.* Collegeville, MN: Liturgical Press.

_____. 1960. *Perspective for renewal.* Collegeville, MN: Liturgical Press.

_____. 1963. Liturgical piety for American Catholics? *Essays in honor of Gerald Ellard,* ed. William J. Leonard. Milwaukee, WI: Bruce Publishing Company.

_____. 1964. *Are parochial schools the answer? Catholic education in light of the council.* New York: Holt, Rinehart and Winston.

_____, with Monsignor Russell Neighbor. 1967a. *There's more than one way: New programs and possibilities in out-of-school religious education.* Mahwah, NJ: Paulist Press.

_____, with Gabriel Moran et al. 1967b. Catechesis for our times. *Bible Today* 28: 1968–74.

_____. 1968-1969. Identity crisis for religious education. *The Living Light:* 4: 6–18.

_____. 1972. *We are all in this together: Issues and options in educating Catholics.* New York: Holt, Rinehart and Winston.

_____. 1974. Trends. *Professional Approaches for Christian Educators* 5: 3.

_____. 1987. The bible, liberation and women. *Professional Approaches for Christian Educators* 18: 145.

Schroll, Agnes Claire. 1944. The social thought of John Lancaster Spalding, D.D. Ph.D. diss., The Catholic University of America.

Sexton, Virginia. 1980. Edward Aloysius Pace. *Psychological Research* 42: 39-47.

Shields, Thomas E. 1888. *Index omnium.* Privately published.

_____. 1895. *Effects of odours, irritant vapours, and mental work upon the blood flow.* Baltimore: Johns Hopkins University.

_____. 1906. *The psychology of education.* Washington, DC: The Catholic Correspondence School.

_____. 1907. *The education of our girls.* New York: Benzinger Bros.

_____. 1908a. *The teaching of religion.* Washington, DC: The Catholic Correspondence School.

_____. 1908b. The method of teaching religion. *Catholic Educational Association Bulletin* 4: 199-237.

_____. 1908c. *Religion: First book.* Washington, DC: The Catholic Correspondence School.

_____. 1909a. Notes on education: The teaching of religion. *Catholic University Bulletin* 15: 65-88.

_____. 1909b. Notes on education: The teaching of religion. *Catholic University Bulletin* 15: 156-80.

_____. 1909c. Notes on education: The teaching of religion. *Catholic University Bulletin* 15: 275-99.

_____. 1909d, Notes on education: The teaching of religion. *Catholic University Bulletin* 15: 400-06.

_____. 1909e. *The making and unmaking of a dullard.* Washington, DC: The Catholic Education Press.

_____. 1911. The teaching of religion. *The Catholic Educational Review* 1: 56.

_____. 1912. *Teachers manual of primary methods.* Third Edition. Washington, DC. The Catholic Education Press.

_____. 1917. *Philosophy of education.* Washington, DC: Catholic Education Press.

Shields, Vincent. 1961. The Catholic university press. *The Catholic University of America Bulletin* 29: 2-4.

Sloyan, Gerard. 1950. Christian concepts in social studies in Catholic education. Washington, DC: Catholic University of America Press.

_____. 1957. The Eucharist and the aims of Christian education. *Worship* 31: 312-19.

_____, ed. 1958. *Shaping the Christian message: Essays in religious education.* Glen Rock, NJ: Deus Books, Paulist Press.

_____. 1960. The international study week on mission catechetics (Eichstatt, Germany). *Worship* 35: 112-18.

_____. 1962. The catechetical scene in the United States. In *The good news yesterday and today,* Joseph Jungmann. New York: W.H. Sadlier.

_____. 1964. Are parochial schools the answer? *Critic*: 5.

_____. 1966. *Worship in a new key. What the Council teaches on the liturgy.* Garden City, NY: Echo Books.

_____. 1967. Catechetics. *New Catholic Encyclopedia.* 224.

_____. 1968. *Speaking of religious education.* New York: Herder and Herder.

_____. 1986. Response to the Berekah Award. *Worship* 60: 304.

Snook, I. A. 1972. *Concepts of indoctrination: Philosophical essays: (International library of the philosophy of education).* London: Routledge & K. Paul.

Souvenir of the episcopal silver jubilee of Rt. Reverend J.L. Spalding, D.D., Bishop of Peoria. 1903. Chicago.

Spalding, John Lancaster. 1877. *Essays and reviews.* New York: Catholic Publications Society Co.

_____. 1879. The blessed virgin Mary. *Ave Maria* (June 21) ix.

_____. 1880. *The religious mission of the Irish people and Catholic colonization.* New York: The Catholic Publication Society.

_____. 1882. *Lectures and discourses.* New York: Christian Press Association Publishing Company.

_____. 1890. *Education and the higher life.* Chicago: McClurg & Company.

_____. 1892a. The Catholic exhibit in the Columbian exposition. *The Catholic World* 55: 580-86.

_____. 1892b. *New World.* Chicago (December 21).

_____. 1894. *Things of the mind.* Chicago: McClurg & Company.

_____. 1895. *Means and ends of education.* Chicago: McClurg & Company.

_____. 1897. *Thoughts and theories of life and education.* Chicago: McClurg & Company.

_____. 1900. *Opportunity and other essays.* Chicago: McClurg & Company.

_____. 1901a. *Aphorisms and reflections.* Chicago: McClurg & Company.

_____. 1901b. *Things of the mind.* Chicago: McClurg & Company.

_____. 1902a. *Socialism and labor and other arguments.* Chicago: McClurg & Company.

_____. 1902b. *Religion, agnosticism and education.* Chicago: McClurg & Company.

_____. 1905, 1969. *Religion and art and other essays.* Freeport, NY: Books for Libraries Press.

Spellacy, Marie Elizabeth. 1984. The evolution of the catechetical ministry among the Mission Helpers of the Sacred Heart: 1890-1980, a case study. Ph.D. diss., The Catholic University of America.

Spring, Joel. 1986. *The American school, 1642-1985.* New York: Longman.

Swartz, Alice Marie. 1997. Gerard Stephen Sloyan: A career in bible and liturgy and a ministry to all people of God. Ph.D. diss., Drew University.

Sweeney, David Francis. 1965. *The life of John Lancaster Spalding.* New York: Herder and Herder.

Thimmesh, Hilary. 1992. Benedictines and higher education: American style. http://www.osb.org/acad/thimmesh.html (accessed February 1, 2008).

Thomas d'Aquin. 2003. *De l'enseignement (De Magistro)* Langres, Paris: Kincksieck.

Veverka, Fayette Breaux. 1993. Defining an approach to education in the United States, 1920-1950. *Religious Education* 88: 523-42.

Viotto, Piero. 1991. L'humanisme dans la réflexion philosophique contemporaine. *Notes et documents* 25: 16-26.

————. 2000. *Introduzione a Maritain.* Roma-Bari, Italia: Editori Laterza.

Walch, Timothy. 2003. *Parish schools: American Catholic parochial education from colonial times to the present.* Washington, DC: The National Catholic Educational Association.

Walsh, M. Rosalia. 1937. *Child psychology and religion.* New York: P.J. Kenedy & Sons Publishers.

————. 1943. The lesson plan in the adaptive way. *Journal of Religious Instruction,* 13 (May, June): 674-80, and 775-85.

————. 1944. *Teaching confraternity classes the adaptive way.* Chicago: Loyola University Press.

————. 1946a. A Confraternity parent-teacher association. In *Proceedings of the Eighth National Catechetical Congress,* 505-08. Paterson, NJ: St. Anthony Guild Press.

————. 1946b. An approach to the public school child. In *Proceedings of the Eighth National Catechetical Congress,* 149-53. Paterson, NJ: St. Anthony Guild Press.

————. 1947. Teaching religion as bond of world unity. *Lumen Vitae* 2: 265-81.

————. 1951a. Training for leadership. *The Catholic Educator* 21: 475-77.

————. 1951b. Use of Confraternity teacher manuals in the Confraternity religion school in *Proceedings of the Ninth National Catechetical Congress,* 115-20. Paterson, NJ: St. Anthony Guild Press.

————. 1952. Cooperation between confraternity classes and the home. *Catholic School Journal* 52: 174-75.

————. 1956a. Advanced and continued preparation and a standard course of study in *Proceedings of the tenth National Catechetical Congress* 110-14. Paterson, NJ: St. Anthony Guild Press.

————. 1956b. School year instruction. *The confraternity comes of age,* 85-97. Paterson, NJ: Confraternity Publications.

————. 1957. *A Confraternity school year religion course: The adaptive way for the teachers of children attending public schools.* Washington, DC: Confraternity of Christian Doctrine.

_____. 1959. *The adaptive way of teaching confraternity classes.* St. Paul, MN: The Catechetical Guild.

_____. 1966. *Teaching religion–the adaptive way: Post Vatican edition.* St. Paul, MN: Catechetical Guild Educational Society.

Ward, Justine. 1947. *Thomas Edward Shields: Biologist, psychologist, educator.* New York: Scribner.

Watson, J. 2004. Educating for citizenship–the emerging relationship between religious education and citizenship education. *British Journal of Religious Education* 26: 259-71.

Whalen, Michael D. 1996. Method in liturgical catechesis: a systematic and critical analysis of the relationship between liturgy and catechesis in the writings of Dom Virgil Michel 1890-1938. Ph.D. diss., The Catholic University of America.

Wohlwend, Mary Verone. 1968. The educational principles of Dr. Thomas E. Shields and their impact on his teacher training program at the Catholic University of America. Ph.D. diss., Catholic University of America.

Woods, Thomas E. Jr. 2004. *The Church confronts modernity: Catholic progressives and the progressive era.* New York: Columbia University Press.

Contributors

JOHN L. ELIAS, Professor of Religious Education and Social Ministry, Fordham University, is the author of *A History of Christian Education* (Krieger, 2002) as well as other books and articles on the history, philosophy and psychology of religious education.

PHILIP FRANCO, Director of Faith Formation, Diocese of Brooklyn, is the author of "Educating Toward Communion: The Traditional Italian *Festa* as a Means of Religious Education," *Religious Education* 102 (2007): 25-43.

ANN M. HEEKIN, Director of Programs and Publications, Center for Christian Jewish Understanding, Sacred Heart University, is the author of "Reclaiming a Lost Leader: Mary Perkins Ryan, Visionary in Modern Catholic Education," *Religious Education* 103 (2008): 196-217.

HAROLD D. HORELL, Assistant Professor of Religious Education, Fordham University, is the author of "The Moral Demands of Contemporary Life and Christian Moral Education," in M. deSouza, K. Engebretson, G. Durka, R. Jackson, and A. McGrady, eds., *International Handbook of the Religious, Moral and Spiritual Dimensions of Education* (Springer, 2007) and "Cultural Postmodernity and Christian Faith Formation," in Thomas H. Groome and Harold D. Horell, eds., *Horizons and Hope: The Future of Religious Education* (Paulist Press, 2003), as well as other articles on religious and moral education.

LUZ IBARRA, Lecturer in philosophy at the University of Iberoamericana in Mexico City, is the author of several articles in the field of education.

LUCINDA A. NOLAN, Assistant Professor of Religious Education and Catechetics, The Catholic University of America, is the author of "John Lancaster Spalding: Catalyst for Social Reform, *Catholic Education* 9 (2005): 178-97, as well as other articles and book chapters on Catholic education and the history of religious education.

JACQUELINE PARASCANDOLA, Librarian, Columbia University, is a religious educator and liturgist.

Index

Abelard, Peter, 4-5
academic freedom, 46-47, 238,
    293-94
*Acerbo Nimis (On Teaching
    Christian Doctrine),* 169-70
Adaptive Way, 171, 174-75,
    184
*Adaptive Way Course of Religious
    Instruction for Catholic
    Children Attending Public
    Schools, The* (Walsh),
    168-69
Adler, Mortimer, 201
adult education
    McCluskey, Neil Gerard, on,
        222, 232
    Ryan, Mary Perkins, on, 250,
        259, 262-63, 265-67, 269
Aeterni Patris, 11
African Americans, 23-24, 162,
    170
Ahr, George, 278
aims of education
    culture, 89-90, 204
    growth of the individual, 141
    Johnson, George, on, 117-22
    as living faith, 173
    Maritain, Jacques, on, 203-05

McCluskey, Neil Gerard, on,
    229-30
Michel, Virgil, on, 138-39
Shields, Thomas Edward, on,
    82, 86-91, 93
American catechetical
    movement, 140-41
American Catholic
    Philosophical Association
    (ACPA), 53
American College of the
    Immaculate Conception
    (Louvain, Belgium), 22,
    197
Americanism, 30-31
American liturgical movement,
    248-53, 281-84
Anselm, 5
anti-Catholicism, 29, 223-24,
    227
apperception, 69, 175-76, 184.
    See also correlation
    principle
Aquinas, Thomas
    contributions of, 4-5, 6-7, 9
    De Magistro, 64
    Maritain, Jacques, on, 191,
        194

Acuinas, Thomas *(continued)*
  Pace, Edward, on, 64
  Shields, Thomas Edward, on, 88
  Summa Theologica, 191, 196
  on teachers, 211
Are Parochial Schools the Answer? (Ryan), 248, 257-58
Aristotelian Thomism, 196
Aristotle, 125, 194, 196, 198
assimilation of Catholics, 166, 256-57
At Your Ease in the Catholic Church (Ryan), 247, 250
Augustine of Hippo, 3-4, 7, 64, 194

Baierl, J.J., 183
Baltimore Catechism
  assimilation exercises in, 179
  feasts and seasons in, 150
  Michel, Virgil, on, 141-42
  Shields, Thomas Edward, on, 96-97
  Sloyan, Gerard Stephen, on, 290-91
  Spalding, John Lancaster, and, 25-26
Bandas, Rudolph G., 168, 183
Barr, Stringfellow, 201
Basil, 3
Beauduin, Lambert, 133-35, 249, 250, 283
Beginning at Home (Ryan), 253
behaviorism, 61
Benedictine Liturgical Conference. *See* National Liturgical Conference
Benedictine tradition, 7-8, 133-34

Benedict XVI, Pope, 283
Bergson, Henri, 191, 194
Bernard of Clairvaux, 6
Better Men for Better Times, 107-08, 123, 126-29
BHRAGS, Inc., 222
Blanshard, Paul, 223
Bloy, Léon, 191
Boys, Mary, 18
Brothers of the Christian Schools, 9-10
Brownson, Orestes, 14, 24, 132
Bryce, Mary Charles, 18, 50, 279
Buchanan, Scott, 201
Buckley, Francis, 18

Caldwell, Mary Gwendolen, 27
Cardinal Principles of Education, 86
Caronti, Emmanuele, 134-35
catechesis. *See also* religious education
  dogma/authority in, 171-72
  explanation/memorization method, 171-72
  history of, 291-92
  kerygmatic movement and, 254-56
  Michel, Virgil, on, 147-53
  Sloyan, Gerard Stephen, on, 284, 286-88
  sources for, 176-79
Catechetical Forum, 248, 262
Catholic Associated Press, 79-80
Catholic Church
  educational mission, 62-63
  in 1940s and 1950s, 271-73

Catholic Correspondence
    School, 78-79
*Catholic Education: The
    Background, Present
    Position, and Future Trends
    of Catholic Education*
    (McCluskey), 232-34
Catholic Educational Review, 53,
    79
Catholic Education Association,
    53
*Catholic Education Faces its
    Future* (McCluskey), 221-
    22, 225
Catholic Education in America
    (McCluskey), 221
Catholic Encyclopedia, 54, 61-63
Catholic identity
    McCluskey, Neil Gerard, on,
        227-29, 233-34
    schools and, 103, 259
    Spalding, John Lancaster, on,
        23
Catholic intellectual life, 15,
    256-57
Catholic religious education
    Protestant influences, 142-43
Catholic Rural Life Bureau,
    166
Catholics
    assimilation of, 256-57
    and non-Catholics, 230-31
    in non-Catholic schools, 14,
        166, 170-71, 182-83
    in pluralistic society, 253-54
Catholic schools. *See also*
    private schools
    distinctiveness of, 106, 115-
    16

history in U.S., 103-04
public support for, 258-59
Spalding, John Lancaster, on,
    28-29
Catholic Sisters College at
    Catholic University, 53-54
Catholic Social Action, 166
Catholic social thought, 29-30
Catholic University, The
    (McCluskey), 234
"Catholic University and the
    Aggiornamento, The,"
    236-37
Catholic University Bulletin, 53
"Catholic University in the
    Modern World, The," 236-37
Catholic University of America,
    15, 76-77
    Department of Education, 78
    Johnson, George, and, 105
    Leo XIII, Pope, and, 70-71
    Pace, Edward, and, 52-55,
        76-78
    Sloyan, Gerard Stephen, and,
        276-79
    Spalding, John Lancaster,
        and, 26-28
    and Thomism, 197
*Catholic Viewpoint on Education,
    A* (McCluskey), 220-21, 225
Charmot, François, 220
Chenu, M.D., 137
Chicago group, 201
Child Psychology and Religion
    (Walsh), 167, 181
Chippewa Missions, 139-40
*Christian Concepts in Social
    Studies in Catholic
    Education* (Sloyan), 277

Christian education. *See* catechesis; religious education
Christian Religion Series, The, 152-53
Christ-Life Series, 251
Christ-Life Series in Religion, The, 150-52. *See also* elementary school
Murray, Jane Marie, 150
Church
  and culture, 256-57
  educational mission of, 11, 62-63, 65-66, 92-93
  as Mystical Body of Christ, 133, 151, 155, 249, 251-53
Ciceronian approach, 5-6
City University of New York, Center for Gerontological Studies, 222
Clement, 3
clergy, education of, 27, 46-48, 71-73, 76, 234
Clérissac, Humbert, 191
Coe, George, 87
Colet, John, 8
Collins, Joseph B., 168, 183
Commission on American Citizenship, 107, 125, 126-27
Complete Works of Jacques Maritain, The (Oèuvres complètes), 194
Confraternity of Christian Doctrine (CCD), 166-69, 262
Congar, Yves, 137
correlation principle, 80, 97, 100-01. *See also* apperception

Correspondence Course for Lay Catechists, The (Walsh), 168
culture, 89-90, 204, 256-57
Curtis, Walter, 169
Cyril of Jerusalem, 3

De Concilio, Janarius, 25-26
Deferrari, Roy, 18
Degrees of Knowledge, The (Maritain), 217
de Lubac, Henri, 137
De Magistro (Thomas Aquinas), 64
democracy, 124-25
De Néve, Father, 23
Deutsch, Alcuin, 133
Dewey, John
  Maritain, Jacques, and, 199-200
  moral education and, 240-41
  Shields, Thomas Edward, and, 80-81, 110-11, 119-20
Diekmann, Godfrey, 168, 250, 284
Distinguish to Unite: The Degrees of Knowledge (Maritain), 192
Divini Illius Magistri, 11
Divino Afflante Spiritu, 285
dogma/authority, role of, 86-87
Dominican Sisters, 251
Ducey, Michael, 247

economic efficiency, 89
education
  for citizenship, 90-91, 124-25

as mission of Church, 11,
    62-63, 65-66, 92-93
parents' right to choose, 230-
    31
"Education and the Future of
    Religion" (Spalding), 30
education as liturgy. *See* liturgy
    as education
Education at the Crossroads
    (Maritain), 12, 190, 193
Education of Man, The
    (Maritain), 201
Education of Our Girls, The
    (Shields), 92
elementary schools, 9-10, 108-
    09, 111-12. *See also The*
    Christ-Life Series in Religion
Ellard, Gerald, 168, 250
Ellis, John Tracy, 237
Erasmus, Desiderius, 8
Eucharist, 155, 294-95
European catechetical
    movement, 172
European liturgical movement,
    134-35, 249, 281-84
European Social Catholicism,
    23
Existential Thomism, 196-97
experimental psychology, 52-
    53, 55-59
explanation/memorization
    method, 171-72

Fahs, Sophia, 87
family in religious education,
    91-92, 181-82. *See also*
    parents' role
Favre, Geneviève, 190
Favre, Jules, 190

Feeney, Leonard, 247
Freire, Paulo, 137
Fuerst, Anthony N., 183-84
Gatterer, Michael, 172-74
Gaudium et Spes, 13-14, 214
Gibbons, James, 26-27, 163
Gilson, Étienne, 192, 196-97
Glennon, John J., 28, 31-32
Gonzaga University, 221, 235
Gredt, Joseph, 133
Griffin, William A., 277-78
Groome, Thomas, 18
Guardini, Romano, 283
Gueranger, Prosper, 282

Haas, Frederick J., 123
Hackett, Estelle, 149-50, 251
Harris, Maria, 18
Harris, William Torrey, 220
Hecker, Isaac, 24
Heeg, Aloysius J., 168, 183
Herbart, Johann, 184
Herwegen, Idlefons, 282
Hesburgh, Theodore, 18, 235-
    37
higher education
    Christian Religion Series, The,
        152-53
    institutions of, 18-19
    McCluskey, Neil Gerard, on,
        221-22, 234-38
    Pace, Edward, on, 59-60, 70-
        71
    Sloyan, Gerard Stephen, on,
        293-94
    Spalding, John Lancaster, on,
        31, 39, 45-46
high schools, 147-49, 152-53
Hildebrand, Dietrich von, 252

Hillenbrand, Reynold, 250
Hofinger, Johannes, 75, 248, 254-55, 288
home visitations, 181-82
How Do I Know I'm Doing Right? Toward the Formation of a Christian Conscience (Sloyan), 280
humanism, Renaissance, 8-9
Humanisme Intégral (True Humanism) (Maritain), 192
Human Rights and Natural Law (Maritain), 193
Hurley, Michael, 24-25
Hutchins, Robert, 201

IFCU (International Federation of Catholic Universities), 221, 236-37
immigrants, ministry to, 48, 164-65
Index Omnium (Shields), 77
intellectual freedom, 30
International Federation of Catholic Universities (IFCU), 221, 236-37
interreligious activities, 221, 223-24
Irish Colonization Association, 24

Jacobs, Elaine Lituchy, 222-23
James, William, 95
Jean Baptiste de la Salle, 9-10
Jehovah's Witnesses, 230
Jensen, Joseph, 279
Jesuits, 9
Jesus, 69, 72, 97-98, 144

Jesus in Focus: A Life in its Setting (Sloyan), 280
John of the Cross, 191
John Paul II, Pope, 198-99
Johnson, George
    aims of education, 117-22
    Better Men for Better Times, 126-29
    and Catholic schools, 105-06
    Catholic University of America, 105
    on education as development, 119-20
    on education of teachers, 113-15
    on elementary school curriculum, 111-12
    on history of education, 108-09
    legacy, 15-16, 129-30
    life, 104-08
    modern theories, 109-11
    moral character education, 118-19
    philosophy of education, 108-13
    progressivism of, 106, 112-13, 115-16
    role of experience in education, 120
    in 1930s and 1940s, 122-25
    service on federal commissions, 106-07
    Shields, Thomas Edward, 104-05
    on sources of truth, 111-12
Jungmann, Josef, 75, 254, 282

Kelley, Marie Virginia, 274
kerygmatic approach, 288-90

kerygmatic movement, 254-56,
    264-65
Kilpatrick, William, 95
Kinshasa Statement, 236-37
Kirsch, Felix, 167
Krus, Felix, 172-74

laity, 136, 160-61, 247, 268
Lancaster, Mary Jane, 21-22
Land O'Lakes Statement, 14,
    236-38
Leo XIII, Pope, 29, 59, 70-71,
    197
Leo XII, Pope, 79
lesson, parts of, 176-81
liberal education
    Chicago group and, 201
    Maritain, Jacques, on, 201-
        02, 204-05
    Newman on Christian, 10-11
    for teachers, 154
Liturgical Press, The, 135-36, 251
liturgical reforms, 254, 283
liturgical summer school, 139-
    41
liturgy
    in catechesis, 255
    lay participation in, 136, 247
liturgy as education. *See also*
    With Mother Church series
    Johnson, George, on, 120-21
    Michel, Virgil, on, 138, 140-
        44, 149-51, 154-56, 160
    Pace, Edward, on, 66-67, 70
    Ryan, Mary Perkins, on, 260-
        61
    Shields, Thomas Edward, on,
        82-83, 92-93
    Sloyan, Gerard Stephen, on, 282

Liturgy of the Church, The
    (Michel), 134
lives of saints, 173
Living Light, The, 261-63
Loyola, Ignatius, 9
Lucker, Raymond, 262
Lumen Vitae (Belgium), 75

Man and State (Maritain), 193
Mann, Horace, 220
Maritain, Jacques
    aims of education, 203-09,
        213
    *Complete Works of Jacques
        Maritain, The (Oèuvres
        Complètes),* 194
    Degrees of Knowledge, The,
        217
    and Dewey, John, 199-200
    *Distinguish to Unite: The
        Degrees of Knowledge,* 192
    Education at the Crossroads,
        12
    Education of Man, The, 201
    *Humanisme Intégral (True
        Humanism),* 192
    *Human Rights and Natural
        Law,* 193
    legacy, 12, 16, 213-14, 217-
        18
    on liberal education, 201-02,
        204-05
    life, 190-94
    Man and State, 193
    *Oèuvres complètes de Jacques et
        Raissa Maritain,* 217
    Peasant of the Garonne, The,
        194, 214-15
    personalism of, 207-09

Maritain, Jacques *(continued)*
  philosophy of education,
    199-202
  Pour une Philosophie de
    l'Éducation, 201
  Ransoming the Time, 193
  on reason as way to seek
    God, 195-96
  Scholasticism and Politics, 193
  on teacher's role, 202-05,
    210-13
  on Thomism, 189-91, 194-
    99, 217
  Todo y Nada (Everything and
    Nothing), 191
  True Humanism, 208
  wisdom, 206-07
Maritain, Jeanne, 190
Maritain, Paul, 190
Maritain, Raissa Oumançoff,
    190-91, 194, 217
Marthaler, Berard, 18, 50, 279
materialism, 57
Mathis, Michael, 247
McClosky, John, 26
McCluskey, Elaine, 222, 223
McCluskey, Mary Genevieve,
    219-20
McCluskey, Neil Gerard
  aims of education, 229-30
  BHRAGS, Inc., 222
  Catholic Education: The
    Background, Present Position,
    and Future Trends of
    Catholic Education, 232-34
  Catholic Education Faces its
    Future, 221-22, 225
  Catholic Education in
    America, 221

  on Catholic identity, 227-29,
    233-34
  Catholic University, The, 234
  Catholic Viewpoint on
    Education, A, 220-21, 225
  critical reflection, 231-32
  educational vision, 232-33
  Hesburgh, Theodore, 235-37
  on higher education, 221-22,
    234-38
  International Federation of
    Catholic Universities
    (IFCU), 236-37
  interreligious activities of,
    221, 223-24
  legacy, 17, 242-44
  life, 219-23
  on moral education, 239-42
  Notre Dame University, 235-
    37
  Public Schools and Moral
    Education, 220, 239
  on public support for private
    schools, 238-39
  on religious freedom, 225-27
  on Vatican II, 221-22
McCluskey, Patrick John, 219-
    20
McMahon, Gerald, 136
McVey, Leo, 167
Mediator Dei, 252-53
Messmer, Sebastian, 51
Michel, Virgil
  on aims of education, 138-
    39, 141
  and American catechetical
    movement, 140-41
  and American liturgical
    movement, 250-51

on *Baltimore Catechism*, 141-42

catechetical manuals by, 147-53

and Chippewa Missions, 139-40

on education through participation, 152-53

on Eucharist, 155

and European liturgical movement, 134-35

on higher education, 154

High School Course in Religion, A, 147-49

legacy, 16, 159-61

life, 131-40

liturgical summer school, 139-41

on liturgy as education, 138, 143-44, 154-56, 160

Liturgy of the Church, 134

on moral education, 156-58

Orate Fratres [later *Worship*], 135-36

personalism, 136-39, 141-42, 153, 158-59

on religious education, 156-59

on role of experience in education, 144-47

teachers' role, 153-56

Mind the Baby (Ryan), 253

Mission Helpers of the Sacred Heart, 165-66, 169-70, 186

modernism, 50

Montessori, Maria, 119

Montini, Giovanni Battista, 193

Moore, Thomas Verner, 59

moral education

Dewey, John, on, 240-41

Johnson, George, on, 118-19

McCluskey, Neil Gerard, on, 239-42

Michel, Virgil, on, 156-58

Pace, Edward, on, 70

and public schools, 239-40

Shields, Thomas Edward, on, 90-91

Moran, Gabriel, 14, 18, 50, 262, 290

More, Thomas, 8

Mounier, Emmanuel, 136-37

Munich Method, 172-73, 183-85, 184

Murray, Jane Marie, 132, 149-50, 150, 152-53, 251

Murray, John Courtney, 12, 223

National Catholic Educational Association (NCEA), 53

National Catholic Welfare Conference (NCWC), 53, 105, 166

National Committee on Education, 107

National Liturgical Conference, 246-47, 251-53

National Liturgical Weeks, 251-52

National Shrine of the Immaculate Conception, Teacher's Division, 167-68

natural sciences in the curriculum, 52-53, 56-57, 112

"Nature of the Contemporary Catholic University, The," 236-38

Neff, John, 201
Neighbor, Russell, 248, 261-62
neo-scholasticism, 12-13
neo-Thomism, 189-90, 196-99, 217
Newman, John, 10
non-Catholics and Catholics, 230-31
non-public schools, 104-05, 117
Notre Dame Institute for Studies in Education, 221
Notre Dame University, 235-37
Novelle Théologie, 137
Oèuvres complètes de Jacques et Raissa Maritain, 217
Offeramus, 136
O'Hara, Edwin, 166
On Teaching Christian Doctrine (Acerbo Nimis), 169-70
Orate Fratres, 135-36, 251, 283
Origen, 3
Oumançoff, Raissa, 190-91, 194
Our Mass, 136

PACE, 248, 265-68
Pace, Edward
  on *Baltimore Catechism,* 141
  Catholic Educational Review, 79
  Catholic Encyclopedia, 54, 61-63
  and Catholic University of America, 52-55, 76-78
  early life and education, 51-52
  on higher education, 59-60, 70-71

legacy, 15-16
liturgy as education, 66-67, 70
moral education, 70
on natural sciences in curriculum, 56-57
as progressive, 49-51, 73-74
as psychologist, 52-53, 55-59
on psychology and philosophy, 57-59
on public schools, 67-68
as scholastic philosopher, 59-61
on seminary education, 71-73
and Shields, Thomas Edward, 53-54, 80
on teachers' qualifications, 60
teaching methods, 65
theory of education, 63-65
parents' role, 181-82, 230-31, 238-39. *See also* family in religious education
Parish Kyrie, The, 136
parochial schools
  Ryan, Mary Perkins, 257-59
Paul VI, Pope, 193, 198, 237
Peasant of the Garonne, The (Maritain), 194, 214-15
Péguy, Charles, 191
Perkins, Charles, 246
Perkins, Elizabeth Ward, 246
Perkins, Mary. *See* Ryan, Mary Perkins; Ward, Mary Perkins
personalism
  Maritain, Jacques, 198, 207-09
  Michel, Virgil, 136-39, 141-42, 153, 158-59

personality, 208
Perspective for Renewal (Ryan), 255-56
Petrarch, Francisco, 8
philosophy and psychology, 57-59
Philosophy of Education (Shields), 80
Piaget, Jean, 85, 220
Pius IX, Pope, 23, 50
Pius XII, Pope, 193, 252-53, 283, 285
Pius XI, Pope, 11, 198
Pius X, Pope, 50, 169-70
pluralistic society, 253-54, 260
Popular Liturgical Library, The, 136, 251
Pottebaum, Gerald, 262
Pour une Philosophie de l'Éducation (Maritain), 201
private schools, 104-05, 117, 224-27, 238-39. *See also* Catholic schools
Professional Approaches for Christian Educators (PACE), 248, 265-68
Program of Affiliation, 79
progressivism
    Johnson, George, 106, 112-13, 115-16
    Pace, Edward, 49-51
    Spalding, John Lancaster, 33, 35
Protestant influences, 67-68, 142-43
psychological method. *See* Munich method
psychology and philosophy, 57-59

public schools
    Catholic students in, 182-83
    moral education in, 239-40
    purposes of, 93-94
    religious education in, 67-68, 121-22, 241-42
    Spalding, John Lancaster, on, 24, 29
Public Schools and Moral Education (McCluskey), 220, 239
public support for private schools
    McCluskey, Neil Gerard, 224-26, 238-39

Ransoming the Time (Maritain), 193
Ratio Studiorum, 9
reason, 33, 36-38, 195-96, 209, 215
recitation, 180-81
Reflections on America (Maritain), 194
Reinert, Paul, 18
Religion, First Book, 99-100
Religion Teacher and the World, The, 168
religious education. *See also* catechesis
    as a continuum, 257-61, 266-67
    experiential approach to, 264-65
    family as center of, 181-82
    historical overview, 1-19
    improved methods of teaching, 68-69
    indoctrination debate, 121

religious education *(continued)*
  liturgy in, 140-43
  Michel, Virgil, 156-59
  as new term, 287
  parents' role, 181-82
  in public schools, 67-68,
    121-22, 241-42
Religious Education
    Association, 221, 224
religious freedom, 225-27, 238-
    39
*Religious Mission of the Irish
    People and Catholic
    Colonization, The*
    (Spalding), 30
revelation
  Michel, Virgil, on, 155
  Pace. Edward, on, 67
  Ryan, Mary Perkins, on, 255,
    262
  Shields, Thomas Edward, on,
    87-88
  Spalding, John Lancaster, on,
    36-37
role of experience in education
  Johnson, George, on, 120
  Michel, Virgil, on, 144-47
  Shields, Thomas Edward, on,
    85-86
Rome Statement, 236-37
Russell, William, 167
Ryan, John, 29-30
Ryan, John Julian, 247
Ryan, Mary Perkins
  and adult education, 250,
    259, 262-63, 265-66,
    269
  and American liturgical
    movement, 250

*Are Parochial Schools the
    Answer?,* 248, 257-58
Beginning at Home, 253
Catholic family in pluralistic
    society, 253-54
Hofinger, Johannes, 254-55
legacy, 14, 17-18, 268-70
life, 245-48
Mind the Baby, 253
PACE, 265-68
Perspective for Renewal, 255-56
on religious education as a
    continuum, 257-61
Speaking of How to Pray, 250
*There's More Than One Way:
    New Programs and
    Possibilities in Out-of-School
    Religious Education,* 263
*We're All in This Together:
    Issues and Options in the
    Education of Catholics,* 265
Your Catholic Language, 250
*At Your Ease in the Catholic
    Church,* 247, 250

Sacramental Way, The, 252
scholasticism, 4-5, 58-61, 171,
    272
Scholasticism and Politics
    (Maritain), 193
school choice, 238-39
*School Year Religious Instruction
    Manual, The,* 168
Scripture in education, 285,
    289
secondary schools. *See* high
    schools
Second Plenary Council, 24
Shahan, Thomas Joseph, 97

Shaping the Christian Message: Essays in Religious Education (Sloyan), 287, 291
Shields, Thomas Edward
aims of education, 82, 86-91, 93
on *Baltimore Catechism,* 96-97, 141
Catholic Educational Review, 79
on Church as educator, 92-93
on correlation principle, 80, 97, 100-01
on culture as aim of education, 89-90
on Dewey, John, 80-81
on dogma/authority, role of, 86-87
on educational processes, 82-86
Education of Our Girls, The, 92
on family in education, 91-92
Index Omnium, 77
Johnson, George, and, 104-05
legacy, 15-16, 75-77, 101-02
life, 77-80
on liturgy as education, 82-83, 92-93
on moral education, 90-91
Pace, Edward, and, 53-54
philosophy of education, 80
Philosophy of Education, 80
on philosophy of religious education, 94-96
as progressive, 49-50, 87, 89

on public schools, 93-94
and religious education, 82
on role of experience in education, 85-86
on teacher's role, 87-88
textbook series, 99-101
Trinity College, 78
on women's education, 91-93
Sisters College of the Catholic University of America, 31, 53-54, 79-80
Sisters of Saint Dominic, 149-50, 251
Slavin, Robert J., 123
Sloyan, Elizabeth, 274
Sloyan, Gerard Stephen
academic freedom, 293-94
Are Parochial Schools the Answer?, 257-58
awards and honors, 280-81
Baltimore Catechism, 290-91
and biblical movement, 285
and Catechetical Forum, 262
and catechetical movement, 284, 286-88
and Catholic University of America, 50, 276-77, 278-79
early life and education, 271, 273-77
on Eucharist, 294-95
on higher education, 293-94
How Do I Know I'm Doing Right? Toward the Formation of a Christian Conscience, 280
and kerygmatic approach, 288-90
legacy, 14, 17-18, 295-96

Sloyan, Gerard Stephen *(continued)*
life, 273-81
and liturgical movements,
281-84
*Shaping the Christian Message:
Essays in Religious
Education,* 287, 291
on teaching methods, 290-92
and Temple University, 279-
80
*Worship in a New Key: What
the Council Says about the
Liturgy,* 280
Sloyan, Jean, 274
Sloyan, Jerome James, 274
Sloyan, Marie Virginia Kelley,
274
Sloyan, Virginia, 274
social studies, 277-78
Socratic method, 5
Spalding, John Lancaster
and academic freedom, 46-47
on aims of education, 35-36,
38-39
and *Baltimore Catechism,* 25-26
and Catholic school system,
28-29
and Catholic social thought,
29-30
"Catholic University and the
Aggiornamento, The,"
236-37
and Catholic University of
America, 26-28
early life and education, 21-23
early ministry, 24-25
on education as life's work,
35-36
on education of clergy, 46-48

on higher education, 31, 39,
45-46
on intellectual freedom, 30-
31, 43
legacy, 15
life as gift, 34-36
on moral development, 38-40
philosophy of education, 32-34
progressivism of, 35
on public schools, 24, 29
on pursuit of truth, 36-38
*Religious Mission of the Irish
People and Catholic
Colonization, The,* 30
and Sisters College of the
Catholic University of
America, 31
on teacher's role, 40-43
on women's education, 43-46
Spalding, Martin John, 21-22,
24, 26
Spalding, Mary Jane Lancaster,
21-22
Spalding, Richard Martin, 21
Spalding Institute, 31
Speaking of How to Pray (Ryan),
250
spiral curriculum, 66
Spiritual Exercises (Loyola), 9
St. John's Abbey, 250-51
St. John's College, 133, 140
Stegmann, Basil, 251
Stieglitz method. *See* Munich
method
storytelling, 176-78, 289-90
Summa Theologica (Thomas
Aquinas), 191, 196
Syllabus of Errors (Pius IX), 23,
50

teachers, education of
    Johnson, George, on, 113-15
    liberal arts in, 154
    Pace, Edward, on, 54, 64-65
    Shields, Thomas Edward, on,
        78
teachers, qualifications of
    as Christians, 212-13
    Johnson, George, on, 114
    and Mission Helpers of the
        Sacred Heart, 169-70
    Pace, Edward, on, 60
    Ryan, Mary Perkins, on, 267-
        68
    Spalding, John Lancaster, on,
        41-43
    Walsh, Mary Rosalia
        (Josephine), on, 185-86
Teacher's Division of the
    National Shrine of the
    Immaculate Conception,
    167-68
teacher's role
    Maritain, Jacques, 202-05,
        210-13
    Michel, Virgil, 153-56
    Shields, Thomas Edward, 87-
        88
    Thomas Aquinas on, 211
*Teaching Confraternity Classes:
    The Adaptive Way,* 168
teaching methods, 65, 68-69
    of Jesus, 69, 72, 97-98, 144
    Maritain, Jacques, 209-10
    Pace, Edward, on, 65
    Shields, Thomas Edward, on,
        88
    Sloyan, Gerard Stephen, on,
        290-92

*Teaching Religion the Adaptive
    Way* (Walsh), 175
teaching role of Church, 65-66
Teilhard de Chardin, Pierre,
    137
Temple University, 279-80
*There's More Than One Way: New
    Programs and Possibilities in
    Out-of-School Religious
    Education* (Ryan), 263
Third Plenary Council of
    Baltimore, 25
Thomas Edward Shields
    Memorial School, 119-20
Thomism, 15-16
    Catholic University of
        America and, 197
    Maritain, Jacques, on, 189-
        90, 194-99
    and philosophy of education,
        214-17
Thomistic revival. *See* neo-
    Thomism
*Todo y Nada (Everything and
    Nothing)* (Maritain), 191
Transcendental Thomism, 197
Trinity College, 53, 78
True Humanism (Maritain), 208
United Nations, 194
*Universal Declaration of Human
    Rights,* 194
university education. *See* higher
    education
University of Louvain, 22, 197

Vatican II
    and *Are Parochial Schools the
        Answer,* 257-58
    and *Gaudium in Spes,* 214

Vatican II *(continued)*
  McCluskey on, 221-22
  and pluralistic society, 260
  results of, 13, 160, 265-66,
    283
  Scriptural study and, 285
Vergerio, Petrus Paulus, 8

Walsh, Mary Concannon, 164
Walsh, Mary Rosalia
    (Josephine)
  Adaptive Way Course of
    Religious Instruction for
    Catholic Children Attending
    Public Schools, The, 168-69
  Child Psychology and Religion,
    181
  Correspondence Course for Lay
    Catechists, The, 168
  early life, 162-65
  legacy, 16-17, 181-86, 186-
    88
  Munich Method, 183-85
  religious life, 165-67
  Teaching Religion the Adaptive
    Way, 175
  writings, 167-69
Walsh, William E., 164-65
Ward, Justine Bayard, 246

Ward, Leo, 55
Warren, Michael, 50
We're All in This Together: Issues
    and Options in the
    Education of Catholics
    (Ryan), 265
With Mother Church series,
    149-50. *See also* liturgy as
    education
Wolter, Placidus, 282
women's education
  McCluskey, Neil Gerard, on,
    234
  Shields, Thomas Edward, on,
    78-80, 91-93
  Sloyan, Gerard Stephen on,
    279
  Spalding, John Lancaster, on,
    43-46
World's Columbian Exposition,
    28
Worship, 135-36, 251, 283
Worship in a New Key: What the
    Council Says about the
    Liturgy (Sloyan), 280

Yorke, Peter, 96-97
Your Catholic Language (Ryan),
    250